Aeneas McDonell Dawson

The temporal sovereignty of the Pope

With relation to the state of Italy

Aeneas McDonell Dawson

The temporal sovereignty of the Pope
With relation to the state of Italy

ISBN/EAN: 9783337043766

Printed in Europe, USA, Canada, Australia, Japan

Cover: Foto ©ninafisch / pixelio.de

More available books at **www.hansebooks.com**

THE TEMPORAL SOVEREIGNTY

OF THE

POPE,

WITH RELATION TO THE STATE OF ITALY;

A LECTURE DELIVERED IN ST. ANDREW'S CATHOLIC
CHURCH, OTTAWA,

WITH ADDITIONAL FACTS AND OBSERVATIONS.

BY

THE REV. ÆN. M^cD. DAWSON,

LONDON:
CATHOLIC PUBLISHING AND BOOK-SELLING COMPANY,
61 NEW BOND STREET.

BALTIMORE:

OTTAWA:
1860.

PREFACE.

Whoever is possessed of any knowledge, is thereby a debtor to his fellow countrymen. This must be my apology for offering to the public the following pages.— The importance of the information they contain, which, to many will be new, may, perhaps, atone for imperfection of style.

In what belongs to History, there can be no claim to originality. Authors of weight and name will recognise, within the narrow compass of this *duodecimo*, the great historical facts, which they have been the first to place on record, or have set forth with all the interest that attaches to an important narrative.

The reasoning employed aims at being sound and conclusive, without pretending to be novel, startling, or brilliant.

The delay in publishing, with its additions, a discourse which was delivered so many weeks ago, is accounted for by the necessarily slow process of printing, in a city, which, although now the metropolis of British North America, was, only some thirty years back, a portion of the unbroken forest.

OTTAWA, APRIL, 1860.

CONTENTS.

	PAGE.
Introductory remarks.—State of parties	3
General view of the Papal Government as regards the Liberty of Italy and of Europe.—Noble efforts of Gregory XVI.—The end of his reign	4
Prospect afforded by the New Pontificate	6
Accession of Pius IX	7
Sketch of the life of Pius IX	9
Pius IX. in America	10
Pius IX. Director of an Hospital	13
Pius IX. Archbishop of Spoleto	14
Mastai, Cardinal,	17
The real enemies of reform unmasked	18
Conciliatory character of Pius IX.—The Amnesty.—Public rejoicings	25
Cardinal Gizzi, Minister.—Further reforms.—The Press.	30
Pius IX. receives the Ambassador of the Sultan	32
Pius IX. and Daniel O'Connell.—Father Ventura's Oration	34
Popular demonstration at Rome	40
The Pope's Sermon	43
Cardinal Ferretti, Minister.—Extraordinary manifestation of the Austrian Government.—Its deference to the wishes of the Holy Father.—Further Reforms.—A Municipal Council instituted.—The Council of State.—A Constitution projected	46
Constitutional Government established	53
The war agitation	54
Revolutionary tendencies.—Count Mamiani, Minister.	59
Parties.—The Italian Radicals.—Count Rossi, Minister.	62

CONTENTS.

PART II.

	Page.
The Spirit of the Age	81
——————Enlightenment	81
——————Justice	83
——————Humanity	86
The Papal Government eminently characterized by its humanity	90
The Temporal Power originating in the wisdom and humanity of the Papal Rulers.—Opinion of the celebrated writer, Balmes	95
Enquiry continued.—The Papal Government essentially humane	96
Humanity of the Pontifical Government in the punishment of political offenders	97
Humanity of the Popes in the administration of Justice	100
Humanity of the Papal Rule.—War	104
The Spirit of the Age.—Education.—The Arts and Sciences encouraged by the Popes.—The Poor, as well as the higher classes, educated by their care.—Remarkable testimony of Mr. Laing and Baron Geramb	107
Wisdom and Humanity of the Papal Government, as manifested by its numerous Institutions for the relief of human misery	117
The Spirit of the Age.—Liberality	127
The Papacy essentially liberal	132
Liberality of the Papacy further considered.—Political Institutions	143
Origin of Civil Power.—Doctrine of a learned Jesuit and other eminent Divines	153
Whether in any case, established power can be conscientiously resisted	157
Liberty of Speech	164
The argument against Papal Rule, founded on the alleged state of the popular mind, considered	171
Rights of peoples.—Pretended rights of factions and inconsiderable sections.—Opinions of "*The Times*".—Numbers and extraordinary increase of Catholics.—Enlightened opinion and noble conduct of Greeks and Protestants	187

CONTENTS.

APPENDIX.

Page.	
81	
81	I.—Count Rayneval's report.—Reform persevered in at Rome after the events of 1848.
83	
86	II.—Principles and Practice of the Papal Church with relation to Slavery and Liberty,—from Lectures by the Rev. Æ. McD. Dawson.
90	
	III.—Origin of the Pope's Temporal Sovereignty.
	IV.—Merciful character of the Pontifical Government.
95	V.—The truth about Perguia.—The Hon. Mrs. Ross' letter.
96	VI.—Science not unfavorable to the progress of the Catholic Church.—Numbers of Protestants probably not increased.—Opinion of Baron Macaulay.
97	
100	VII.—Value of the *popular* vote for annexation to Piedmont.—Foreign Intervention.—Italian correspondence showing that the revolted and annexed Provinces have been coerced.
104	
	VIII.—Popularity of Pius IX.—Letter from Rome.
107	IX.—The popular vote for annexation.—Foreign Intervention.—Note from the Holy See to the French Government.
	X.—The Marquis of Normanby.—Value of his testimony.
117	XI.—Admirable sentiments of good Protestants.—Two remarkable letters quoted.
127	
132	
143	
153	
157	
164	
171	
187	

THE T

WITH RE

INT

In consid
that there a
political cha
called, who
their ally th
tiff, Pius IX
and to pron
the enjoymc
that there is
and the hap
revolutiona
Mazzini, ni
sions, at th
means. Ev
must be sw
the Red Re
their nume
the only fri
the case, he
country.
Other and
Italy. A
when their
must it be
only been
of the rash
it be univ
men of th
and who
its cause.
profession

THE TEMPORAL SOVEREIGNTY
Of the Pope,
WITH RELATION TO THE STATE OF ITALY, &c.

INTRODUCTORY REMARKS,—STATE OF PARTIES.

In considering the state of Italy, it must be borne in mind that there are two classes of persons who desire or favour political changes. The moderate party, if *party* they can be called, who represent the general voice, not unduly claim as their ally the present sovereign of Rome, the illustrious Pontiff, Pius IX. They deem it their highest honor to encourage and to promote such social arrangements as will best secure the enjoyment of rational liberty; believing, in all sincerity, that there is no surer guarantee for the peace, the prosperity, and the happiness of nations. The socialist, red-republican, or revolutionary faction, who own as their chief the lawyer Mazzini, aim also, if credit may be given to their loud professions, at the establishment of liberty, but by very different means. Every existing institution, whether civil or religious, must be swept away, in order to make room for their utopia, the Red Republic. The leaders of this party endeavour by their numerous writings to make it appear that they are the only friends of Italy and of Italian freedom. If such were the case, hopeless, indeed, would be the state of that distracted country. It is not, however, left to their tender mercies.— Other and more beneficent genii watch over the destinies of Italy. And the hour is now, to all appearance, near at hand, when their guardian care will meet with its reward. Nor must it be supposed that the true friends of Italian liberty have only been aroused from the sleep of ages by the wild clamour of the rash and desperate men who labor so zealously to make it be universally believed that they, and they alone, are the men of the times,—the only men who can save their country, and who devote themselves with self-sacrificing patriotism to its cause. Let us not be dazzled, far less won to them by their professions. By their works only can we judge them.

GENERAL VIEW OF THE PAPAL GOVERNMENT AS REGARDS THE LIBERTY OF ITALY AND EUROPE.—NOBLE EFFORTS OF GREGORY XVI.—THE END OF HIS REIGN.

But first, let us look, as is meet, to those purer regions, where wisdom and moderation have ever been in the ascendant. It is no new thing with the Popes to exert their talents, their influence, their power n the cause of Italy. By their mild but firm rule they at first mitigated, and, finally, overcame the tyranny of the early Emperors. At a later day, who could have struggled or who was there to struggle as did the Popes, against a more recent but no less fatal oppression?—who else than the Popes could have taught the Emperors of Germany, who labored so perseveringly to establish their power in Italy, that no foreigner should lord it over that lovely land? What other influence than that of the Papacy could have raised up and fostered to maturity that more modern Germanic Empire, which has scarcely ever ceased to make its return of grateful duty to the Holy See? And where, we may well enquire, would be Italy, its people, its religion, and its hope of liberty to-day, if the Roman Pontiffs, as if moved by the voice of Heaven, had not marshalled around them the chivalry of Europe, to resist and to repel the barbarism and infidelity of the Moslem invader? And later still, almost in our own day, who, of all Europe's sovereigns, alone stood erect, the champions of liberty, amid the vanquished and prostrate nations? Those holy pontiffs of imperishable memory—Pius VI. and Pius VII. No sword was drawn in their defence. No armed men were near to guard them, and yet, they held their ground. Even more, in their panoply of moral steel. like the martyrs of the early times, they fought the battle of their day. They conquered as the martyrs conquered, and with the weapons of the martyrs.

By the extraordinary reaction which followed the fever of the great French or rather European revolution, power all but absolute was everywhere established,—such are the triumphs of the sword. Liberty will not thus be won. The haughty goddess will not soil her robes by suffering herself to be dragged in 'the victor's train. The violent need not court her. She is of heavenly origin, and like the ruler of the Heavens, she abhors blood.

It need not surprise us, therefore, if the sacred cause of liberty was not advanced by the sanguinary career of the revolutionists; and if only some impediments were swept away by the battles and the victories of the formidable armies that had struggled so valiantly and so long against the most terrible of all political convulsions.

Revolutionary excess ends at length, and the necessary restraints of authority are once more recognized in the world. In due time the depositories of this authority invoke that liberty, which appeared to have fled, and for ever, from their counsels. Of her powerful aid, they would fain avail themselves. But the Pontiff Sovereign must lead the way—must trace out by his example, the path of safety, in which the nations shall be called to walk. Certain measures of reform are discussed and sanctioned in the cabinets of Europe. The Sovereign of the Church's States will be the first to undertake them. The other sovereigns offer their support and their encouragement. They even urge the necessity of the reforms he has in view. Not, indeed, that his State stood more in need than other states, of political improvement.* But, all

---

* Rome was not quite in a desparate state in the time of Gregory XVI. Let the most celebrated man of the liberal school bear witness. Few will question the testimony of Silvio Pellico. It was as follows: "The eight months I have spent at Rome, (under Gregory XVI.,) in 1845 and 1846, have abounded in delightful impressions. *It can never be sufficiently told, how well this venerable city deserves to be visited, and not in passing only.* How the good and beautiful abound in it! whilst notwithstanding, certain men write and speak about Rome with hostile prejudices, hoping thus to lessen its authority!"

Alluding to this same visit of eight months towards the close of the reign of Gregory XVI., Pellico writes: "I continue to be quite deligted with Rome both as regards men and things. In the small book *Dei Doceri*, I have shewn my inclination to avoid being absolute in my judgments, a too common error, especially with minds that dogmatize passionately. By such Rome is often unjustly judged.

Several types of social customs must be considered as moderately good; and we cannot condemn as decidedly bad anything but barbarism, irreligion, and a superabundance of knaves and fools. These odious elements are by no means over-abundant in this country; and in the midst of evils that are unavoidable everywhere, I observe great intellectual power, much goodness, cultivated minds, gracious and sincere generosity. Whoever comes to Rome will be morally well off as regards intelligence; he will be so likewise on account of the sociability of the inhabitants. The Romans are a jovial people. But even their joviality

States are alike subject to time and circumstances; and all of them must, as period succeeds period, remodel themselves—adapt themselves anew to the new wants, the new wishes, and the new habits of men. Of this the venerable Pontiff is not ignorant. Nor is courage wanting to him. He commences in good earnest, although not without hesitation and misgiving, and in part accomplishes the important task. But "*periculosæ plenum opus alexætractat, superposito cinere doloso.*" His path is beset with dangers. True liberty has more enemies than despotism itself; and these its enemies—the enemies, as well, of all social progress—will take care that it shall not yet prevail. Pope Gregory is unable to proceed. Age now lays its chilling hand upon him: and he who had laboured long and zealously and successfully in the cause of humanity; —he who more than once by his irresistible influence, had enforced the adoption of salutary reforms, even in the most despotic States;—he who,' urged by the cry of the afflicted, had stayed the arm of tyranny. and bid the mightiest Potentates desist from persecution,—the venerable Gregory,—sinks at last under the weight of his many years. His long day of toil draws rapidly to its close; and he leaves to the vigorous hands of his successor, the great—the stupendous work, that could not in his own time have been accomplished.

PROSPECT AFFORDED BY THE NEW PONTIFICATE.

And now commences that Pontificate which will be ever memorable in the world's annals. Already it reflects, even at its birth, the new glory that awaits it. The hopes and aspirations of millions crowd around its cradle. Will these hopes be disappointed? Will this glory be dimmed? So

---

is as admirably subject to good order as it is graceful, and does not impair the natural goodness of their disposition.

But perhaps, I am wrong, and it were better I should assume a frowning aspect, and behold only attempts on life, importunate beggary, useless priests and monks, and reserve my praises for those happy nations, where there are no crimes, no inequality of fortune, no misery. Impassioned men declaim, exaggerate, disfigure, lie. For my part, I am neither an optimist nor a pessimist. It is impossible to speak with certainty of the moral of a country, if we speak of it too soon. I know that here at Rome, I find amiability, science, and good sense. It seems to me that everything is much the same as in other civilized countries."

pray its enemies. But they will not be gratified. Weigh them; number them. Their influence as against that of the Pontiff Sovereign, is a nullity. Compared to the countless hosts that guard and uphold all that appertains to the honour of the great Pontificate, they are as a grain of sand. Dearer than gold, to his people, is the least privilege of the Holy Pontiff; and sacred in their sight is the most inconsiderable appendage of his temporal state. Were the hostile factions more numerous by tens of thousands than they dare pretend to be, they could not be favoured with success. Their designs would inevitably be frustrated, and their hopes blasted. An institution dear to humanity throughout so many centuries, cannot perish in our time—cannot yield to the violence of a passing hurricane. The Providence of God watches over it as well now as in the trials of former ages. The model sovereignty—the object of Heaven's care, will be sustained. It will flourish as in the days of old; and the wish and the scheme of the wicked shall be confounded. *Desiderium paceatorum peribit.*

ACCESSION OF PIUS IX.

The accession of the reigning Pontiff to the Papal Chair, was no ordinary event. Nor was it brought about in an ordinary manner. The Cardinals assembled in solemn conclave, are anxious to elect a chief Pastor and Sovereign who will not be disinclined to carry out certain changes and improvements—improvements in the civil government of the Papal States that appear to be called for as well by public opinion, as by the wants of the times. There are, indeed, some members of the sacred college who incline to conservative, although not extreme conservative principles. But the greater number, and, to the utter confusion of their calumniators, let the fact be proclaimed, have nothing more at heart, than to place at their head, a reformer Pope. The votes are chiefly divided, at first, between an eminent member of their body, whose zeal and active exertions in the cause of reform, had crowned him with popularity,—Cardinal Gizzi, and the illustrious Bishop of Imola, Count Mastai Ferretti, whose liberal tendencies were not unknown.*

The distinguished representative† of more conservative views has also a few votes. But the Cardinals have not yet been two days in conclave when more than the requisite number of suffrages elevates Cardinal Mastai to the Popedom. The new Pontiff is hailed by the representatives of the Catholic world. In the sacred assembly perfect unanimity prevails. Thus is placed in the chair of Peter an eminent member of a family celebrated for its liberality. Thus, without one dissentient voice, is raised to the Pontifical throne a Bishop characterised no less by sacerdotal zeal, and disinterested, self-sacrificing charity, than by his enthusiasm in the cause of improvement, and his anxiety to establish such reforms in the state he is called to govern as are best calculated, as well to secure its stability, as to promote the material progress, the prosperity, and the happiness of the people.‡

In the face of this event calumny stands condemned. In vain will it discourse, henceforth, on the narrowness of view, the illiberality, the incorrigible ultra-conservatism of the Roman cardinals.

The Pope elect, as if anticipating the days of trial that were destined to reveal so soon qualities in no way inferior to the heroism which encircles with imperishable fame the memory of two Pontiffs, almost his cotemporaries, assumes the name of Pius. And if the martyr fortitude of the VIth and VIIth, who bore this name, blighted and broke down the ephemeral but galling tyranny of their day, what may not be hoped for liberty, order and good government, from the truly heroic

---

* It is related that Pius IX. long before his accession to the Pontifical throne, had written a paper which might be called a programme of the necessary reforms, and sent it to Gregory XVI.

† Cardinal Lambruchini had fifteen votes. Thirty-six for Cardinal Mastai immediately preceded the acclamation of the undivided conclave. The Conclave opened 14th June, 1846. The election was concluded on the second day.

‡ On the 80th August 1846, Silvio Pellico wrote as follows: "All are agreed in saying that Pius IX. is the Pope our time required. Let us offer prayers for him. He has need of signal assistance in order to surmount so many political, religious and administrative difficulties. His is an arduous undertaking. But a Pontificate which commences so auspiciously affords the best hopes to the whole Catholic world."

courage of which the ninth Pius has already given such frequent and such noble proofs? What do we not hear every day about the weakness, the timidity, the pusilianimity of Roman Pontiffs?—and who but a Roman Pontiff would not have quailed before the enemies it has been his lot to encounter,—enemies more reckless, if possible, and scarcely less formidable than those conspirators against peace and order, who, at the end of the last century, strewed their path with ruin, and made the earth desolate?

It is difficult to understand what motive there can be for the rebellion which rages so fiercely in the States of the Church, and which has already wrested from the Sovereign Pontiff a third part of his territory. Are we to look for the cause of this unnatural strife, in the conduct of the Cardinals who surround the Papal throne, and who are the legitimate advisers of the Sovereign? Of their own free choice, as has been shewn, they raised to the Pontifical chair, one of their number, who, they were not ignorant, would not fail to introduce into the Government, every necessary measure of reform. And, besides, the Counsellors of the Ruler are not to be confounded with the Ruler himself. To the chief, then, we must look. And, may there not be in the character or policy of the Pope, good reason for the conduct of his people, —for the extraordinary efforts which some, at least, of his subjects, and not without foreign aid. have made, in order to subvert his temporal dominion?

Or, might it not be the unanimous wish of his people, let his rule be never so paternal, that he should no longer reign over them as their temporal Prince? And, to what extent, if at all, would the alleged change in the popular mind, bear out and justify the violence by which a few men are endeavoring to rob of his inheritance, the successor of St. Peter and of so many Pontiffs?

SKETCH OF THE LIFE OF PIUS IX.

Not only from what has been said, but, also, from the information you were already possessed of, you will have formed an idea of the character of Pius IX. A few traits of his early life, as well as of his Pontifical and political career, will shew more clearly still, what opinion we ought all to entertain of the man, whose office, in the estimation of three millions at least, of the most civilized portion of the human family, is of such high importance, and is necessarily calculated to sway the destinies of mankind.

Whilst the young Count Mastai was pursuing his studies at the ecclesiastical academy, the celebrated Theologian, Graziosi, moved by the charity, the gentleness, and the piety of the future Pontiff, was heard one day to exclaim, " that the Abbe Mastai had the heart of a Pope." No sooner is he elevated to the office and dignity of the christian Priesthood, than he verifies to the full, the words of his learned professor. He devotes himself to the service of the poor. The truly christian zeal of Giovanni Borgi, had founded out of his own resources alone, an hospital for destitute orphans, with a view to rescue them from blighting idleness and crime, the inseparable attendant of extreme poverty. Mastai, in his early youth had laboured in the cause of this industrial school. Now that he is a Pastor of souls, he devotes himself without reserve. The charge of this interesting establishment is conferred on him by Pope Pius VII. During five years, he ceases not to bestow his fortune, his care, and all his energy in promoting the material and spiritual prosperity of an institution to which, by means of salutary reforms, and the well directed impulse imparted to professional education, he gives a new existence; he becomes the idol of these little children to whom he is more as a father than a master. He lives with them, and knows them all by name. Nor does he lose sight of them when they are engaged in the various pursuits of life.

PIUS IX. IN AMERICA.

Abbe Mastai is now called to more arduous duties; he is appointed member of a mission to the recently erected and yet untamed republics of the new world. He embarks on the 5th October, 1823, together with Monseigneur Muzzi, the Bishop Vicar Apostolic of Chili, Peru, Mexico, and the other States that had succeeded in emancipating themselves from the yoke of Spain, and the Abbe Sallusti, Secretary of the Legation. The *Heloise*, which bears the important freight, is exposed during three months to all the perils of the ocean. And not only are the pious voyagers in danger from the winds and waves. When near the Coast of America, they are taken, notwithstanding their sacred charecter, at one time, for accomplices in the rebellion against Spain; at another they are attacked by a ship of filibusters who cannot allow to pass unmolested, the Italian flag. And now in order to reach their place of destination, Santiago, they must traverse the Pampas and the vast ranges of the Andes. It may easily be conceived how great are their exertions, and how severe the privations they are reduced to! They travel on foot, all day, and sometimes even during the night, amid the burning sands, and through the great untrodden forests of South America. They have no other comfort, than their trust in God, no other recreation than that inexhaustible cheerfulness, which is the never failing privilege of a good conscience. In the most terrible sufferings, when almost perishing from hunger and thirst, the pious travellers edify one another, by reciting verses of the psalms, and this prayer in common, whilst it sustains their minds, alleviates also their bodily fatigue. At other times they lighten their toilsome path by calling to mind the finer passages of Virgil or of Tasso; and by thus charming the imagination, they sometimes forget their sorrows. For three months the Vicar Apostolic and his companions submit, with patience truly exemplary, to the toils and privations of this perillous journey. They enter at length the territory of Chili, disguised in a manner by no means calculated, as has been well observed, to offend republican austerity.

Such devotedness to a cause, ought not to pass unrewarded. But, unlooked for difficulties arise, not the least of these is the capricious disposition of the people. The newly erected republic is jealous of its recently acquired power and privileges; and to such lengths does it carry its views of the rights of the State, that a *concordat* becomes impossible. Every point is disputed; and to this is added a mean and contemptible system of annoyance; they even grudge and deny to the legation the costs of subsistence, which they had engaged to defray. These unworthy proceedings reduce the representatives of the Sovereign Pontiff to the most humble resources. They are obliged to rely upon the alms of the charitable. A new scruple occurs to the chiefs of the State. They pretend to take the Bishop Vicar Apostolic for an adventurer, and several months are spent in idle verifications. The Bishop preserves his equanimity, and the Abbe Mastai sets an example, and is as it were, a living counsel of resignation. Wearied out with this continual war, the legation resolves to leave; and just one year after their departure from Italy, its eminent members set sail from the shores of America, without having concluded anything, or having obtained any result.

How happy were not those republics in their enjoyment of unbounded liberty! There was only wanting to them a principle of life. They are fallen, and no process known to men can galvanize them into new existence. Well would it have been for them if, at the opportune moment, "the acceptable time" that comes once to all, but may come a second time to none, they had listened to the voice of truth and reason, and had availed themselves, if only for their temporal good, of an influence which raised up the thrones and republics of Europe, and completely renewed its social state.

This mission, otherwise so fruitless, was not lost to the Reverend Count Mastai. It had been the means of developing the admirable qualities which he possessed. It had afforded him the opportunity of seeing many cities, as well as the manners and customs of many peoples. These lessons of travel were not addressed to an ordinary mind. His views were enlarged, elevated and refined by contact with so many rising or fallen civilizations, so many different peoples, and by the spectacle of nature, that admirable handmaid of the Divinity, with her varied splendors and her manifold wonders, astonishing no less in the immensity of the ocean than in the vast forests of the new world

The mind appears to grow as the sphere of material life extends. Vast horizons are adapted to great souls, and prepare them for great things. The Abbe Mastai had thus received in his youth two most salutary lessons, which are often wanting to the best tried virtues of the sacerdotal state:—the lesson of the world which Mastai had received before the time of his vocation to holy orders, and the lesson of travel, which disengages the mind from the bondage of local prejudices.— Both of these wonderful teachings he had admirably understood.

On his return from Chili, Count Mastai entered on the career of ecclesiastical preferments. Leo XII., who had been particularly struck by the penetration and good sense of which he had given proof in this difficult mission, appointed him Canon of *Sancta Maria in via lata*, and raised him to the dignity of Prelate. The Roman purple was on this occasion more than ever adorned by the solid virtue and the learning of him on whom it was conferred.

PIUS IX. DIRECTOR OF AN HOSPITAL.

The humble but important services the Count Mastai had rendered to the hospital Tata Giovanni, were not forgotten at Rome: and he who had been faithful in his charge over a few things, is now called to a more extended sphere of duty. Pope Leo XII., unwilling that such rare talents should lie buried, nominated Canon Mastai, president of the commission which governed the great hospital of *St. Michael a Ripa Grande*. This is one of the greatest institutions of charity which Rome or the world is possessed of. A whole people dwells within its vast precincts. It is at once a place of retreat for aged and infirm men, an immense professional school for poor girls, and a sort of workshop on a great scale for children that have been forsaken. The greater number learn trades. Some who give proof of higher talents, apply, at the expense of the hospital, to the study of the fine arts. This hospital is in itself a world, and the government of such an establishment requires almost the qualities of a statesman. At the time Mastai was named to this charge, the budget of the hospital stood in need of unremitting care, and the utmost capacity of a financier. Nor were these qualities wanting.

At the end of two years, all the resources of the institution were in admirable order: bankruptcy was far from its doors; the deficits in its income made up, its receipts abundant.— And far from impoverishing the hospital by giving to the apprentice workmen a share in the fruit of his labour, Mastai had shewn by this measure, that just is in admirable accordance with economy, and that the best houses are not those which make the most of the labour of their inmates, but those which encourage industry by allowing it what is just. In the space of two years, the orphans had amassed a small sum which guaranteed to them an alleviation of their misfortunes, whilst the proceeds of the hospital had doubled. Mastai thus acquired a reputation for administrative talent of the highest order.

ARCHBISHOP OF SPOLETO.

In the Consistory of 21st May, 1827, Canon Count Mastai was named Archbishop of Spoleto. This city was the birth-place of Leo XII. No other present the Holy Father could have made to his country, would have better marked his solicitude and affection.

The sojourn of Archbishop Mastai at Spoleto, will be ever memorable there. During that stormy period of five years, his presence appeared to draw down upon the people the visible protection of Heaven. Wrath was treasured in every mind. Some exclaimed against abuses, whilst others dreading reform, clung pertinaciously to the past. Civil war was raging in the people's minds, before it had yet appeared in the streets. Spoleto divided into two hostile camps, resembled one of those Italian cities of the middle age, where stood in presence, and armed from head to heel, the undying enmities of the Ghibellins and the Guelphs. The fire of civil war was smouldering within its bosom, ready on the slightest occasion, to burst into a flame. Thanks to Mastai, opportunity was wanting. Spoleto may not remember without emotion, what diplomacy his Christian zeal induced him to employ in order to appease wild passions; how delicately and perseveringly he laboured to reconcile those Italian feuds, to calm the dire spirit of revenge, to bury the sense of wrong in the oblivion of forgiveness. And on occasion of the terrible rebellion of 1831 and 1832, it was well seen during the bloody insurrection of those days, and the pitiless repression which ensued, what a man may do, with the two-fold authority, with which virtue and the estimation in which he is held, invest him. Once and only once, insurrection appeared before the walls of Spoleto. But it was when vanquished, and pursued by a whole army, it came to beg for shelter and for bread. The Archbishop, not unmindful of the Gospel, saved the lost sheep. Without a moment's delay, he went to the Austrian general and prayed him to desist, taking it upon himself to disarm the rebels, and thus, satisfy the demands of war, without having recourse to useless cruelties.

Returning to Spoleto, he harangued the insurgents, and immediately saw, laid at his feet, those arms, which the Austrian troops could only have torn from the dead bodies of the men who bore them. In disarming, he saved the rebels.

Goodness was his characteristic. How well the following trait displays it: A superior agent of the Roman police exhibited one day, triumphantly to Archbishop Mastai, a list of the principal conspirators; he had bestowed great pains in preparing it, and took much credit to himself for the success of his labours; he made no doubt that his zeal would meet with a magnificent reward. It pained the Archbishop to behold such joy manifested in his presence. As the agent was still rejoicing over his performance and good fortune, the prelate read over, with a look of anxiety and terror, the melancholy catalogue. All of a sudden a secret thought brought a smile to his lips. "You know nothing about your business;" said he, "when the wolf intends to devour the sheep, he takes care to avoid warning the shepherd;" at the same moment a flame is seen on the hearth, and the fatal catalogue disappears in smoke. This was a fault, no doubt, and the Archbishop, as is related, had to account for it to the Sovereign. It was a fault, indeed, but such only as the Saints are guilty of. Was it in expiation of this crime, that some years later the holy Archbishop was without a friend in his hour of trial? Where were, then the sheep that he had saved? The *wolf* was more merciful.

That same year, it pleased the Sovereign Pontiff Gregory XVI. to transfer Archbishop Mastai to the see of Imola. A deputation from Spoleto, in vain beseeches the Holy Father to leave the good pastor to the affection of his people. The City of Imola is less considerable, but the diocese is more populous and richer. Nomination to the Episcopal chair of Imola leads directly to the Cardinalate. It has also thrice given to the Catholic Church its chief pastor.

The people of Imola still cherish the most pleasing memories of their Bishop. The numerous institutions, which owe to him their existence, are the best monuments that bear witness to his Episcopal zeal and Christian charity. The virtue, of which the most reverend Bishop Mastai was so bright a pattern, had no sourness in it, no outward shew of austerity; nor was it forbidding and intolerant, but sweet and gentle; words of forgiveness were always on his lips, and his hand was ever open to distress. He laboured assiduously to reform, wherever reform was wanting, but, what rarely happens, without alienating affection from the reformer. It was his constant study to elevate the character of the Clergy, and he ceased not to encourage, among them, learning as well as piety. Into the Diocesan Seminary, which was always the object of his most anxious care, he introduced some new branches of study—of these were agriculture, practical as well as theoretical, and a general knowledge of the medical art. There was yet wanting to the Clergy of his Diocese, a common centre, where they could meet for mutual edification and instruction. To this purpose, he devoted his own palace, and founded there a *Biblical Academy*. The members of this academy met once a month, in order to discuss, together, some subject connected with the sacred writings. None can be ignorant, how powerfully such meetings contribute to promote the study of the scriptures, pulpit eloquence, and the great science of Theology.

Nor, in his new position, did the holy Bishop forget his first care; the orphan. An orphanage at Imola is due to his munificence. In order to obviate the dangers to which students were exposed, who, whilst they studied at the Seminary were not inmates, and enjoyed not the safeguards of its discipline, he founded an institution, called *"the convitto,"* where these poorer alumni of his Seminary were boarded, without charge.

Anxious also to provide for the comfort of the lowly poor, and to guard against all wasting of their humble means, he reformed the hospital of Imola, and set over it, the Sisters of Charity,—that incomparable order, which owes its existence to the most benevolent of men—St. Vincent de Paul.

Of his liberalities, there was no end. Solely, at his own expense, he repaired the tomb of St. Cassien, and decorated the Chapel of our Lady of Dolours, in the Church of the Servites.

MASTAI, CARDINAL.

Thus did the Servant of God unconsciously prepare for the greater ministry,—the higher destiny, that Providence had in store for him.

It may well be conceived, that such a prelate lived in the affections of his people. Accordingly, when he was raised to the high dignity of Cardinal by Pope Gregory XVI, on the 14th Dec., 1840, the greatest honors were spontaneously heaped upon him. Congratulations in prose and in verse, illuminations, fireworks, demonstrations of every kind marked the joy that everywhere prevailed. This popularity, however great, was but a prelude to that which, at a later period, it was his fortune to enjoy.

These details of the history of Pius IX are by no means foreign to our subject. The Pope, it has been said, is unfit to reign as a temporal Prince. Is this unfitness to be looked for, granting, for the sake of argument, that it exists, in the person of the reigning Pontiff? Let any one who reads the foregoing sketch of his life, reply. What high administrative talent does it not evince? what goodness? what kindly consideration for, even, the least of the people!—what love for all? Was it possible that such a man should not be an enemy to every abuse, that tended to lessen the people's happiness, or impede the march of their material prosperity? Have we not seen how anxious he was to reform, wherever reform was called for, and how successfully he laboured in every office which he held, to renew the face of things; to found new institutions, suited to the circumstances, the ideas, and the necessities of the age, or to adapt what already existed, to the wants and exigencies that had arisen?

Those qualities, and above all, this determination to reform, were not unknown to the most learned Cardinals, when as we have seen, they elected Count Mastai to the highest office in the Catholic Church, and to that temporal Sovereignty, by which it is accompanied. Reform was loudly called for, in the Roman State. The Cardinals, by choosing Mastai, decided for reform. Who then shall say, that in the sacred college, is to be found that hostility to the cause of reform—the cause of Rome,—the cause of Italy, which has been such a fruitful source of evil in our time?

THE REAL ENEMIES OF REFORM UNMASKED.

Who then, are the real enemies of reform? What if it were those very men, who so loudly call for change, and claim to be the only reformers of the age? We have just read the history of the Pope. Let us also read theirs and ask it to make reply.

The men here alluded to, are the members of the ultra liberal, socialist, or red republican party. Of this party mention has already been made at the commencement of this discourse. It may not be superfluous to lay before you some further details of their well known history—details that are admirably calculated to throw light on their character and designs.

These socialists form a secret society, the members of which are bound together by the most fearful oaths. This society has ramifications all over Europe. One day, we read of some great political movement, they have originated at Rome. Their agents are assembled there, from all quarters of the civilized world—not a very difficult matter in a city to which strangers resort every year in thousands. These socialists write, talk, agitate—a few citizens speedily fall into their toils; and lo! it is the Roman people, who are roused at length to a sense of their degradation. Such a clamour for change, for progress, for lay government, arises, that half the world must needs believe that the Romans are thoroughly tired of their Priest Ruler, and have unanimously resolved to bear with him no longer. At another time, we hear of great popular commotions at Turin, to which the secret societies have resorted in great numbers. With these commotions, of course, the good socialists have nothing to do. It is the people—the emancipated people rejoicing over their new found liberty, and encouraging their young king, whom experience has not yet taught its salutary lessons, to make war upon the Pope, seize upon his territory, usurp all his temporal rights, cast his Religion, root and branch, out of the Sardinian States, in the first place, and in due course of time, out of every province of Italy.

In these associations which, if we may believe them, aim at nothing less than the regeneration of society, we are entitled to look for high principles of government, superior statesmanship—political views, at least in harmony with, if not in advance of the spirit of the age. What their principles are, will best be learned from the mode of government, pursued among themselves. An important, perhaps the principal, section of the socialist body—"young Italy," which owns for its chief, the lawyer Mazzini, enjoins its members to carry firearms and a poniard. Does any one refuse obedience to the head of the society, or divulge his secrets, he is mercilessly put to death. A secret tribunal condemns the victims, and appoints the executioners. The member who should refuse to execute the decrees of the society, would be punished with death, as a violator of his oath. If a victim, marked out for vengeance, escapes, he will be everywhere pursued, and *sacrificed by an invisible hand, even although he should take refuge in the bosom of his mother, or in the sanctuary of God.* Each secret tribunal is competent not only to judge the members of the association, but, also, to cause to be put to death, all whom it shall have condemned. Numerous facts attest, that these statutes are not an empty threat. "Young Europe" was founded on the 15th April, 1834. It was composed of

"Young Italy," "Young Germany," "Young Poland," and, somewhat later, of "Young Switzerland," also. Two of its first founders were massacred that same year, by order of the society. These were Nast and Stromayer, the former for unfaithfulness in the transaction of their financial affairs; the latter, for indiscretion. In 1835, a student, named Lessing, was likewise assassinated at Munich. More recently, four Italian refugees, who were quite willing to fight against the Italian Princes, would not accept the sanguinary doctrines of the Mazzinian sect, and openly delared that they would not. The secret tribunal assembled at Marseilles, under the presidence of lawyer Mazzini, condemned two of the four to the lash and the galleys, and the two others to death. A copy of this judgment was seized, and still exists. As the condemned parties were domiciled at Rhodez, to the sentence was added the following clause: "The President of Rhodez will make choice of four members who shall execute the present sentence, and who shall be under strict orders to do so, within twenty days. He who should refuse, would incur death, *ipso facto*." A few days afterwards, one of those who had been condemned, M. Emiliani, passing along the streets of Rhodez, was attacked by six of his fellow-countrymen, who struck him several times with a poniard, and made their escape. The assassins were arrested, and condemned, by a French Jury, to five years' imprisonment. M. Emiliani, still suffering from his wounds, was leaving the Court of Assizes, with his wife, when both he and the lady were stabbed to death, by a wretch named Gaviati. This murderer was arrested, although not without difficulty. He was tried, condemned, and made to suffer the punishment due to his crime. Meanwhile, the advocate Mazzini returned to Switzerland, as the satiated tiger, after a scene of carnage, returns to his den, and coolly resumed his work of social destruction. (Wars and Revolutions of Italy, in 1848 and 1849, by Count Edward Lubienski and M. Rhorbacher.)

In the middle age, there was in the mountains of Lebanon, a Mahommedan sect of assassins, under the orders of a chief called, the Old Man of the Mountain. In these our times, even, the grossly pagan tribes of India have had their sects of Thugs. But, the mind is lost in horror and amazement, when obliged to contemplate an association of political murderers in the very centre of European civilization, and amid the noon-day light of the nineteenth century.

But, in order to rule they must be constituted rulers. For this end, the weapons of flattery and misrepresentation, together with every species of falsehood, are at their command. These weapons they use skilfully and without scruple. To all classes of society they hold out the most fallacious hopes.— Thus did the socialist chief, in a document brought to Turin in Nov'r, 1846, set torth the principles by which his followers must be guided :—

"In great countries by the people only can the work of regeneration be carried out. In yours (he is addressing the Italians) by the princes. They must absolutely be gained to our side. And, they can easily be won. The Pope will pursue the cause of reform by principle, and from necessity. The king of Piedmont from the hope of wearing the crown of Italy; the Grand Duke of Tuscany by inclination no less than imitation ; the king of Naples by force; and the lesser princes will have other things to think of than reform. Avail yourselves of the least concession, in order to gather together the masses, were it only to express your gratitude. Festivals, songs, public meetings, numerous relations, established between men of different shades of opinion, are calculated to bring out ideas, and to impart to the people the knowledge of their strength, and render them exacting. The concurrence of the great is necessary, indispensable, in order to originate notions of reform, in a feudal country. If you have only the people with you, mistrust will arise at the very outset, and they will be crushed. If they be under the guidance of men of high rank these persons will be as a passport to the people. Italy is still what France was before the revolution. It must, therefore, have its Mirabeau, its Lafayette, and so many others. A great Lord may be won to the cause by material interests. He may also be gained by vanity. Let him play the foremost part so long as he chooses to remain with you. There are few who would persevere with you to the end. It is essential that the final object of the great revolution be concealed from them.— Let them never see more than the first step. In Italy, the clergy is rich in property and the faith of the people. They must be dealt with as regards these two interests, and, as far as possible, their influence must be turned to account. If you could in each capital create a Savonarola, we should advance with giant steps. The clergy are not averse to liberal institutions. Endeavour, therefore, to associate them in this first work, which must be considered as necessarily the porch of the temple of equality. Without them the entrance,—the sanctuary, itself, remains closed. Do not attack either the possessions or the orthodoxy of the clergy. Promise them liberty and they will, at once, join your ranks. It is now nearly two thousand years since a great philosopher, Christ, preached fraternity, which the world is still in quest of. The clergy hold only one-half of the socialist doctrine. Like us, they profess fraternity, which they call charity. But their hierarchy and its habits make of them a pillar of authority, that is, of despotism. We must take what is good in their doctrine, and leave aside what is evil. Manage to make equality prevail in the church, and everything will prosper. Clerical power is personified in the Jesuits. The odium attaching to this name is already a power for the socialists;—make use of it."*

Such are the doctrines of the secret societies of Italy, as set forth by their chief, two years, only, before the accession to the Popedom of Pius IX. They had already their ramifications all over the Peninsula, seeking everywhere to extinguish religion, prosperity, and every existing right. Mazzini says distinctly, in the two first articles of the anti-social society, 1st, That the society is instituted in order to bring about the indispensable destruction of all the governments of the Peninsula, and to erect into one state the whole of Italy, with a republican government. 2nd, That on account of the evils arising from absolute government, *and those still greater evils which flow from constitutional monarchy*, we must labor with united

---

* Guerres et revolution d'Italie; par le Comte Edward Lubienski, p.p. 44 and 47.
Balleydier Hist: de la Revolution de Rome. Introd; &c., &c.

efforts to constitute a republic, one and undivided."—(Balleydier.) Thus, no existing form of government will be allowed to remain. What, then, will be the nature of the Mazzinian republic? Another socialist chief, Ricciardi, will inform us. "In order to govern the people," says he, "there can be no question of a popular assembly, which is fluctuating, undecided, and slow in its deliberations. But there must be *a hand of Iron*, which alone is capable of ruling a people hitherto accustomed to divergencies of opinion, to discord, and what is still worse, *a people corrupt, enervated, degraded by slavery.*" —(Balleydier.) What an exchange! The mild sway of the reforming Pope, the gentle rule of the Grand Dukes, must give place, not to a constitutional monarchy, nor yet to a rational republic, but to a *hand of Iron!* Alas for Italy! if ever it should fall into the grasp of this government of the Iron hand! It may not be out of place now to enquire as to the practice of the men who are so anxious to renew the face of society. We have seen that within their own body they have no hesitation in acting as they teach. They hold the doctrine, as false as it is rigid, that the least offence against established laws ought to be punished, even as are the greatest crimes,—with death. Mismanagement of their funds, want of prudence or of care in keeping their counsel, the leaving of their society for better courses, are crimes, which, the history of the time assures us, can only be expiated in the blood of the perpetrators. Of this terrible practice,—this ruling with a " hand of iron," in their own community, numerous instances might be adduced. But the fearful examples already noticed, may well suffice.

In the world, they aspire to remodel, they find occasional victims. Does a prince fall beneath their "hand of iron," it is no doubt to encourage other princes, to place himself and his people under their yoke, and so learn by experience how preferable is their peculiar form of government, as well to the best constitutional monarchy, as to the most admirably organized republic. How many sacrifices have they not offered in these our days, to the Moloch of their idolatry! In vain will they plead that it is the blood of tyrants and oppressors only, that they have sought. Of what tyrrany was the young Duke of Parma guilty?—what steps in the way of oppression, was it possible that so youthful a sovereign should have taken, when without a moment's warning he was consigned by these cowardly assassins to an untimely grave? What had the late King of Naples done, to incur their wrath? He was not so imbecil, as to be *led by vanity* to second their plans, and for this crime of omission, perhaps, his life was aimed at. He who had spared so many lives, the lives of traitors and conspirators who had compassed the death of so many of his people and brave soldiers, was doomed to lose his own life. But an unseen hand averts the cowardly blow, and as if in defiance of the ever-living conspiracy against all states, a monarch, dear to his people, is permitted to reign until the natural term of his career on earth.

The heir of the house of Hapsburg, young and chivalrous though he was, could not hope to escape their mean attempts. The *hand of iron* fain would smite him, too. But the generous son of a generous land is near, and the dagger of the coward falls powerless. The great Emperor of the French, in like manner, impervious to vanity, as yet, must be removed from the political arena. With what care are not the instruments of destruction prepared! All the talent of the secret government, one would say, is employed to compass the death of one man. But, whilst many perish by his side, he remains unhurt, amid the ruin and the blood that surrounded him. In what cause was this blow struck? In the cause of the people? But Louis Napoleon Bonaparte was the people's choice. In the cause of the fallen constitutional monarchy? But that monarchy was gone. And can it, for a moment, be supposed, that they who were the enemies alike of monarchy and constitutions, would have endeavoured to recall it into being! In what interest, then, were the deadly grenades thrown? In no other, surely, than that of anarchy, confusion, ruin. From the midst of this political chaos, it was hoped, would arise the *Red Republic*; and its authors, mounting the whirlwind they had evoked, would ride triumphant, and with "iron hand," direct the storm.

That such was their aim, their conduct towards the reforming Pope, but too well shews. And, as no better illustration can be found of the principles of the Red Republic, than the part its supporters bore, in the Roman revolution of 1848, it may not be uninstructive to revert to that event. The chief actors in the melancholy scenes of that time, are the very men who "play such fantastic tricks before High Heaven" to-day, disturbing all Italy, and rendering abortive, every plan for the establishment of constitutional government.

CONCILIATORY CHARACTER OF PIUS IX.—THE AMNESTY, PUBLIC REJOICINGS.

The first thoughts of Pius IX, on his accession to the Papal throne, are thoughts of mercy. From inclination, morh than policy, but, not without a view to conciliate the discontented portion of nis people, he resolves to recal to their country, all political offenders. A congregation of Cardinals is appointed to investigate this important matter. The Pope convenes them at the Quirinal. Each of them, when asked what he thought, appeared to share the opinion of his Holiness, admired his benevolence, praised his kindness. When the votes were taken, black balls only were found in the urn. This unexpected difficulty meets with a prompt solution. The Pope takes off his white *calotte*, (a small skull cap,) and placing it on the black balls, observes that "they are now all white!" By this fine trait of wit and feeling, the amnesty became law. By this amnesty, all criminal proceedings, on account of political offences, were at once suppressed. Persons accused of such offences, as well, as all who were already condemned, were liberated from prison, or restored to their country, on the sole condition, that they should henceforth fulfil the duties of good and faithful subjects. Fifteen hundred exiles returned to their families, who had long since lost all hopes of seeing them again. The cases of a small number of offenders only were reserved. To them even, hope was not forbidden.

The preamble of the decree was all in the Pope's own handwriting. The following quotations from it will shew what a noble address it was,—how worthy the sovereign, and the Pontiff!

"At the time when the public joy occasioned by our accession to the office of Sovereign Pontiff, caused us to experience in our inmost soul, the most lively emotion, we could not avoid entertaining a feeling of sorrow when we remembered that a great number of families amongst our people, could not take part in the general rejoicing, deprived, as they were, of domestic happiness. * * * On the other hand, we cast a look of compassion on the numerous and inexperienced youth, which, although carried away by deceitful flatterers, in the midst of political troubles, appeared to us guilty rather of allowing itself to be led astray, than of deceiving others. On this account, it was, that from that moment, we cherished the thought of extending a friendly hand, and offering peace to such of these dear, but misguided children, as should come to us, and give proof of their sincere repentance."

These generous words were not lost upon the people. They were fully appreciated, no less than the great act of grace, by which they were accompanied.

The evening was far advanced, when the decree was posted up. It is, nevertheless, observed amid the increasing darkness. No sooner is the word *amnesty* read, than a cry of joy—of triumph—of enthusiasm is heard. People hasten from their houses,—the passers-by stop in crowds, to read by torch light the cabalistic words. The citizens assemble in masses.— There is but one feeling: they embrace, and even weep for joy. Deeply moved, intoxicated with delight, their gratitude must find expression, and the cry is heard: "To the Quirinal!" Arrived at Mouate Cavallo, with one acclaim, they hail the Pontiff: "Long live Pius IX.! Long live our holy Father!" And this heartfelt acclamation redoubles, when the noble figure of the Pontiff is seen advancing amid the blaze of innumerable torches, lighted up with that sublime joy, which springs from consciousness of noble deeds. Twice over, the immense space in front of the Quirinal Palace is filled with an ever renewing throng;—twice over, the Holy Father imparts his benediction to the devout and grateful people. These crowds are succeeded by the more distant population, now moving forward in dense masses, rending the air with their joyous acclamations, and hastening to express their gratitude to the Holy Father—the Father of his people. But, it was late; and Pius IX., worn out—overwhelmed by his emotions, had withdrawn to his oratory, and was pouring into the bosom of his God, the overflowing of a heart inundated with happiness. Meanwhile, without the palace were waiting with respectful anxiety, ten thousand men. But, let Count Rossi speak. At that time Ambassador from France to the Papal Court, he was the witness and the historian of this great scene:

"Suddenly the acclamations are redoubled. I had not yet understood on what account, when some one called my attention to the light, which was shining through the window blinds at the farthest end of the Pontifical Palace. The people had observed that the Holy Father was traversing the apartment, in order to reach the balcony. It was speedily thrown open, and the Sovereign Pontiff, in a white robe and scarlet mantle, made his appearance, surrounded by torches. If your Excellency (M. Guizot—at that time—minister of the French king, Louis Philippe) will only figure to yourself a magnificent place, a summer night, the sky of Rome, an immense people moved with gratitude, weeping for joy and receiving with love and reverence, the benediction of their Pastor and their Prince, you will not be astonished, if I add, that we have shared the general emotion, and have placed this spectacle, above every thing that Rome had as yet offered to our contemplation. Just as I had foreseen, as soon as the window was closed, the crowd withdrew peacefully and in perfect silence. You would have called them a people of mutes; they were satisfied."

Another ovation awaited the Pontiff next day, on his return f... the church of the Lazarists whither he had gone to celebrate the feast of St. Vincent de Paul. The corso was carpeted with cloths richly decorated with the Papal colors, hung with silk, with velvet, and strewn with flowers. A crowd of young men in the place Colonna hastened to unyoke the horses of the Pope's carriage. And it was no slight shock to the modesty of the Holy personage, to see men and Christians drawing his chariot, in something like the style of a Pagan triumph. But it would have been in vain to endeavor to stay the full tide of popular feeling. Its source, besides, was pure and unexceptionable.

"The amnesty was not everything," wrote M. Rossi; "but it was an important step. The new furrow has been opened, and the Holy Father will assuredly continue it, notwithstanding the obstacles that will not fail to be thrown in his way."

These difficulties were indeed formidable. The influence of the extreme conservative party, the unscrupulous proceedings of the socialists, must be alike contended with. Meanwhile, the demands of the time are urgent. Concessions are necessary. The condition of the people must be improved, while anarchy has to be carefully guarded against. Revolution must be discouraged by wise reforms, and a new and self-sustaining political system established. To this end, there must be created in the Pontifical States a sound public opinion, which will render them proof against the vicissitudes incident to newly-emancipated populations, and will at the same time secure the existence of the temporal sovereignty of the Holy See, and enable it to keep its ground without the aid of foreign arms. Such were the objects the enlightened and liberal Pontiff had in view. The state of Italy, the peculiar position of the Pontifical states, the character of modern civilization, the spirit of the age,—all conspired to produce new wants, and, at the same time, made it a matter of the greatest difficulty to meet them. "This difficulty," observes Balmes, "it was impossible to surmount by chaunting patriotic hymns, any more than by having recourse to Austrian bayonettes."

By none was this better understood than Pius IX. It is related that long before his accession, he had prepared and sent to Gregory XVI., a programme of the necessary measures of reform. Be this as it may, he was no sooner Pope than he commenced the salutary work with no ordinary vigor and resolution. At the commencement of his reign, no general measure, with the exception of the amnesty, was practicable. But by all that characterizes a wise, and just, and humane, and liberal government, was this early period distinguished. The punishment of imprisonment for petty debts is in the estimation of the Pontiff as unjust as It is cruel and odious, answering no better purpose, for the most part, than the gratification of private spite; and by a generous contribution from his own funds, he throws open the prisons of the capitol. Anxious to encourage virtue, as well as to relieve indigence, he distributes twelve thousand Roman ecus, in the form of dowries, among the young women of poor families, whose poverty renders an honourable settlement difficult, and promotes collections in favour of such of the amnestied parties as are in need. But for his more important financial reforms, must the State be ever grateful. The revenue was alarmingly deficient. Without a great change ruin is inevitable. He first proposes that his faithful clergy should make a sacrifice, and, let the revilers of the Priesthood hear it, every convent engages to pay ten *scudi*, yearly, and each parish priest a *scudo*, during three consecutive years. He himself sets the example of the most rigid economy, as well by reducing the scale of his own establishment, as by retrenching those rich sinecures, which were, in a manner, engrafted on the temporalities of the Papacy. What is, if possible, still more admirable, he shews the most enlightened sympathy for all the sciences, which contribute to the material and intellectual well-being of the populations, such as physiology, natural history, political economy, and mathematics. Nor was he unwilling that his people should avail themselves of the knowledge of foreigners. He even intimated his intention to re-establish the celebrated scientific academy, *Di Lincei*. By such isolated acts as these, only, was it possible for him, as yet to evince the elevated and liberal tendencies of his mind in which were blended boldness with moderation, views of reform with all that became his position, and was adapted to the wants of the country and the age.

CARDINAL GIZZI, MINISTER—FURTHER REFORMS—THE PRESS.

It is not the least considerable merit of constitutional monarchies, that they secure to a country the services of the most popular statesmen. Pius IX., although not yet, in the strict sense of the term, a constitutional monarch, was resolved that his people should enjoy all the benefits of a free and liberal government. Acting on this principle, he called to his counsels a member of the sacred college, whom real liberality had rendered popular. When Legate of Forli, Cardinal Gizzi had opposed the establishing of an arbitrary court, and thus won for himself the sympathies of all rational reformers. He was looked upon as a pattern of loyalty, of sincerity, of patriotism. Nor was he wanting in any other quality of the statesman. Of a patient and enquiring mind, he was incapable of coming hastily to a determination. But, when once resolved, he could not easily be moved from his purpose. The only fault of such a ministry, if fault it could be called, was, that it promised more than it was in a position to accomplish. Placed between two parties, each of them extreme in its views, it was not supported by a sufficiently numerous and powerful body of judicious and moderate reformers. Some writers lay it to the charge of Pius IX., that he did not commence by forming such a body. This does not appear reasonable. The materials were wanting. The old conservatives were confirmed in their principles, by the radical faction, which sought the immediate destruction of every existing right; and these last, by opposing and preventing the formation of a reform party, which, like Gizzi and Pius the Ninth, would have been an impersonation of clemency and justice, became as a drag on the great engine of the State, actually supporting the retrograde policy of an aristocracy, which naturally dreaded, and in such a state of parties, had too much reason to dread change, whilst, at the same time, they impeded the march of safe and salutary reform, and even rendered impossible any great measure of improvement.

Meanwhile, the Pope, surrounded by so many difficulties, is not discouraged. No doubt, he must have experienced—and the history of the time bears witness, that he often did experience—that interior and secret anguish which, in a well regulated mind, dare not find expression, and is no sooner felt than it is contended with, and overcome. Tranquil and serene, he proceeds with energy and perseverance.

In no city is the education of the people so abundantly provided for, as in Rome. Pius IX., nevertheless, discovers that still greater facilities for instruction may yet be called into existence. He establishes in the city a central school for the education of the youth of the operative classes. It is a school of arts and manufactures, as well as a military institution, in which the pupils are qualified to be master tradesmen, or subordinate officers in the army. Under the ministry of Cardinal Gizzi, many useful schemes received the approbation and the signature of the Pontiff. Numerous commissions also were appointed—commissions for the study of railway communication in the Pontifical States—for the reformation of criminal and civil procedure—for the amelioration of the municipal system, and the repression of vagrancy.

There was scarcely as yet a periodical press at Rome. The ministry required time, for the preparation of a law, which should establish it, and regulate the degree of liberty it should enjoy. Meanwhile, the Pope in anticipation of the law, and the labours of his ministry, authorized the founding of a few journals. The "Contemporaneo" was first established; next came the "Bilancia," the "Italico," the "Alba." These newspapers fulfilled at first the expectations of the nobleminded Pontiff. They spoke only of improvement. They advocated only reform. They had no argument, as yet, for subversion. Their enthusiasm and their *vivats* were all for the reforming Pope. They had not yet discovered the excellence of the socialist Utopia.

The legislation of Christian Rome has always been as liberal towards the Israelite people, as the circumstances of the times and the prejudices of society would permit. In regard to this people, the State of the Church has invariably been in advance of all other states. Whilst all over Christendom, the Jews were treated as a proscribed and accursed race, at Rome the arms of Christian charity were ever open to receive them. The policy of the Pontiffs, superior to mere worldly wisdom, never failed to afford them shelter and hospitality. If certain restrictions were imposed,—for instance, that they should dwell in a certain part of the city,—is it fair, is it liberal, to cite this circumstance as a proof of Papal illiberality? If the Popes gave them a dwelling place in Rome, it was necessary, also, that they should protect them; and how could this be more effectually done, than by assigning to them a portion of the city, and imposing such regulations as were calculated to lessen the chances of quarrels between them and the rest of the citizens? Who but a Pope, even in this age of the world, could have regulated as Pius IX. has done, that the Jews should have the privilege, like the other citizens, of establishing their habitations, wherever they had a mind to dwell, that they should be governed by the same laws, and treated in every way as the rest of the people? Who but Pius IX. could have given to the Jews, without a murmur on the part of his Christian subjects, an equal share in his liberal donations? It adds not a little to the praise of his generosity that he also liberated them from the custom, which time had consecrated, of coming formally, every year, to pay tribute at the Capitol.

This labour of Christian love could not fail to be appreciated. Modern Jewry actually beheld, in the Holy Pontiff, the looked for Messiah. The old Rabbins, more considerate, affirmed only that the Pope was a great Prophet. The chief of the synagogue, Moses Kassan, composed, in honour of Pius IX., a canticle, distinguished by poetic inspiration, in which he blessed the Pope, for having gathered together in the same barque, all the children whom God had confided to him,—for having snatched from the contempt of nations, and gathered under his wing, a persecuted people.

PIUS IX. AND THE SULTAN.

It will be remembered that Christian powers had not yet espoused the cause of the falling Empire of Mahomet; that for great political ends, the Cross had not yet been seen in the same field of strife, in union with the Crescent; when on the

20th of February, 1847, the portals of the Quirinal were thrown open to the Ambassador of the Sublime Porte. To the Jews, the Rome of Pius IX. was as a new Jerusalem. Islamism from its tottering throne at Constantinople, looked towards it, with rapture and with hope.

One object of the Embassy was, to come to an understanding with the Pope, as to placing the Christians of the Levant under his Pontifical protection. This guardianship the Government of the Sultan would have infinitely preferred to the armed intervention of the great Powers. Whatever may have been the secret purpose of the Embassy, it was something quite extraordinary, to behold Chekif Effendi at the Quirinal. No wonder if all Europe was in ecstacy. The presentation was very solemn. The Ambassador saluting the Pope in oriental style, addressed to him a magnificent oration, richly interspersed with metaphors, the Diamonds and the Pearls of his country's eloquence. The Sublime Porte was compared to the Queen of Sheba, and Pius IX. to King Solomon. Whatever may have been the style, the sentiments expressed in his speech were appropriate and affecting. Pius IX. replied by assuring him that he was anxious to cultivate friendly relations with the Sultan, his master. Three days later, Chekif Effendi took his departure from Rome, carrying with him on his breast, as a *nishun*, (decoration,) the portrait of the Holy Father.

In consequence of the embassy, which was more than mere show, or an interchange of friendly sentiments, Pius IX. lost no time in re-establishing the Latin Patriarchate of Jerusalem. This was nothing less than a revolution in the traditions of European diplomacy in the Levant. The Latin Patriarch, in compliance with the request of the Porte, was bound to reside in the city of Jerusalem. In this confidential position, he was the natural protector of the Catholics of the Eastern world. He was, if it may be so expressed, a consul, appointed by the Holy See, to defend the interests of Religion,—interests as important, surely, as those of trade. The first Patriarch, named by the Pope, was Monsignor Valergo, who had formerly been a missionary in Persia.

PIUS IX. AND DANIEL O'CONNELL.

(*The most Eloquent of Italian Preachers, Father Ventura.*)

The greatest advocate of Liberty modern times have produced,—that illustrious Irishman Daniel O'Connell,—attracted by the magnetic power of kindred feeling, resolves to visit Rome. Not only is he anxious, whilst kneeling reverently at the shrine of the apostles, to participate before the close of his earthly career in those abundant benedictions which have never ceased to be poured forth, in that sacred spot; but he desires also, with a fervor which can find place only in the nobly moulded soul, whose love of liberty, and whose patriotism are unfeigned and pure, to hold communing with one who was, no less than himself, a friend of liberty, and whose exalted ation, and whose high duties towards mankind at large, hindered him not from labouring, as did Ireland's patriot, to liberate his country, not, indeed, from such cruel bondage as that under which the land of O'Connell had for so many ages groaned, but from the no less dangerous tyranny of abuses, which, like weeds that grow most luxuriantly in the richest soils, must needs be frequently rooted out.

But the last hope of the Patriot was doomed to disappointment. Scarcely had he set foot on the shores of Italy, when the strength of his once herculean frame declining rapidly, forbad him to proceed. Genoa received his parting breath, and Rome will gather up as a relic of incomparable price, that heart which, cold and inanimate though it be, is eloquent in death, and grandly emblematic, as it is borne by friendly hands to commingle with the consecrated dust of Heroes, Patriots, Saints and Martyrs, of all that he had been to whom it was the centre of material life, and to whose generous impulses it had so long and so faithfully beat responsive.

That son of "the Liberator" who bore his name, together with the Reverend Doctor Miley, who had so kindly ministered to him in his last hours, now hasten to Rome, and seek the presence of the Holy Father. "The halls and ante-chambers of the Quirinal "are filled with groups of personages in every style of costume, from the glittering uniform to the cowl, and all before them, in the order for reception." The name of O'Connell—magic word!—brought them, notwithstanding, at once into the presence of his Holiness. "Since that happiness, I had so longed for," said the Pontiff, "was not reserved for me, to behold and embrace the hero of Christianity, let me at least have the consolation to embrace his son." He then, writes Dr. Miley, drew the son of O'Connell to his bosom, and embraced him, not unmoved, with the tenderness of a father and a friend. Then, with an emotion which stirred our hearts within us, this great Father of the Faithful poured out his benign and loving soul in words of comfort, which proved that it was not new to him to pour the balm of Heaven into broken and wounded hearts. "His death," the Pontiff said, "was blessed. I have read the letter in which his last moments were described, with the greatest consolation." The Pope then proceeded to eulogize the Liberator, as the great champion of Religion and the Church, as the Father of his people, and the glory of the whole Christian world. "How else" observed Monsignor Cullen, now the eminent Archbishop of Dublin, who was present, "could the Pope have spoken of him, than he has done, even if he had been the bosom friend of the Liberator, as well as the ardent admirer of his career."

It would be an omission, if we failed to call to mind in what terms the venerable Pontiff, on this memorable occasion, referred to Ireland. The thought of O'Connell was one with that of Ireland. In death, even, they could not be parted. The living image of grief and bereavement still before him, the Holy Father cannot refrain from giving expression to his paternal sympathy. "And," writes Dr. Miley, "while he spoke of the sufferings of the Irish, of their fidelity, of his solicitude and his hopes regarding them, it was beautiful and impressive beyond my power to describe, to observe that countenance, which, like a mirror, reflects the charity, the compassionate care, the fortitude, with a hundred other sentiments Divine, which are never dormant within his breast."

Pius IX, anxious that nothing should be wanting that was calculated to honor the memory of O'Connell, gave orders himself for the celebration of the funeral obsequies, and intimated his will and command that they should be celebrated in his name. "The achievements, also, of his wonderful existence, I wish to be celebrated, and made known to the world—not that this is necessary, because," (said the Pontiff with a sublime look and gesture) "his grand career was ever in the face of Heaven—he ever stood up for legality—he had nothing to hide; and, it was this, with his unshaken fidelity and reverence for religion, that secured his triumphs."

It would be unjust towards the people of Rome to omit saying, that they vied with the chief Pastor, and the Magnates of their country and of Europe, in doing honor to the memory of O'Connell. "From the Campus Martius, and the Roman Forum,—from both sides of the Tiber,—and from all the seven hills, and their interjacent valleys, this people, who grow up from infancy, with the trophies of thirty centuries of greatness round them on every hand, assembled with enthusiasm to supplicate for the eternal happiness of Ireland's liberator, and to exult in the wonders he had achieved, as if he had been their own." (Dr. Miley).

But the greatest homage of all, was the incomparable oration delivered in his praise, by the Bossuet of Italy, the friend and fellow-student of Pius IX.,—the most illustrious preacher, Father Ventura. A passage or two may convey some idea of a panegyric, which was all so eloquent,—which was listened to with rapture by the vast congregation that had gathered round the cenotaph of the immortal Patriot.

"It is, then, because these two loves,—the love of religion, and the love of liberty,—common to all good Princes, to all great minds, to all truly learned men, to all elevated souls, to all generous hearts, might be said to be personified in Daniel O'Connell,—because in him they manifested themselves in all the perfection of their nature,—in all the energy of their deeply felt conviction,—in all the potency of their strength,—in all the splendour of their magnificence, and in all the glory of their triumph; it is because of all this, that this singular man, who was born, and has lived at such a distance from Rome, is now admired,—is now wept for by you, as if he had been born in the midst of you. Hence it is that this great character, this sublime nature, has awakened all your sympathies."

In alluding to the lessons O'Connell derived from history, the orator spoke in the following terms, of the darkest epoch in the annals of France: "He saw with his own eyes monarchy compelled to degrade itself, and to inflict its death-wound with its own hand; he saw the throne that base courtiers had dragged through the mire, defiled by the grip of parricidal hands, and buried, fathoms deep, beneath a sea of blood; he saw the best of kings expire upon a scaffold, the victim, not less of other men's crimes than of his own weakness; he saw that vice was hated, as if it were virtue, wickedness uplifted, as if it were morality,—atheism proclaimed aloud, as if it were religion; that the "Goddess of reason" (or rather a vile strumpet) was recognized as the only Deity, and honored with hecatombs, of human victims; the people decimated and oppressed by vile tyrants, in the name of the people; whilst beneath the shade of the tree of liberty was instituted universal slavery; and that the most christian, as well as the most civilized of all nations, had fallen down to the lowest limits of impiety and barbarism.

"Now, God having so disposed that the young O'Connell should be witness of these events,—the most celebrated and the most instructive to be found in the annals of history,—they served to inspire him with the greatest horror for tumults and rebellion; they persuaded him that there is nothing more insane, and, at the same time, more pernicious than to proclaim the rights of man, in trampling upon those of Heaven,—in establishing liberty on the ruins of religion,—in making laws, under the dictation of passion, or through the inspiration of sacrilege,—and, finally, they convinced him, that *to regenerate* a people, religion is omnipotent—philosophy of little or no avail."

This celebrated oration was not only a tribute offered in the temple of the most High, to liberty and O'Connell, —it was at the same time, the noblest homage to religion.

"What more moving spectacle, than to see the greatest man in the united kingdom,—to see him, who was the object of Ireland's devotion, of England's fear, and of the world's admiration, kneeling with the people, before the altar, practising the piety of the people, with that humble simplicity, that recollection, that devoutness, and that modesty, which supercilious science, and stolid pride abandon, as things fit only to be followed, by those whom they disdain, as the people?"

In alluding to the insolent abuse, poured out upon O'Connell, by an intolerant, upstart, ignorant, and may we now hope, utterly defunct Toryism, which assigned to him the title of "king of the beggars." The Orator admirably says: "Poor, miserable, and most pitiful fatuity, which, while intending to mock, actually did him honor. For, what Sovereignty is more beautiful, than that, whose tribute is not wrung from unwilling fear, but that is a voluntary, love-inspired offering? What Sovereignty is more glorious, than that, whose sword is the pen, and whose only artillery, the tongue; whose only courtiers are the poor, and, its sole body guard, the affections of the people? What Sovereignty more beneficent than that, which, far from causing tears to flow, dries them; which, far from shedding blood; stanches it, which, far from immolating life, preserves it; which, far from pressing down upon the people, elevates them; which, far from forging chains, breaks them; and, which always maintains order, harmony, and peace, without ever inflicting the slightest aggression on liberty? Where is the monarch, who would not esteem himself happy, in reigning thus? Of such a Sovereignty, we may with truth say that, which was said of Solomon's, that none can equal its grandeur, its glory, and its magnificence."

All in doing homage to O'Connell, the learned orator, gives the most admirable lessons to his fellow countrymen.

Alluding to the ultra-radical faction, which was already causing so much alarm at Rome to the cause of Liberty and Reform, Father Ventura spoke these incomparable words: "But these degenerate citizens, if citizens they can be called, who meditate the ruin of their country, are very few. The people, however, the true, real, Roman people, by their spirit of order, of obedience, and of love for their Prince, have become the admiration of Europe and the world. They regard such ideas and principles with horror, a horror which compels these occult fabricators of rebellion to cover, as with a mask, themselves and their doctrines of disorder and of blood. The exquisite good sense of the Romans prevents them from being captivated by the snares, or deluded by the hypocrisy of such persons. Their good sense leads the Romans to identify liberty with order, and never to regard as separated and adverse propositions, that which is for their own good, and that which is consistent with their fealty and obedience to their sovereign. Rome has conjoined with the most scrupulous legality the enthusiasm of love. It seeks through a loving agitation, as Ireland sought by a legal agitation, the reform of abuses, which time and passions, as they have ever done with all things, have engrafted upon, and then altered the nature of the ancient constitution of the States of the Church,—that being a constitution which rendered perfectly reconcilable with each other order and liberty. And, since it is impossible that the language of a people who love their sovereign should not be understood by a sovereign who is all love for his people; since it is impossible that hearts moved by a mutual affection should not perfectly understand each other, then, we may believe that thou, O! Rome, dost prepare for thyself the noblest boast that nation ever yet made; for if men do not plot against thee, are not able to stop thy progress, cannot deceive thee, and will not betray thee, then canst thou add this bright page to thy history, that which posterity shall marvel at as they read it,—that thou hast been able to obtain, nay, to gain, as if it were a conquest, true Liberty; and that the only means and only instruments in procuring so great a gain were the ways of love.

"I say '*true Liberty*'; for as there is real gold and fictitious gold, so is there true Liberty and a false Liberty. Oh! how very beautiful is that! and oh! how very abominable is this! Oh! how majestic is that! and oh! how terrible is this! As that diffuses around it peace and grace and calm, so does this disseminate, wherever it is implanted, terror, dismay and horror. The brows of one are illuminated with the splendid halo of order, and those of the other are covered with the red cap of anarchy. One holds in her hand the olive branch of peace; the other waves the torch of discord. One is arrayed in robes white as those of innocence, and the other is enveloped in the dark, blood-stained mantle of guilt. One is the prop of thrones; the other a yawning abyss beneath them. One is the glory and the happiness of nations; the other their disgrace and their punishment. The latter bursts out of hell, as if it were a poisonous blast, issuing from the jaws of the Devil himself; whilst true liberty descends sweetly and gently upon the earth, as if the spirit of God had sent it down to us. a holy and a blessed thing, from Heaven. *Ubi spiritus Domini ibi Libertas.*" Need we wonder if, at such words as these, the immense auditory could no longer control their emotion?— A general murmur of approbation was heard throughout the vast temple, and was breaking out into loud applause when the preacher, mindful of the reverence due to the Holy place, hastened to repress it. Let us thank the people of Rome for this noble testimony. This public, unequivocal, and solemn declaration of their real, general, and sincere sentiments, leaves no doubt that it is genuine liberty they aspire to. Would that they had had experience,—a political education,—that would have enabled them to eschew the dangers that lay in their path!

POPULAR DEMONSTRATIONS AT ROME.

To us it appears extraordinary that a whole city should have assembled to hold high jubilee over each instalment of the great boon that was in preparation for them. They had only stepped a few paces, as yet, within the land of promise, that was destined to be all their own. And yet, as a new landscape discloses its beauties to their view, and at every new step in their progress towards a secure and permanent possession of the soil, they stop to rejoice, and give themselves up without control, to the intoxication of delight. The traveller who should thus pursue his journey, would assuredly run great risk of losing himself, and of perishing by the way; and the general who should, in this manner, hope to achieve the conquest of a country, would undoubtedly afford opportunities to his enemy of discomfiting his army, and overthrowing all his hopes of conquest. Are politicians only, or peoples, when they hope to attain political importance, privileged with exemption from the common lot? History speaks not of any such exemptions. Is it unwarrantable, then, to conclude that the people of Rome would have acted more wisely than they have done,—if having confidence, as is well known they had, in the best of Sovereigns, they had left to him, and to the Ministers whom, with all the consideration of a constitutional Monarch, he called to his counsels, that work of reform which was so benevolently and so wisely begun, and which, in the estimation of all but an impatient people, was proceeding with a rapidity which has no parallel, in the annals of any country? Nor were these tumultuous assemblings, on occasion of every popular measure, expressive, as they were, of gratitude and devoted affection to the Pastor and the Prince, without danger to the cause of reform. The secret enemies of the Pope, who foresaw that by so many wise and popular measures he would undoubtedly secure to himself a strong, a peaceful and a glorious reign, availed themselves of the popular enthusiasm, to train and discipline to their will a people naturally so good and unsuspecting. These men came at length to give the watchword, and according to their wishes, and the views which they found it suitable to insinuate into the popular mind, the uneducated and inconstant multitude expressed joy or discontent, as they defiled in imposing masses before the mansion of the Pontiff.

Thus was formed a sort of Government out of doors which, if it did not, as yet, always oppose, at least powerfully controlled the official authority. The most popular minister, Cardinal Gizzi, felt it necessary to require, by a circular letter or proclamation, that these noisy demonstrations should cease. It was too late. The people, as if in defiance of this mandate, hasten in immense crowds to the Quirinal,—salute, as usual, the Pope with enthusiastic *vivats*, and express their detestation of his Ministry,—a Ministry recently so popular,—and which, if it did not by its great activity do much to acquire, had done nothing to forfeit its popularity. "*Viva Pio nono! Pio nono solo!*" was now the cry.

Whilst the ministry of the Pope, on the one hand, was in the estimation of the people intolerably dilatory in preparing measures of reform, the Pope himself did not escape the accusation of sacrificing to his zeal as a temporal ruler the higher duties he owed to religion and the church. He was breaking with inviolable tradition, said one class of revilers, whilst others maintained that so enthusiastic a reformer of the State, must be a revolutionist in the Church. In his encyclical of 9th November, 1846, which has been read and applauded throughout the civilized world, Pius IX. disposes forever of these vain imaginings. To reform the dogma, and revolutionize the discipline and government of the church, would only destroy it. To propose such a thing is a stratagem of the infidel, or of the wolf who, in sheep's clothing, would insinuate himself into the fold. It is nothing short of sacrilege, to hold that religion is susceptible of progress, or improvement, as if it were a philosophical discovery, which could advance with the march of science. The Holy Pontiff enumerates also, in his encyclical, the principal grounds of faith, and exhorts all Bishops to oppose with all their zeal and learning, those who, alleging progress as their motive, perversely endeavour to destroy religion, by subjecting it to reason. He condemns religious indifference, eloquently defends ecclesiastical celibacy, and, mindful that the church is the teacher of the great, as well as of the humble, he enforces the obligations of Sovereigns towards their subjects, whilst he inculcates the fulfilment of all the duties the people owe to their rulers.

In this, as well as in an encyclical of earlier date, Pius IX. expresses his predilection for the religious orders. Whatever abuses time might have introduced into their discipline, he was anxious, for their preservation and prosperity, to extirpate. To some he offered the most admirable suggestions. Other establishments he honored with personal visits, thus evincing a truly pastoral zeal for the wellbeing of institutions so precious to religion.

But, indeed, Pius IX. although occupied with political affairs, that would have wholly engaged any ordinary mind, never for a moment forgot that he was the Bishop, as well as the Sovereign of Rome. It had, for some time, been an occasion of grief to him, and in private, he had been heard to express his sorrow, that certain bad habits obtained among the Roman people,—such as that of profane swearing, and the neglect of children's education. In order to check these evils, he had recourse to a measure as striking as it was unexpected. Since the time of Gregory VII., no Pope had ever appeared in the pulpit. So unusual an occurrence would naturally have attracted an immense assemblage, which by crowding the church, might have disturbed the tranquility of the place, and prevented due attention from being paid to the Word of Peace and Truth. At half past three o'clock, just as the audience were expecting to see Father Ventura enter the church, the Pope himself made his appearance. This was in January, 1847. The sermon was short, but it produced an extraordinary result. "In this city, the centre of Catholicity, there are men who profane the Holy name of God, by blasphemy. All you who are here, receive from me this commission. Publish everywhere that I have no hope of such men. They cast in the face of Heaven the stone which will one day recoil upon them and crush them. I am anxious, also, to speak to you of the duty of fasting. Many fathers and mothers come to make known to me the sorrow which they experience, on beholding the demon of uncleanness exercise such a destructive empire over our youth. The Lord himself, in the Holy Gospel, assures us, that only by prayer and fasting is it possible to overcome this demon, who poisons the sources of life, and works the ruin of immortal souls." The Holy Father concluded a sermon which, in few but expressive words, embraced the great duties of a christian life, by a fervent prayer for Rome and the State. "Look down upon this vine, O Lord, which thy right hand hath planted! Look upon it in mercy, and remove from it the hand of iron which weighs so heavily upon it. Pour into the bosom of the rising generations those two most precious attributes of youth, modesty and a teachable mind. Listen to my prayer, Oh! Lord! and bestow upon this congregation, on this city, and on all people, thy most gracious blessings!"

This noble and pious language, sustained as it was by the most appropriate gesticulation, and rendered, if possible, still more expressive, by that indescribable expression of goodness which lighted up the countenance of the Holy Father moved even to tears and sighs this finely feeling people. The occasion, also, came to the aid of eloquence. The whole congregation were filled with enthusiasm.

The Holy Pontiff had need of the consolation such a scene afforded. Assailed by two parties, each of them extreme in its views, he must have often despaired of the cause he had in hand. The ultra-conservatives, holding in horror the very idea of reform, made it their study to confound, in the popular mind, the beneficial measures which the Pope was introducing into the Government of the State, with radical changes in the very essence of religion itself. The socialist faction, on the other hand, excited the people, and increased their impatience, by representing that the ministry, by studied delays, were only abusing the confidence of the Sovereign, and betraying the cause of reform. To the former party was ascribed an infamous libel, in which the Holy Pontiff was designated as an *intruder, an enemy of religion, the chief of young Italy.* This publication was seized in the hands of a *colporteur*, and only showed too plainly who those secret and cowardly enemies were, whose valour was conspicuous only in the war of calumny. The miserable porter offered at once to disclose the names of the authors. Pius IX. declined his offer, generously forgave the wretched man, and even bestowed upon him some pecuniary aid, in order to induce him to relinquish his detestable trade.

Whilst lamenting the great evils arising from the existence of these two extreme parties, it is pleasing to have to recount the efforts made by a still more numerous body, the real friends of the Pope, who were most anxious to aid him in carrying out the measures of reform he had in view. These faithful and patriotic citizens, on whom too much praise can never be bestowed, organized a powerful force, that kept the excited populace in check. Consisting of the Burghers of Rome, encouraged and headed by the great nobles, such as the Borghese, the Rospigliosi, the Rignano, the Piombino, the Aldobrandini, this national guard was able to preserve order in the city when, on occasion of celebrating the anniversary of the memorable amnesty, it was seriously threatened by the factious. Would that this party—the party of reform, the party of order—had known how to keep its ground, in the face of new dangers that were to arise so soon!

CARDINAL FERRETTI MINISTER.—EXTRAORDINARY MANIFESTATION OF THE AUSTRIAN GOVERNMENT.—ITS DEFERENCE TO THE WISHES OF THE HOLY FATHER.—FURTHER REFORMS.— A MUNICIPAL COUNCIL INSTITUTED.—THE COUNCIL OF STATE. —A CONSTITUTION PROJECTED.

The declining health of Cardinal Gizzi now rendered it necessary that he should relinquish a post that was every day becoming more onerous and difficult. There was another Cardinal, whose high character had endeared him to the Romans. Not only was he possessed of learning and great abilities. He was energetic and resolute, faithful, straightforward, and self-sacrificing. When the dread scourge of Cholera had impoverished his episcopal city, Cardinal Ferretti gave up, for the relief of the sufferers, all he possessed,—money, clothing, plate, furniture, and remained in his emptied palace, as destitute as a pauper. Pius IX did not appeal to him in vain. On the 26th July,

1847, the new Secretary of State arrived at Rome. The citizens gave him an ovation.

Shortly before his arrival, the news had been received that Austrian troops were marching on Ferrara, a city of the Papal States. They were entitled by the treaty of 1815 to garrison this fortress, as well as that of Comachio. This was all the excuse they could allege for displaying in the Pope's States, on occasion of the threatened disturbance at Rome, on the 16th July, the pomp and circumstance of war. This military parade was only the prelude to greater daring. On the 13th August, General Count Auesperg occupied all the posts of Ferrara. This was a serious usurpation of the Papal rights. The most energetic remonstrances were immediately addressed to the Cabinet of Vienna. Austria endeavoured to justify its proceeding, by a wide interpretation of its right of occupation, by alleging the disturbed state of the public mind at Rome, and by insisting on certain precedents. But, it was in vain. The Diplomacy of Ferretti, contended, successfully, with that of Metternich. And Austria, yielding, with the best grace possible, to the representations of the Holy Father, evacuated Ferrara.

Meanwhile, the Pope, nowise disquieted by the Croat troops, proceeded slowly, but perseveringly, with the work of reform. Cardinal Ferretti laboured assiduously, to realize the great views of the Pontiff. He promised that before the end of the year, two great political and administrative institutions would be called into existence. And accordingly, so early as the month of October, two state-papers appeared, the one instituting the municipality of Rome with the designation of *Senate*; the other, decreeing an assembly that should be, to a certain extent, representative, under the name of *Council of State*, (*Consulta*.)

Rome had not, until now, enjoyed, like the other cities of the Pontifical States, a municipal magistracy. The new Senate was to consist of a Senator, eight colleagues, and a hundred members. The Pope reserved to himself the first nomination of the members of this body. It was, afterwards, to renew itself by free election. The preamble, written in the Pope's own hand, was remarkable for wisdom and liberality:—"When we were called by Divine Providence to govern the church and the State, our paternal solicitude was at once directed towards every one of the populations subjected to our government, but chiefly towards this celebrated capital, their elder sister, to which it is consoling for us to devote our watchings and our labours. What was, above all, important, and what, we think, will be a subject of joy to all, is the restoration to this beloved city of its ancient glory of communal representation, by granting to it a deliberative council. The study of this project has been particularly pleasing to us, and we have not allowed ourselves to be discouraged by any difficulty.

This admirable decree was published on the 2nd October. On the following day was held a national festival. The population were in raptures, and made every manifestation of gratitude to the Holy Father, for an institution which recalled the ancient memories of Rome, and restored it to its place and rank among modern cities. The Cardinal Prince Altieri, as President, opened the first session of the Municipal Council by a speech, in which he paid marked homage to Pius IX. "He considers not," said the President, "whether the work be difficult. He sees its utility, and makes no hesitation." The council, almost unanimously, called to the post of Senator, Prince Corsini, who was, at that time, devoted to the policy of Pius IX.

Scarcely was the new form of civic government established, when a measure of more general importance engaged the attention of the Holy Father and his ministers. The *Consulta,* or Council of State, was decreed. This was a deliberative assembly, and a national representation. It was not itself sovereign, but possessed the right to offer counsel to the Sovereign. It consisted of twenty-four counsellors, whose President was a Cardinal Legate. Each counsellor was chosen by the Pope, from a list of three candidates, named by each Province of his States. The

Consulta was divided into four sections, whose duty it was to prepare laws relating to the various departments of finance, home affairs, public works, justice. It was regulated, moreover, that these four committees should hold a general meeting on certain days, in order to discuss the draughts of intended laws which they had separately prepared.

On the 15th November, 1847, the national representatives assembled for the first time. Their place of meeting was the throne room of the Quirinal Palace. Cardinal Antonelli, the first President of the *Consulta*, adopted a respectful allocution to the Holy Father. Pius IX., well aware that the creating of this institution had awakened exaggerated and premature hopes in the minds of a portion of the people, and that some of the Deputies were not disinclined to encourage them, deemed it necessary, in his reply, to define in a very decided manner, the true character and functions of the national representative body: "It is chiefly" said he, " in order that I may become better acquainted with the wants of my people, and that I may better provide for the exigencies of the State, that I have called you together. I am prepared, in time, to do everything, without, however, diminishing the sovereignty of the Pontificate. That man would be grievously mistaken, who should behold, in the functions you have to fulfil, or in your Institution itself, his own Utopias, or the commencement of anything incompatible with the Pontifical Sovereignty." Assuming a sterner tone, he reproached his people for the ingratitude they had already begun to manifest. "There are some persons who, having nothing to lose, wish for disorder and insurrection, and go so far as to make a bad use of our concessions even. To such are these words addressed; let them consider well their meaning."

In this assembly there was a commencement of representative government. Deputies from the Provinces assemble—deliberate. They bear a speech from the crown, they present an address in reply. In due time, this germ of constitutional monarchy will be developed. But the Sovereign will not proceed rashly. The full measure of reform, he is well aware, must like all great works, be the fruit of time, of much labour, and patient consideration.

The French Ambassador Mr. Rossi, conceived that it was already time to introduce a lay element into the political administration of the Papal States. After due deliberation, the Holy Father called some distinguished laymen to the ministry, thus sacrificing time-honored traditions, not so much to the wishes of his friends and allies, as to the spirit of the age, which, whether right or wrong, will have men of the world, to deal with the world.

Italy, although divided into several States, looks to Rome as its centre and its Capital. Whatever occurs in the celebrated City, is at once known throughout the whole peninsula. Such important and unlooked for reforms could not fail, as they were communicated, deeply to affect the Italian mind. Public opinion is aroused. The most profound sympathy is everywhere felt and expressed. Liberty revives, under the auspices of religion. It emanates, as a new blessing from the cross. The chief of Religion, the Father of the Faithful, has become its High-Priest. His name is held in benediction. His praises are sung, not only by the Italian populations, but by every civilized nation. It is no longer violence, no longer insurrection, that contends for liberty. The greatest of all Sovereigns has proclaimed its reign. It is not indebted to any secret society. It relies upon society at large. It rests secure, and immovable, on the firm foundation of enlightened public opinion. Philosophy, in the person of M. Cousin, hails its advent; the statesmanship of France, represented by M. Thiers, extolls its champion; and Protestantism, for once forgetting its illiberal prejudices, re-echoes with enthusiasm the warm vivats of reformed Italy. Pius IX, meanwhile, enjoys his reward; not in the flattering echo of the myriad voices that sound his praise, but in the one still voice of approving conscience. He is consoled, moreover, by the consciousness that the cause he has in hand, will one day prove triumphant.

Every new concession, meanwhile, appeared only to excite a desire for further change. True, the people were satisfied, and frequently expressed their gratitude with no less sincerity than enthusiasm. But there were those among them who, whilst they took part in the tumultuous expressions of satisfaction which so frequently occurred, were far from being sincere. This socialist faction, which aimed at nothing less than *the republic, one and undivided*, over which should prevail for ever *the hand of Iron*, availed themselves of the numerous assemblages that could not now be regulated or lessened in number, to gain new friends, to increase the popular excitement, to discipline it, so as to bring it, through some favorite demagogues, completely under their control. We shall see, in the sequel, with what a dangerous weapon they were thus provided. But for their machinations, and the power they were every day acquiring, there can be no doubt that Pius the IX. would have established a system of government as free as was at all compatible with the existence of his sovereignty, which he was not at liberty to abdicate. And what greater freedom could any people aspire to? Does not history proclaim the truth that liberty is more fully enjoyed, and more securely and more permanently, under the fostering auspices of a constitutional monarchy, than in the best regulated republics?— And yet, this form of government does not cease to be a monarchy. It does not cease to possess such privileges and prerogatives of kingly dignity, as are essential to it, as are necessary elements in its constitution. And this was all the monarchy Pius IX. desired to retain, and which it was obligatory on him never to relinquish. What, besides this, did he care for? Never was there a less selfish sovereign, nor a man of more upright mind, or of sounder judgment. No prince was ever less jealous of his prerogative, and however strongly he was resolved to hold to essential rights, he never would have shrunk from any legitimate concession. Whatever was suitable, useful to his people, and conformable to a well informed and sound public opinion, he was ready to grant. But the complete secularization of power in his states—the establishment of the Red Republic—he could not for a moment contemplate.

Scarcely had the consultative government entered upon its functions, when Pius IX. entertained the idea of rendering it completely representative. This important measure was the subject of frequent conversations with M. Rossi, who was at that time the ambassador at Rome of the French constitutional monarchy. In January, 1848, M. Rossi wrote to his government: "It is a problem which, after much reflection, I consider may be solved. The divisions of sovereignty in the world have been numerous and diverse. And as they lasted for ages, we might even try one more, beginning by separating entirely the temporal from the spiritual—the Pope from the King. Only it would be necessary to leave wholly to the spiritual, and the clergy, matters which with us are mixed." A few days afterwards, the ambassador communicated this more decided intelligence—"The Pope will shortly give the constitution. It is his serious and constant study."

M. Rossi strongly recommended that this great measure should be at once adopted. . . adoption, he conceived, would put an end to agitation—a most desirable result, when it is considered how fatal to the cause of liberty and reform might any day become those tumultuous assemblages, which, constitutional government once established, must necessarily cease. The Pope shared the opinions of the diplomatist.

These hopes and aspirations were, as yet, far from being realised. A new difficulty unexpectedly arose. On the 5th of March, 1848, a courier arrived at Rome, with the startling intelligence that the Constitutional monarchy of France was fallen, and that the Republic was established at Paris.— No greater misfortune could have befallen Rome. The public excitement was, beyond measure increased, and hopes enkindled that could never be realized. The people, from being at first enthusiastic, had become turbulent. The new events in France exercised a still more fatal influence, and anarchy prevailed. The republican party, whom the proclamation of the constitution would have paralyzed, were now in the ascendant. What had been done at Paris might be done at Rome. So they believed, and so they induced the inexperienced multitude to believe. But this belief was only an idle, even a culpable dream. It could not be guiltless, surely, to resolve on sacrificing thousands upon thousands of precious lives for an

Utopia,—a system of things that could never be realised.—Events have since shewn that in France itself, which was entirely free to make whatever political arrangement it pleased, a republic was not possible,—even a rational Republic, such as was established at the downfall of the citizen monarchy, in preference to the Red Republic. How, then, should it be possible to build up in Rome an extreme system, in opposition to the wishes of the whole Christian world,—in opposition, even, to the people of Rome themselves, who, when free from undue excitement, were the firm supporters of the sovereign, who had already granted them so many liberal institutions,—institutions that were in perfect harmony with their ideas, and admirably adapted to the exigencies of the time? There was no need as yet, that the Catholic nations should come to the aid of their chief. They had only, in defence of his sovereignty, *to appeal from Rome drunk to Rome sober*,—from Rome intoxicated with unwonted draughts of liberty, to Rome in its normal state,—to Rome, cool and calm, and intellectual, even as in the days of her ancient glory, when her sages and grave senators sat by her gates, sorrowing but dignified, even in defeat. With the like countenance ought modern Rome to have met the tide of republican invasion, far more destructive than the war of mighty legions, which could only cast down her material walls.

At Rome, the city of the Popes, a socialist republic was impossible. It never would have been able to obtain the countenance, or even the recognition of European governments.—Not Austria and France only, but also every other Catholic nation would have exerted all their influence against it. Nor in doing so would they have acted unjustly. But for the residence of their chief Pastor there Rome would long ago have ceased to exist, or would be known only as an insignificant village, scarcely perceptible on the map of Europe. How often has not the celebrated city been rescued from destruction by the direct agency of the Popes? How long have they not governed it with wisdom, and blessed it with prosperity? If there be any such thing as prescriptive right, undoubtedly it is theirs. If there be any right, better founded and more strong, than that of conquest, such right unquestionably belongs to the saviours of Rome. They have saved it for the Christian world, for mankind, for the church. It is no man's property. It cannot be let, like a paltry farm, to those who shall bid the highest, in vain promises and delusive hopes of liberty.

Should its people of this generation pretend to give themselves away, their forefathers of all preceding ages would indignantly protest against their act; their children of the generation to come would curse their memory; all reflecting men of the present time, would accuse them of black ingratitude,—ingratitude to the mighty dead among their Pontiffs, to whom they are indebted for their name, their city's fame, its very existence in modern times;--ingratitude, above all, to that ruler who has offered them, who has bestowed upon them, liberty, and who would only rescue them to-day from tyranny, --the tyranny of faction, even as his predecessors, in bygone times, snatched them from the cruel grasp of barbarism.

CONSTITUTIONAL GOVERNMENT ESTABLISHED.

As yet, the people of Rome had no idea of anything beyond the representative and constitutional government, which, as we have seen, the Holy Father had made up his mind to institute. They are anxious, however, that his views and theirs should be carried into effect. Accordingly, the Senator, (Mayor,) Prince Corsini, and the eight principal members of the municipal council, are commissioned to make known their wishes to the Pope. His reply was dignified and candid. In declaring his intention to grant the constitution which they asked for, he took care to intimate, in the most decided manner, that he was not making a concession to the urgency of the moment, but accomplishing his premeditated purpose : " Events," said he, " abundantly justify the request which you address to me in the name of the Council and Magistracy of Rome. All are aware, that it is my constant study, to give to the Government that form which appears to me to be most in harmony with the times. But, none are ignorant, at the same time, of the difficulties to which he is exposed, who unites in his own person two great dignities, when endeavoring to trace the line of demarcation between these two powers. What, in a secular government, may be done in one day, in the Pontifical can only be accomplished after mature deliberation. I flatter myself, nevertheless, that, the preliminary labours having been completed, I shall be able, in a few days, to impart to you the result of my reflections, and that this result will meet the wishes of all reasonable people."

On the 14th of March, accordingly, Pius IX. published *the fundamental statute for the temporal government of the Holy See.* This was a straightforward and most complete inauguration of constitutional Rule. It was according to the model of the French liberal monarchy of 1830, modified, so as to render it capable of adaptation to the Pontifical Government. It consisted of a responsible ministry and of two chambers, one appointed during the lifetime of its members,—the other elective. The function of these Chambers was to vote laws, which were to be prepared by a Council of State. The college of Cardinals was to be a permanent Council, whose duty it should be to sanction, in the last instance, the decisions of the Legislative Chambers. Such was the principle of the Statute, by which the subjects of the Pope were brought by undisputed right within the sphere of constitutional States. A few days later was promulgated the nomination of a ministry, three-fourths of which were laymen, under the Presidency of the Secretary of State, Cardinal Antonelli. This was, indeed, reform, and a constitution. What more could Pius IX. have done, to advance the interests and meet the wants and wishes of his people?

THE WAR AGITATION.

But n w, at the moment the excellent Pontiff was entitled to a rich reward, in the gratitude and devotedness of his people, his real difficulty began. Diplomacy at the close of the European war in 1815, had subjected to German rule, as is well known, certain portions of Italy. By war, only, some populations thought, could this fact of diplomacy be recalled. How little did they consider, that by such a course, they set themselves in opposition, not to one great power only, but to all the powers of Europe. Experienced statesmen would have told them,—and one statesman, at least, did tell them,—that what diplomacy, in obedience to circumstances, had done, it would with its wonted pliancy, have undone, when urged by a new and extraordinary state of things, differing widely from that in which it had decided upon the arrangements that still existed. New emergencies having arisen, the learning and the skill of statesmen ought, in the first instance, to have been appealed to. As between individuals, right reason requires that all the means of adjusting a quarrel should be employed; so between nations, there is no device of statesmanship that ought not to be had recourse to before an appeal is made to bayonets and blood. How successful such a course of conduct might have proved, and how beneficial to the cause of Italian liberty, is more than sufficiently shewn by the great result obtained by diplomacy, when Austria, insisting on treaties, displayed the flag of war at Ferrara. O! but in that case, the Pope was the chief diplomatist. And would he not have been so again, when there was question, not of one city, only, but of many of the greatest cities, and fairest States of Italy? Nor would he have found "the Barbarians" more hard to deal with. Austria, barbarous enough to ignore that exquisite refinement which deems it fashionable to despise Religion and its Priests, would have shewn her reverence for the Pontiff; and if he had required it, would have withdrawn every soldier from Italian soil. What was it, a little later, that made Austria forbear, when the French Republic marched its troops to the banks of the Tiber? And what was it, later still, that induced the chief of that great Empire to sacrifice the richest of Italian provinces, and grasp in amity the hand of him who had, so needlessly and so recklessly, become his enemy? Was it the superior diplomacy of France? In diplomacy, the land of Metternich had no need to yield the palm. Was it the carnage of Solferino? That fatal but honourable day brought to his tents the head of a shattered army, to sue for peace. What, then, was it? If, indeed, anything, in addition to his horror of shedding blood, it was, undoubtedly, his reverence for the Roman Pontiff. Was it not an essential condition of the peace, that the Holy Father should remain in undisturbed possession of all his States? But, even before the warlike operations of 1848, and the field of Novara, was there not enough to shew with what success a wise diplomacy might, even t' n, have been attended? But, the voice of Italy is for war. The Italians will have war at any price. The people, even, who own the sway of the Pontificate, although governed by a prince who can conquer without war, must give battle to "the Barbarians." The socialist agitators have persuaded them, and no other counsel will prevail.

On the 23rd of March, the Colyseum presented an unwonted spectacle. It was a grand but ill-omened scene. The entire people had assembled in the ancient arena, under the leadership of their tribunes, who had decided on agitating in so great an assembly, the question of war. They were resolved that it should be settled by acclamation, hoping thus to influence the Holy Father,—to induce him to abandon his system of neutrality, by this immense display of opinion and excitement, by this popular enthusiasm—this intoxication of patriotism. At an early hour, the great meeting was congregated.— Nobles, burghers, soldiers, princes, everybody. Priests, even, were there, in tolerable numbers,—monks of every order, ecclesiastics of every college, members of every congregation. It was a monster club in the open air, in which the question of the "crusade" was to be solemnly discussed. What a grand spectacle would it not have been, had it not been arranged before-hand by skilful demagogues who were masters in the art of preparing revolutionary displays! Whatever sincerity there may have been in the assembly, there was none in the actors of this great scene. If this had been really an improvisation of public opinion, nothing could have been more grand. As it was only a theatrical display of parts, learned to order, there could have been nothing more contemptible. There was in it, moreover, something sad and sinister—a set of actors, practising on the popular mind to-day, in order to discover what they might safely attempt to-morrow.

A rostrum or tribune overlooks the arena. Near it, were observed all those agitators who were destined to become, at a later period, so notorious in the commotions of the time. Among them was Padre Gavazzi, a Barnabite monk, whose puerile vanity made him aspire to distinction, and who was already distinguished by his pretentious eloquence, bombastic style, confused ideas, and a mind still undecided as to the limits of orthodoxy, which, a little later, he stepped beyond. He was the great preacher of *the Crusade*. Next came the shepherd poet, Rosi; Prince Canino's Secretary, Masi; a young French monk of the order of Conventualists, Dumaine; Generals Durando and Ferrari; the Journalist, Sterbini, afterwards so fatally popular, and of course, the demagogue, Cicerruacho, who was at first enthusiastic in the cause of the Pope, but who now burned for war, and ere long imparted to the revolution a character of shifting fanaticism and absurd sympathies. The day was spent in magnificent addresses, modelled according to the antique types, urgent exhortations to war, poetical orations, rounds of applause, rapturous demonstrations. The result was, lists for the enrolment of volunteers, the establishment in the different quarters of the city of tables for receiving patriotic offerings, and a threatening demonstration against the Quirinal, where it was intended to force the Pope to bless the colours for the expedition against Austria.

The Holy Father could no longer controul the movement. His orders were still respected, but not obeyed. The people were at heart rebellious, although preserving as yet a show of reverence. They were no sooner out of his presence, than they transgressed his most sacred commands. In authorizing the enrolment and the departure of volunteers, Pius IX. had distinctly specified that it was his intention and his will, that the expedition should be exclusively defensive, that it should protect the territory, but avoid passing the frontier.— Notwithstanding these formal orders, his name was made use of in order to deceive the populations. This was worse than rebellion—it was perfidy. General Durando's first act, on arriving at Bologna, was to issue a proclamation, in which, falsifying the wishes of Pius IX., he adduced the authority of the Pontiff in order to give a colour to the war. "Radetsky," said he, "fights against the Cross of Christ. Pius IX. has blessed your swords, in union with those of Charles Albert. * * "This war of civilization against barbarism, is not merely national, it is a Christian war. * * "With the Cross, and by the Cross, we shall be victorious: God wills it."

By such perfidious conduct, the character of the Pontiff was seriously compromised. Hence, it became necessary to publish that admirable document, the encyclical letter of 29th April, 1848.

"Men are endeavoring," said the Holy Father, "to disseminate suspicions that are injurious to the temporal administration of our States. It is our duty to prevent the scandal that might thus be given to the simple and unreflecting." Pius IX. then proceeds to declare that he is resolved to expose clearly, and to proclaim loudly, the origin of all the facts of his Government. He refers to the *memorandum* of 1831, which was the collective counsels of the European Cabinets to the Apostolic See, in favour of the necessary reforms. Gregory XVI. adopted some of these reforms. Circumstances, and the danger of the times, caused the rest to be adjourned. Pius IX. considered that it was his duty to complete what his predecessor had begun. On other points, he does not disclaim having taken the initiative. He had pardoned extensively, and he congratulates himself upon it. He repels the calumny which would ascribe to these reforms the general movement of Italy towards its enfranchisement. He attributes this agitation to events that were accomplished elsewhere, and which became facts of overwhelming influence for the whole of Europe. Finally, he protests that he gave no other order to his soldiers, than that which required that they should defend the Pontifical territory. He cannot be held responsible, if amongst his subjects there are some who are influenced by the example of other Italians. He had given his orders distinctly. They had been transgressed.

In this same document, alluding to the war with Austria, the Pontiff says: "They would have us declare war against

Austria. We have thought it our duty to protest formally against such a resolution, considering that, notwithstanding our unworthiness, we hold on earth the place of Him who is the author of peace—the friend of charity; and that, faithful to the Divine obligations of our Apostolate, we embrace all countries, all peoples, all nations, in a like sentiment of paternal love. Nor can we refrain from repelling, in the face of all nations, the perfidious assertions of those who desire that the Roman Pontiff should be the chief of the government of a new republic, consisting of all the peoples of Italy."

"Moreover, we earnestly exhort, on this occasion, these same Italian peoples to keep particularly on their guard against these treacherous counsels. We conjure them to remain devotedly attached to their princes, whose affection they have experienced. To act otherwise would be not only to fail in their duty, but also to expose Italy to discord and factions.— As regards ourselves, we declare once more that all the thoughts and all the efforts of the Roman Pontiff tend only to increase every day the kingdom of Jesus Christ, which is the Church, and not to extend the limits of the temporal sovereignty, with which Divine Providence has endowed the Holy See, for the dignity and the free exercise of the sublime apostolate."

The Holy Father could not have vindicated more eloquently the essentially pacific character of that Religion, of which he is the chief, and the representative on earth. Nor was it possible to offer wiser or more authoritative counsel to the Italian populations. But, it was already too late. The voice of friendly warning was unheard, amid the din of strife and revolution. And, need it be added, the cause of liberty perished for a time, the victim of its own excess.

REVOLUTIONARY TENDENCIES—COUNT MAMIANI, MINISTER.

A party at Rome had succeeded in rallying the populace around them. This civic power, whatever it might have proved 'in the field, was formidable at home. Under the skilful management of its leaders, it now gave law to the Pontifical Government, and yet, was not the Pontiff powerless. An ordinary sovereign would have been crushed; abdication would have been his only resource; but to such a pass the Pope is not yet reduced. Does the socialist party endeavour to thrust upon him unacceptable measures, he repels them. Do they and their myrmidons vociferate for war with Austria, the Pope is able still to say, there shall be no war; and his people do not engage in the crusade. A few, indeed, of the more excitable of the Roman youth, like the field. But, effeminate as they are ardent, at the first sight of a *Barbarian* tent, their courage cools, and they return to their hearths, to discourse in magniloquent terms, of the tented fields that they have traversed, the savage hordes they have encountered, the dangers they have escaped.

In one thing, however, the party who had the command of the people succeeded : they forced a ministry on the reluctant Sovereign. This, however unreasonable in the circumstances it unquestionably was, does not shock so much our constitutional ideas. Of the principle of this act, we may not be entitled to complain.

But neither can we approve the conduct of a faction which, being anything but constitutional, imposed a minister of their principles on a prince who had, of his own accord, become constitutional. Count Mamiani was one of those whom the clemency of Pius IX. had restored to their country. Of all the parties thus favoured, he alone refused to bind himself, in honour, to the Holy Father, never to abuse the favour, and to remain always good and faithful subjects. His abilities were considerable. He was well informed, cool, and resolute, but without any fixed principle in politics. He would have been as ready to set up a red republic, as a constitutional monarchy. His political conduct was guided more by events and circumstances, than by any well-conceived idea of what is right and fitting. He was one of those liberals of Italy who might be truly compared to the Necker of the French Revolution. Mazzini and his followers were the ultra-radicals — the Robespierre of Italian politics.

The Mamiani ministry was a necessary result of the popular commotions. It was also a protest of the excited populace against the Encyclical of the 29th April. In the troubled days that preceded his nomination to the ministry. Mamiani had formally declared, in his harangues to the people, that no priest should be called to public functions; that Pius IX. should, indeed, remain at the head of the Government, but that they should obtain from him the recall of his encyclical address, and a declaration of war against Austria; that a new expedition should speedily set out, and that an official bulletin of the great war should be published every day.

These warlike and revolutionary declarations, so pompously made, could not fail to excite the enthusiasm of the multitude, already in such a state of excitement. But in such things, it is more easy to speak than to act: and this the popular Tribune found to be the case, when he was elevated to the ministry. He then forgot the fine lessons he had studied to impress upon the people. Whether sincerely or not, he still, however, insisted on the Austrian war. This may have been necessary for his popularity. But it was chimerical in the face of two powerful adversaries—the Pope, on the one hand, who by his name, his character, his virtues, was still powerful; and, on the other hand, the representative body, which was appointed to assemble in the beginning of June. When the Parliament met, there was an end, indeed, to the government of the streets; but new difficulties arose. Cardinal Altieri delivered, on the part of the Sovereign Pontiff, an energetic and moving exhortation in support of unity and concord. He also expressed his hope that the deputies would shew their good will, by concurrency with the ministry, in rendering this new adaptation of the constitution compatible with the Pontifical Government. Next day, 9th June, Count Mamiani came to the Tribune, with an oration which expressed more the ideas of the ministry, as individuals, than as the representatives of their sovereign. Such conduct may have been the result of inexperience. They had but little knowledge of constitutions. But when they gave out that the opinion they expressed in favour of war, was also that of the Pontiff, thus endeavouring to give the sanction of a venerated name to designs that were highly detrimental to the Pontificate, we look in vain for an excuse. It was their policy. But what of that?

The new constitution, in more judicious and honest hands, might have proved successful. Such was the thought, as well as the wish, of many well-informed men. But the war question proved its ruin. It was the idea of Italian patriotism at the time, that all true patriots must fight for their country. The Mamiani ministry must reconcile this warlike spirit, with the pacific character of the Pontificate. The Pope can defend himself. But sound theology and the traditions of his sovereignty forbid him to wage war on any people. His ministry will solve the difficulty. As Pope, they insist, he may still decide for peace, condemning the shedding of blood; whilst, as temporal sovereign, he will let his ministers do as they please, and they will declare for war. It was, indeed, a weak government that had need to rely on such wretched sophistry. Were the Pontiff and the temporal sovereign two distinct persons? Or, when ministers wage war, can the Prince, whose representatives they are, be considered as neutral? During the few months that this ministry remained in power, they were in constant opposition to the sovereign, whose repugnance to war could never be overcome. Popular demonstrations of the most threatening kind were frequently made, in favour of war. But as regarded the sovereign, they were powerless:

"Justum, et tenacem propositi virum
Non civium ardor prava jubentium,
* * * *
Mente quatit solida."

The mind of the Pontiff could not be moved from its rightful purpose. But the ministry was shaken. Sophistry and inconsistency were its only remaining bulwarks, and, as was for sometime obviously inevitable, it fell.

PARTIES—THE ITALIAN RADICALS—COUNT ROSSI, MINISTER.

Before entering upon the last scene in which, according to the plan of this discourse, we shall be called upon to witness the efforts of Pius IX. in the cause of reform, it may not be superfluous to consider the political opinion of the time. Although differing widely in many important matters, from the distinguished writers, Gioberti, Balbo, D'Azeglio, it would be unjust to deny them the credit of having imparted new

vigour, if not its first impulse, to the cause of reform in Italy.
They did not rashly hasten to the wished-for goal. The
greatest degree of political liberty they thought it in vain to
aspire to, all at once. The wished-for end they conceived would
be best attained, by judicious and well-timed reforms, and by
such institutions as might be afterwards developed, when the
Italian populations, unaccustomed as yet to constitutional
forms, should be capable of a larger measure of freedom.
Nothing can be conceived wiser than their view of educating
the people for liberty, before conferring upon them the
precious boon. Their idea of commencing their career of
reform by waging war upon Austria, does not appear so
deserving of praise. Was not the Cabinet of Vienna one of
those which joined in recommending reform to the late Pope?
Why then reject so powerful an ally? But, the Germans—
the "Barbarians"—were odious to the Italian people. Might
they not have been disabused of this prejudice? Education
only could do this. And as they were to be politically educated at
length, would not the eradication of illiberal prejudices have
formed a profitable branch of study? Pius IX., as we have
seen, was a reformer in practice, as well as theory. Austria
offered no impediment to his patriotic labours. On one
occasion only, did that powerful Empire shew a disposition
to interfere. It was when Rome and its sovereign were
threatened by popular commotions. And then, even, on the
representation of the Holy Father, Austria laid down her
arms.

So lately as the early part of the year 1848, the opinions of
these constitutional reformers, with whom, as politicians, so
little fault can be found, were shared by almost the whole of
Italy. They were, at the same time, the most powerful party,
in numbers, in authority, in talent. The Republicans were,
at that time, an imperceptible minority. In a few months
everything was, in appearance at least, completely changed.
Talent, respectability, authority, were still on the side of the
moderate reformers. The Red Republic, meanwhile, had the
command of numbers. How this came to pass, it may not,
perhaps, be impossible to explain.

In all populous countries there are numerous people who, being without fixed principles in politics, or without any political principle at all, depend on other men for the opinions by which, for the moment, they shall be guided. Such was the case with the Romans, as well as many other Italian populations. It was not then, difficult for skilful leaders to fashion for such people, as they pleased, principles of policy and political programmes. Even those who were tolerably well grounded in constitutional ideas, but not wholly decided, the Radical leaders tried to gain to their side by persuading them to compromise certain points, to adopt new designations, modify their opinions, agree to coalitions, enter into ingenious arrangements. The result was, that, as is usual in such circumstances, the most extravagant views came to prevail with the multitude. The French Revolution of February 1848, which overthrew the constitutional monarchy, came opportunely to the aid of the Italian Red Republic. A little reflection would have shewn them the extreme peril to which France exposed herself, by her most unconstitutional proceeding, in tearing down by violence a system in many respects so good, and which, simply because it was a constitution, was capable of new developments, new adaptations, and greater excellence in every way, than without the constitutional element, it can ever hope to attain to. But, they beheld only a new step towards liberty, and the Italians, they declared, must follow in the wake of enlightened France, and seize the glorious prize that was at length within their reach. Thus were the people advised, and thus were they led astray. The moderate reform party, themselves excited by the enthusiasm which events had inspired, observed not the snares which the radical leaders had laid for them, and were completely caught in their toils, whilst they conceived that they were only working out their own idea. They even thought to gain Mazzini, whilst, in reality, Mazzini was proselytizing them. Gioberti and his more immediate friends, not certainly without faults on their side, were abandoned by the crowd.

We have already bestowed some notice on Mazzini and his views. Calling to mind what has been already said regarding him, there need be no hesitation in pronouncing him the evil genius of modern Italy. In his book, "Italy in its Relations with Liberty and Moral Civilization," which was published in France, where he was an exile, in 1847, he formally declared that "Young Italy" was the only party that could exercise any decisive influence on the destiny of the country (Italy). He treated, at the same time, with sovereign contempt, the ideas and the hopes of the reform party. In his mystic republic, only, was to be found, he conceived, *the principle of unity, the ideal formula of actual progress.* This theory was the idol at whose shrine he offered sacrifice. His followers were also his fellow-worshippers. He was their High Priest. And such was the nervous excitement of some of his fellow-countrymen, that he exercised over them a control which they could not resist. They were fascinated by his brilliant utopias. He was no longer a legislator, a politician, a philosopher, only; he was a man of inspiration, a prophet, the Mahomet of a new Hegira. His sayings were oracles. His doctrines were enunciated in sententious and poetical language; and from his place of exile, they were disseminated over the Italian peninsula.

Allusion has already been made to the generosity of Pius IX., in recalling from banishment so many who had violated the laws of their country. However well these men may have appreciated the boon, and there is no doubt they were, at one time, sincerely grateful, it is not surprising if, as is usual in the case of persons circumstanced as they were, they remembered more the severity which punished than the goodness which forgave them. Mazzini dissembled for a time. It has even been suggested that he was sincere at first, and had nobly resolved to sacrifice his peculiar views to the cause of Italy. It was not long, however, till the newspaper, *Italia del Popolo*, revealed the sectarian and the fanatic. The popular mind was poisoned by its ravings, and filled with mistrust. Sects and parties were raised up anew, to be once more the ruin of ill-starred Italy.

"*Unita e non unione. Assemblea del Popolo Italiano e non dieta.*" Unity; not union. The assembly of the Italian *people; not a Federal Diet."* Such was the daily theme of Mazzini's journal. The multitude ceased not henceforth to vociferate, as directed by the revolutionary leader, "Live the Constituent Assembly"! as they had formerly shouted for Pius IX., and reform. What this meant, they did not very well understand; but it was believed to be something extreme —a boundless measure of liberty; and for the populace, this was enough: it could mean nothing less, they conceived, than unity, the most complete, and a republican government. But could there have been anything more impracticable and more preposterous? How subject to the yoke of a popular convention so many different peoples? They were all Italian, it is true; but each had for ages past, possessed its distinct nationality, its national laws, customs, manners, prejudices, predilections and antipathies. Nor were their interests the same. What would be for the good of one state, might prove ruinous to another, or even to all the other states. The Liberal Government of the Grand Dukes had endeared their rule to the Tuscan people. Piedmont and Naples were devotedly attached to their respective monarchies. The people of the Papal States, with the exception of the populace of Rome, whose numbers were so much increased in 1848, by the influx of strangers--men of republican opinions, industriously culled from foreign populations—were devoted to the mild and clement rule of their Pontiff-Sovereigns, and they had been favored of late with signal proof that the sacred monarchy itself was capable, without detriment to its real power and dignity, of the most extensive popular reforms. Must all these moderate and well regulated monarchies which were constitutionalizing themselves every day more and more, be overthrown? The Mazzinian idea required nothing less than this. At the time of which we are speaking, the sacrifice of so many rights would have cost torrents of blood, and would not, perhaps, have been accomplished. The torch of civil discord would have blazed from end to end of unfortunate Italy. And if the ancient monarchies were destined to fall, new and more despotic forms of kingly rule would, in all probability, have arisen in their place.

At this time the Italian populations, by assuming an imposing attitude—by acting in concert and with united influence, might have obtained not only the forbearance, but the aid even of their powerful neighbours, in developing such of their institutions as already contained germs of freedom, in extending constitutional rights which already existed in monarchies that were far from being despotic. But in the confusion of popular demonstrations and party cries, the "still small voice of reason" was unheard. The revolutionary leaders reiterated their war harangues, and Italy, by directing its arms against its sovereigns, inflicted a fatal blow on its own political existence.

The plan for uniting Italy, proposed by the moderate reform party, was much less open to objection, and with modifications adapting it to each state, might, if carried into effect, have been attended with the best results. They would first of all have cemented the union between the rulers and the people, by recommending to the former moderation, and to the latter the more difficult virtue of patience, they would have adjourned the idea of absolute unity, and of a popular convention for establishing and maintaining it: instead of such an assembly they would have had a federal diet, an admirable plan of which was reduced to writing by the Reverend and learned Rosmini. The Pope, the King of Sardinia, the Grand Duke of Tuscany, and the other Princes, would thus have been united in an offensive and defensive league. Such were the bases of this arrangement, and if there were nothing in its details which could interfere with the sacred character and office of the Sovereign Pontiff, few of those who hold constitutional principles, in politics, would have objected to it. Eminent writers of the liberal school have expressed their approbation. M. Laboulaye, in his learned comments on Count Balbo, says: " It was necessary that the Princes should be induced to take an interest in the independence which concerned them so much, by forming a confederation, like the *Zolverein*, which has so powerfully contributed to the union and the greatness of Germany. A confederation is undoubtedly that organization which is most suited to the character and the history of Italy,

and it is also the best means of reviving Italian nationality
and of checking Austria." It is scarcely necessary to add,
that when there should be question of restraining Austria,
there would be at hand an influence which Austria respects,
and to which that mighty Empire and its disciplined legions
would have sooner yielded than to all Italy in arms. Without
some such arrangement, there was no better lot for Italy than
civil war and national disgrace.

Events, meanwhile, hasten on with alarming rapidity.
The Red Republic maintains its idea. The danger with which
Italy is threatened from without, does not, in the least,
moderate its efforts. Its labours, too, are attended with the
only results they were calculated to produce. Italy remains
divided. The of Charles Albert cannot alone cope
with the formid e power of Austria. An united people
might have stayed the tide of battle. The imposing spectacle
of their union would even have influenced a foreign cabinet:
and the legions of Radetsky would never have marched across
the Mincio. But it was otherwise ordained. Men rushed
into every excess. Terrible chastisement followed in their
track. *Perish Italy, rather than our idea*, said the socialist
leaders; and, as if fate had combined with the phrenzy of the
Red Republic to destroy a people, Italy was crushed by the
invader. But what cared they? What was it to them, that
their country was brought low, and its princes humbled in the
field of Novara? This downfall of the Sardinian monarch—
this defeat of Italy, was to them a victory. One more
impediment was removed. "*The war of Kings is at an end,
—that of the people commences,*" said Mazzini; and he
declared himself a soldier. But Garibaldi did not long
command him. His warlike enthusiasm was soon exhausted.
The war of the people also ended in defeat; and Mazzini, tired
of the sword, resumed his pen, and attacked once more the
moderate reformers, who alone had fought like brave men in
the Austrian war. The war of words was more congenial to
the revolutionist: and he made haste to issue a new publication. In this writing he raged against the moderate reformers
as a "set of traitors, as anti-chamber Machiavels who had

muzzled the popular lion for the benefit of kings and aristocracies." These *Machiavels* were such men as Count Balbo, who had given his five sons to the war of independence; M. d'Azeglio, who had been in the campaign with Durando, who had had a leg broken by a ball at Vicenza, whilst defending Monte Benico with two thousand men against twelve thousand Austrians. M. D'Azeglio, still smarting from his wounds as well as from the insults of these reckless politicians, replied in a pamphlet, which appeared under the title of "Fears and Hopes." He was at no pains to spare those club soldiers, those tavern heroes and intriguers, who waged war so cleverly against the men who were standing under the enemy's guns. "For my part," he says in this pamphlet, "I do not fear your Republic, but despotism. Your agitation will end with the Croats." And so it fell out. The prediction was but too well realized. A French writer, M. Mignet, expresses these sentiments at some length, and with remarkable eloquence: "A party as extreme in its desires as in its doctrines, and which believes that it is possessed of nothing so long as it does not possess everything, and which, when it has everything, knows not how to make anything of it; imagined the establishing of a republic in a country which is scarcely capable of attaining to representative monarchy, and where the only thing to be thought of, as yet, was territorial independence. This party divided the thoughts, weakened the efforts of the country, and caused mutual mistrust to arise between those governments and peoples, which were reconciled under constitutional liberty, and had an understanding against the common enemy. They thus compromised the deliverance of the land. The king of Naples, threatened by an insurrection in his capital, retained his troops that were on the point of marching to the theatre of war; the Pope ceased to give encouragement; the king of Piedmont already in full march, hesitated; and Italy, agitated, without being free, became once more powerless, because she was disunited, and beheld the Austrians reappear as conquerors, and re-establish themselves anew as masters, in the recovered plains of Lombardy." These striking words confirm the view I have always entertained,—that the extreme party have, all along, been the ruin of Italy. Radetski, thanks to their sinister operations, having reconquered upper Italy, the socialists hastened towards Rome, spreading terror as they approached, even as if they had been an army of Goths or Vandals. Adding themselves to men of the same opinions, who were dissatisfied, and whom nothing could satisfy, they occasioned an inconceivably great agitation of the people, causing continual disquietude, and exciting inordinate hopes. They inoculated the masses with their baneful principles, which forbade all transaction with the Papal Government. They brought every thing that could be thought of, in aid of the fatal work of dispossessing the Holy Father, as they had already done all that lay in their power to overthrow monarchy in Piedmont. Many moderate reformers became their dupes. We have already seen what popular manifestations were organized at Rome, in the commencement, in honor of Pius IX. The extreme party succeeded in obtaining possession of this powerful machine, and they worked it with consummate skill. The masses, once under agitation, are at the disposal of the most resolute. The reformers allowed themselves to be ensnared. They continued singing their patriotic hymns, the *Roman* MARSEILLAISES, without observing that Radicalism was imperceptibly taking the crown of the causeway, and that the popular demonstrations had entirely changed their character. These, "Young Italy," had at first employed as a threat,—latterly they were an arm in its hands. It now governed in the streets, making a tribune of every milestone. There was only wanting to them a centre, or general head-quarters of insurrection, from which should go forth the word of command,—the signal for every rising of the people. This was the celebrated *Roman circle,*—a sort of convention without commission,—a travelling cohort of two or three hundred agitators, who carried from town to town, the dread and dismal flag of the Red Republic. It was this mob-power, as we have seen, that had, against the inclination of the Holy Father, brought into power the Mamiani ministry. Weak and irresolute, this minister broke the ranks of his own party and passed over to "Young Italy." They dictated to him on every occasion. War with Austria they especially urged upon him, knowing well that the Pope would never agree to it, and by his refusal would lose his popularity. The constitution was at an end. The minister was at the orders of a party out of doors, and no longer the organ of the Sovereign. The Pontifical authority, however much it was still venerated, was in reality no better than an empty name. The Republic reigned, and now only waited for the moment, but too certain at last, when it should be openly recognized. The Mamiani Government, in the meantime, was daily losing ground, and now in its death agony and impotent for good, it persisted, with incor rigible perverseness, in adding to the confusion that prevailed, by repeated declarations of war against Austria. They were ready, like patriots and heroes, to fight for their country; but with all their vanity they hastened not to be enrolled. Whilst they were thus vainly boasting, the few who had volunteered and taken the field, returned from Vicenza, which had been bravely but fruitlessly defended during two days. The Forum warriors only setting out in time to meet their wounded brethren, and give them the honors of a triumphal entry. The war was evidently nothing else than a weapon of offence against the Holy See. Every day, besides, brought the news of fresh disasters. The war-cry was becoming every moment more inopportune. King Charles Albert, driven from the Mincio to the Oglio, thence to the Adda, thence to Milan, was recrossing the Piedmontese frontier, humbled, despairing and heart-broken. Piedmont, meanwhile, was preparing, in the silence of her humiliation, for a last effort.

In these trying circumstances, and with a sad foreboding of more serious evils yet to come, Pius IX., who had tried several ministries without success, had recourse to the well known statesmanship of M. Rossi, and proposed to the former Ambassador of France, that he should become the chief of his council. M. Mignet, the eloquent biographer of Count Rossi, gives a thrilling account of the difficulties and dangers of the position: " M. Rossi at first hesitated; he knew what formidable problems there were to solve. To conduct according to constitutional principles, a government that had been heretofore absolute ; to administer by the hands of laymen, the affairs of a country that had been hitherto subject to Ecclesiastics ; to unite in an Italian league, a state that had been almost always opposed to a political union of the Peninsula ; in a word, to establish all at the same time, a Constitutional Government, a Civil Administration, a National Federation, were not the only difficulties that he would have to overcome. The minister of a Prince, whose confidence others would dispute with him, a stranger in a country, where he would exercise public authority, he would be liable to be left without support notwithstanding his devotedness, and without approbation notwithstanding his services ; to be attacked as a revolutionist by the blind advocates of abuses, and disavowed as an enemy of liberty by the impassioned partisans of chimeras. He continued to decline for a considerable time. The conditions which he at first proposed to the Sovereign Pontiff, not having been accepted, M. Rossi thought that he had escaped the lot that was in store for him. But the Pope, after having essayed in vain a new ministry, pressed him more urgently, in the month of September 1848, to come to his aid, offering him at the same time his full confidence and unlimited authority. M. Rossi accepted." At this period, Count Rossi was sixty years of age. His life had been spent in the midst of political agitation. He had suffered much, and also learned much at the severe school of experience. More than once he had been an exile, and had thus acquired a claim to several countries. Banished the Peninsula in 1815, on account of the part he bore in the cause of Italian liberty, he had resided at Geneva and at Paris, and had left in each of these cities a bright reputation. As a writer on political economy and jurisprudence, he displayed the most extraordinary knowledge of these sciences, great intellectual power, and superior penetration. Relying upon principles and theories, he did not, however, ignore facts, nor refuse to accommodate the lofty forms of science to practical requirements. Nor was the knowledge of mankind wanting to him. He was not one of those rigid theorists who would make nature itself yield to their opinion. To Pius IX. he was an invaluable counsellor, when the affairs of Italy were at so terrible a crisis, and anarchy prevailed at Rome. With these rare endowments, there were not conjoined in the person of Rossi, those outward graces which tend so much to win favor for the public man. His manner was cold and reserved. His keen lynx-like gaze caused no inconsiderable embarrassment. Familiarity with science, and diplomatic habits, had imprinted on his forehead gravity that bore the appearance of superciliousness and disdain. He studied not to please, preferring to command by strength of will and the authority of superior intellect, rather than by the attraction of amiable qualities and the charm of the affections. His mind was that of the statesman, but he possessed not that seductive exterior which fascinates the crowd and disarms hostility—none but his own family knew how really good he was, how tender minded, even whilst these admirable qualities were concealed by a cold and repulsive exterior.

Count Rossi was firmly resolved to preserve the Sovereignty of the Holy See: "The Papacy," he wrote at the time, "is the last living glory of Italy!" His great abilities were applied with incredible zeal and ardor to the important work with which he was entrusted. We read with astonishment what he was able to accomplish in less than two months. And there was still more in preparation. The things to which he at first chiefly devoted his attention, were the interior government of Rome, the state of the finances of the Holy See, and the territorial independence of Italy. He saved the Pontifical treasury from all danger of bankruptcy by obtaining three millions of ecus from the Roman Clergy. Thus relieved from all disquietude as to finance, he applied his mind to the important task of adapting the Government to the new institutions, of causing that to become a fact, which had already a legal existence,—a constitutional Pontificate. To this end, he prepared a series of legislative measures, in order to determine with precision the sphere of action of the different powers, and so confine within certain limits the disorderly force of popular movements. He at the same time projected the civil re-organization of the Roman States, bearing well in mind that good laws are the best guarantee for freedom, and the strongest check to arbitrary power. An Italian in feeling as well as in blood, his patriotism led him to consider how he should best introduce into the political machinery which he was building up, the sound and liberal theories of Gioberti and Rosmini, by negotiating at Turin, at Naples, and at Florence, a confederation which should unite all the Italian States, respecting the forms and institutions peculiar to each state, but fixing between them certain relations in time of peace, determining their military contingents, and regulating their common action in case of war. He gained for this great undertaking the favor of the Pope, and thus to Pius IX. belonged the glory of an important initiation, from which might have proceeded one day, with time, the emancipation and regeneration of Italy. Time, however, was wanting; and anarchy again held sway.

Hitherto the Legislative Chambers had only wasted time in unprofitable debates. For their meeting of the 15th of November, 1848, Count Rossi prepared a bold but conciliatory address. They were now no longer to hear the ambiguous and factious words of a maniac, but the true language of constitutional government. Rossi assumed the attitude of a grave and resolute minister, the counsellor of his sovereign, and the exponent of his views; not the slave of the people, and the organ of their passions. This address was never delivered. It commenced with the following words:—
"Scarcely had his Holiness ascended the Pontifical throne when the Catholic world was filled with admiration at his clemency as a Pontiff and his wisdom as a temporal sovereign. * * * The most important facts have shown to mankind the fallacy of the groundless predictions of that pretended philosophy which had declared the Papacy to be, from the nature of its constitutive principle, the enemy of constitutional liberty. In the course of a few months, the Holy Father, of his own accord, and without aid, accomplished a work which would have sufficed for the glory of a long reign. History, impartially sincere, will repeat,—and not without good reason,—as it records the acts of this Pontificate, that the Church, immovable on her Divine foundations, and inflexible in the sanctity of her dogmas, always intelligently considers

and encourages with admirable prudence, such changes as are suitable in the things of the world." The remainder of the oration was a bold and luminous exposition of the ideas and the policy which M. Rossi had it in charge to carry out. He appealed to the Chamber for the necessary aid of their loyal concurrence, and bound himself in honour to observe faithfully the Constitution.

But there were men who had sworn that the Constitution should no longer exist. This Constitution and the ministry which sustained it were, indeed, formidable impediments to the schemes of the radical faction. Both were the objects of the most violent attacks, as well in street meetings as in the republican journals. The minister remained undaunted. "To reach the Holy Father," said he, "they must pass by my lifeless body." Such a noble determination only rendered him more odious to the revolutionists. On their return from a scientific Congress at Turin, where the name of science was abused in order to conceal their plots, the leaders of the Red Republic decreed the death of Rossi. Mazzini, in a letter which was published, had declared that it was indispensable that he should die. In one of the Clubs of Rome, they selected, by casting lots, the assassins who should bear a hand in the murder of Rossi; and the principal actor in this crime actually practiced on a dead body in one of the hospitals. The day on which the parliament was to meet, 15th November, was the time fixed for the foul deed. Meanwhile repeated warnings reached the ears of the intended victim. Some of the conspirators, struck with remorse, had made revelations; others boasted cynically, that they would soon be rid of the oppressor. The Duchess de Rignano conjured the Minister to avoid leaving the house. Words of warning equally solemn, from other quarters, were alike slighted. Nothing could alarm the Minister. If he indeed believed in a plot, he hoped to disarm the fury of the conspirators by his courageous bearing. He now hastened from his house to the Quirinal Palace, and spoke words of comfort to the Pope, who was in a state of great anxiety. Pius IX. recommended that he should keep on his guard, and imparted to him his benediction,

4

which he then received for the last time. At the door of the Pope's apartments he met an aged priest who beseeched him to remain: "If you proceed," cried he, "you will be murdered." M. Rossi paused a moment. "The cause of the Pope," he said, "is the cause of God;" and he proceeded. A guard of carabiniers, contrary to orders, were treacherously absent from the approach to the Representative Chamber. As the Minister ascended the stairs he was surrounded by a group of conspirators. At first they offered insult; then one of them struck him on the shoulder. Turning indignantly towards this assassin, he exposed his neck to the poniard, which, waiting for the opportune moment, now dealt the fatal blow. The minister fell, deluging with his blood the steps at the very threshold of the Legislative Hall.

The Chamber listened in silence to the account of the murder that was committed at its doors. Not one of all Rome's secular representatives raised his voice in condemnation of this monstrous crime. They passed at once to the order of the day. In the place at the foot of the stairs the civic guard was in arms on duty; but nobody arrested—nobody shewed the least intention to arrest the murderer. The criminal, unpunished, was led in triumph through the city by his accomplices, who were joined by some dragoons and carabiniers or gendarmes. They sang a new hymn—" Blessed be the hand that slew Rossi." The dagger of the assassin was exposed to public veneration, crowned with flowers, in the Café of the fine arts. The populace in their phrensy insulted the widow of the murdered Minister. By an excess of irony, they called upon her to illuminate her house. The newspapers expressed their approval of the crime, as the necessary manifestation of the general sentiment. The whole population by its silence, if not by actual participation in these demoniac rejoicings, became accomplices in the foul deed.

Together with the noble Rossi perished, and perhaps for ages, the cause of Rome, the cause of Italy. What might they not have gained if the minister had been allowed to fulfil his task? Constitutional government would have been established on a solid and lasting basis; the wild agitation of the streets would have subsided, the excited passions of the revolution would have been awed into composure, on beholding the sound, regular and beneficial working of free political institutions. But, by an act which history will never cease to stigmatize, the only man whom the authority of his name and talents and experience rendered equal to the stupendous work of building up, on new principles, the social fabric, is struck down, and Europe which had hitherto looked on with sympathy, recoils in horror. Liberal men throughout the civilized world had long been deeply interested in the state of Italy. In their zeal for her cause they could pardon the ill-controlled agitation of her children, their greatest excesses, even, when they first began to enjoy—to enjoy before they knew how to use it, liberty, that was so strange to them. But with crime and its results they had no sympathy. A state of things, inaugurated by assassination, could only be perpetuated by violent means. The humanity of Europe was shocked. As regarded Rome, the die was cast. She had rejoiced in unhallowed violence; and by the legitimate violence which Divine Providence in due time brought to bear against her, she was punished.

It was in vain now to think of the constitution. By the same blow which struck Rossi down, was the great cause of well-regulated liberty overthrown.

Meanwhile the conspiritors made haste to profit by their crime. There was question in the chamber of sending a deputation to the Pope, in order to express to him the regret of the representatives for what had happened. This was opposed and prevented by Prince Canino.* The revolutionists now

---

* In 1815, the Bonaparte family were without a name in that Europe, where they had possessed so many thrones. One man had compassion on them and acted generously. Pius VIII. welcomed them to his States. A member of this family, Lucian Bonaparte, NAPOLEON's brother, having always shown great faithfulness to the Holy See, Pius VIII. conferred upon him the title of a Roman Prince and the principality of Canino. Lucian's son has not been gifted to walk in the footsteps of his honorable father. Balleydier in his history of the Roman revolution, thus portrays him: "Versed in dissimulation, Charles Bonaparte had under the preceding Pontificate, acted two very opposite characters. In the morning attending in the ante-chambers of the Cardinals, in the evening at the Conciliabula of the secret Societies, he laboured to secure, by a double game, the chances of the present, and the probabilities of the future. He had often been seen, going piously, to the Vatican even, to lay at the feet of Gregory XVI., homage which his heart belied." No doubt in 1847 and 1848, he thought himself an abler man than his father, as he marched poniard in hand, at the head of the malcontents of Rome.

formed a sort of permanent club, which was anxious to make a great demonstration, and required that the civic guard and the army should join them. When all was in readiness, a mob that had been for some time organized for the purpose, marched to the Quirinal, the Pope's residence, and pointed their cannon against the gates. From the neighbouring houses muskets were discharged. A ball struck Monsignor Palma, who expired at the feet of the Holy Father. One of the gates was set on fire, but the Swiss guards succeeded in extinguishing the flames. They threatened to put to death all the inmates of the Palace, with the exception only of Pius IX. himself, if he would not yield to the requirements of the revolution. Balls which fell in his chamber, proved but too well that the Pope, even, would not have been spared. Reduced to this extremity, Pius IX., who had hitherto refused to accept a ministry, the mere naming of which was an insult to him, at last, but only with a view to save the lives of the people around him, submitted. Mamiani with his former programme, and in addition to it, the constituent assembly, consisting of the representatives all Italy; Doctor Sterbini, Guœtti, and some four other names equally unacceptable, constituted this radical administration. They wished to add the venerated name of Rosmini; but this learned divine refused to take any part in their proceedings.

When, on the 17th November, several deputies proposed that a deputation of the Representatives should be sent to Pius IX. in order to express to him their devotedness and their gratitude, Prince de Canino prevented so laudable a thing from being done, declaring that it would be imprudent, and that they might have reason to repent it. "Citizen Bonaparte," as he delighted to be called, farther said, that the Italian people were indisputably the master now, and that they well knew how to humble the Parliament, the ministers, and the thrones, which should oppose their energetic impulses.

During this terrible crisis the Pope was abandoned by all save a few friends, the officials of his palace, his faithful Swiss guards, and the foreign ambassadors. Among those who remained with him were six noble guards, and the cardinals, Soglia and Antonelli. Such was the whole court and army of the great Pontiff who was so lately the idol of his people and the hope of mankind. In this all but desperate condition he never lost confidence. He was all along self-possessed and serene. He was pained only by the ingratitude of his people.

The ministry of subversion had scarcely extorted from the Pope his reluctant consent to their existence when the Holy Father, solemnly, and in the face of Christian Europe, as represented by its ambassadors,* protested against this ministry and all its acts. The multitude, intoxicated with their delusive success, and the leaders who aspired to guide them, were still celebrating their victory; the frequent discharge of firearms and the loud vociferations of the crowd were still reverberating through the venerable edifices of Rome, when the Holy Father addressed the following words— speaking the while with indescribable emotion—to the ambassadors, by whom he was surrounded: "Gentlemen, I am a prisoner here. Now that I am deprived of all support and of all power, my whole conduct will have only one aim—to prevent any, even one drop of fraternal blood from being uselessly shed in my cause. I yield everything to this principle; but at the same time, I am anxious that you, gentlemen, should know, that all Europe should be made

---

* These ambassadors and diplomatists were Martinez Della Rosa, the ambassador of Spain, with the Secretary of the Embassy, M. Arnao; the Duke d'Harcour, ambassador of France; the Count de Spaur, ambassador of Bavaria; the Baron Venda Cruz, ambassador of Portugal, with the Commandant Huston; the Count Bautenleff, who represented at that time the Emperor of Russia and King of Poland; Figuereido, ambassador of Brazil; Liedekerke of Holland, and several other diplomatists, of whom not one was an Italian. There was at Rome also on the occasion, although not in the appartments of the Pope, a British Statesman, who was not an ambassador, inasmuch, whatever may have been his business at Rome, he had no recognized mission, if any mission at all, to the Sovereign of Rome. He was rather officious, than official, and, whether he had commission or not, he held, as is well known, serious communications with the enemies of the Pope. Lord Minto was enthusiastically received by the secret societies of Rome. The people, forgetting at the time the way to the Quirinal, went to serenade him. Lord Minto frequented "the popular circle," (a band of three hundred chosen agitators, whose office it was to carry the torch of discord into all the cities of the Papal States, and of Italy,) and the offices of the socialist newspaper. He went so far as to receive courteously Cicervacchio, and made verses for his son Cicervacchietto. (Rohrbacher.)

The Earl of Minto was not, however, a faithful exponent of the opinions of British Statesmen. Few of them, fortunately, hold the subversive doctrines that were countenanced by his lordship, when representing at Rome, the least respectable portion of the Whig party.

aware that I take no part, even nominally, in this government, and that I am resolved to remain an absolute stranger to it. I have forbidden them to abuse my name ; I have ordered that recourse should not be had even to the ordinary formulas.'' Thus did the Pontiff abdicate provisionally until more happy days should dawn upon his country. The representatives of the powers received with respect and emotion which found expression in tears, the protestation of Pius IX., who was reduced to be a prisoner in his own palace, and a hostage of the Revolution.

Thus ended for the time, and to his inexpressible regret, the career of the statesman Pope. What he may yet be able to accomplish in the better days which, may we hope, are yet in store for him, none can venture to foretell. But if Rome and the Roman States—if all the kingdoms, principalities, and republics of Italy, have not yet been favoured with the wished-for measure of liberty, no blame can be imputed to the Pope of our time, who as we learn so clearly from the study of his political career, has nothing more at heart, as a temporal sovereign, than to reign as the constitutional head of a constitutional government.*

* Vide APPENDIX.

THE TEMPORAL SOVEREIGNTY
Of the Pope,
WITH RELATION TO THE STATE OF ITALY, &c.

PART II.

THE SPIRIT OF THE AGE.

It would, indeed, be difficult to find anything in the character or political career of Pius IX., which could lead to the conviction that the Pontifical sovereignty of Rome ought to give place to a red, or any other form or colour of republic. But, it may not perhaps be in accordance with the spirit of the age, that the Pope should reign, whilst the men who are so anxious to fill his place remain in obscurity.

What then is the spirit of the age, from which we are taught to expect so much? Will any intelligent well-informed man call in question the reply, that the time in which we live is characterized by its greater love of knowledge, its moderation, its liberality, its spirit of peace and humanity, no less than by the desire that justice and fair-dealing should everywhere prevail? At whose hands, then, are we to look for the government that shall be most in accordance with these views and sentiments which now so generally obtain? Will it be found with the Pope, who rules, according to knowledge, with wisdom, moderation, and humanity; or with the retrograde faction, that would throw back the world of the nineteenth century to the darkest epoch of Pagan barbarism, and in characters of blood, inscribe the laws of Draco on the tablets of modern Europe?

I. ENLIGHTENMENT.

This age of the world, more, perhaps, than any preceding period, is distinguished by its love of knowledge. At what time was science so generally, so earnestly, and so advantageously cultivated? None will pretend, indeed, that mankind have as yet even made the conquest of all science. But at what earlier epoch was more progress made, greater success achieved? Was there ever a period when the pursuit of knowledge was held to be so honorable, or when its votaries were universally encouraged, and crowned with rewards? That science, above all, as difficult in its acquirement as it is important in its results,—the science of man—is now more than ever an object of study; and with good reason, assuredly: for is it not the groundwork of political science, the science of government, upon which depends the happiness of nations? Now, who in past ages, as well as the present time, have shown themselves the friends of science? None more than the Popes. Deny this, and you blot out, not pages, not volumes only, but all history.

Not only have the Popes in every age encouraged science. They have themselves excelled in many of its branches. The world is indebted to them for important discoveries. The reformation of the Kalendar, alone, would add lustre to any ordinary dynasty.

But, on the other hand, what has science to expect from the men who are so anxious to overthrow the venerable Sovereignty? Just as much as in a by-gone age was gained, or could now be hoped for, from a reign of terror—from the reign of "the hand of iron." This much we know, that these men are deficient in the knowledge of man, in the science of government. Who but such politicians could for a moment suppose that the world of to-day would submit to a rule of tyranny and fear? In some of the lesser States such a system may be established, and may for a time prevail. But they read not aright the signs of the times—they understand not the spirit of the age, who maintain that a government of this extreme and ferocious character is adapted to the wants, the feelings, the state of progress, the habits, or even the prejudices of the men and nations of our epoch. In an important and vital matter, therefore, the science of the socialist faction is at fault. That knowledge which, above all others, they ought to possess, who aspire to rule mankind—the knowledge of the true principles of government, of sound political economy—

they have not yet mastered; nor are they likely soon to learn it. They are at the wrong school. Not the school of the age; but a school which the age condemns.

THE SPIRIT OF THE AGE—II. JUSTICE.

Another manifest and striking characteristic of the age, is the desire, as general as it is laudable, that justice should prevail. Now, to all who are in the least conversant with the history of the Civil Government of the Roman States, there is nothing better known than that it has always been distinguished by its love of justice. Nor was this a vain and barren theory. The rule of the Popes, in all ages, may be described as, justice in action. What was it, that first recommended it to the favor of mankind—that, so to speak, forced it into political existence? that constrained it, though reluctant, to assume the Government of Rome? That love of justice, which is inseparable from its spiritual character; that stern impartiality which accepts not persons, which knows not man from man. "Discite Justitiam, moniti," said the Pagan sages to the rulers of their time and creed. But sooner than take the lesson, these rulers abdicate their power, and abandon Rome. And thus, together with the reign of justice, is established the temporal authority of the Christian High Priest. How carefully these new sovereigns refrain from war! It is not upon record, that they ever engaged in a war of aggression, or ever, consequently, in an unjust war,* if we except the armaments they encouraged and promoted, not for their

---

* A very profound Statesman, Count Joseph de Maistre, in speaking of the difference between the Roman and other European governments says: "It is a very remarkable circumstance, but either disregarded or not sufficiently attended to, that the Popes have never taken advantage of the great power in their possession, for the aggrandizement of their States. What could have been more natural, for instance, or more tempting to human nature, than to reserve a portion of the Provinces conquered from the Saracens, and which they gave up to the first occupant, to repel the Turkish ascendency, always on the increase? But this, however, they never did, not even with regard to the adjacent countries, as in the instance of the Two Sicilies, to which they had incontestible rights, at least, according to the ideas then prevailing, and over which they were, nevertheless, contented with an empty sovereignty, which soon ended in the *Aaquenée*, a slight tribute, and merely nominal, which the bad taste of the age still disputes with them."—*Du Pope*: Book II., Chap. 6.

own protection only, but for the safety, the liberty, and the Religion of all Europe. They have no place, whatever, in the annals of carnage and devastation. More than once have they saved their people from war and its attendant horrors. But where is the people who can say that the dread scourge was ever inflicted on them by the Pontiff Rulers?

Examine more closely still the Government of the Popes. In their internal administration, how strictly just! The nation cannot be named, in the tribunals of which greater pains are taken to distribute justice with an equal hand. And, does the government, at any time, stand in need of extraordinary pecuniary aid, there is no iniquitous and violent seizing of the property of any class or corporation in the community, no undue increasing of the taxation, no extortion, no cruelty, no injustice in the collection of the existing taxes. A voluntary grant is at hand, as well to meet the exigency of the time, as to render more firm and indissoluble the bond that binds the people to their sovereign. Justice in the Roman States is practiced even to scruple. Who will not say that it was justice, and more than justice, on the part of the Papal Government, to pay from its own resources, the debts of the unauthorized and revolutionary governments of 1848, debts incurred for the most part in setting at defiance—in waging war against the legitimate Ruler of the country?

In merely temporal States, no doubt, justice has prevailed, and does prevail; but in no other State has its practice been for many centuries—even from the foundation of the State to its latest hour, the invariable rule. Under no other constitution, however liberal, has the necessary severity of justice been so wisely moderated by mercy, but without diminution of its rightful privilege. " Earthly power doth then shew likest God's when mercy seasons justice."

Such is the perfection of justice. Let it now be decided (the deliberative effort will not be great) who they are who approach nearest to this standard,—whether the Popes, who have been so cruelly reviled, or the socialist republican party, who, whilst they lay claim to superior political wisdom, carry their views of justice far beyond anything of which ancient or modern Rome bears record, *pursue to extremity the victim of their secret judgment, and inflict the fatal blow, even should the object of their vengeance have sought refuge in the bosom of his mother, or in the Sanctuary of God.*

It must not, however, be supposed that justice is altogether foreign to these gentlemen. When there is question of certain interests, they pay court to the Goddess, and make her all their own. If when they are in power, parties complain of the absence of justice, or groan under its excessive application, they know how to make amends. They do themselves *justice*. In speaking of Signor Cipriani, the socialist and rebel ruler of the Emilian Provinces—that portion of the Pope's territory in which rebellion is temporarily triumphant—journals friendly to the revolutionary cause have been pleased to say :— " Scarcely were his powers confirmed by the assembly, when he at once doubled his salary, which is now 1000 écus per month, (£214 sterling,) and allowed himself 70 écus more for his monthly travelling expenses. In the course of a few days, moreover, he caused to be paid to him 30,000 francs (£1200 sterling) by way of *secret* service money." Little better, indeed, could be expected of the son of a slave merchant, who himself, writes the same journal, " in his youth, bought and sold unhappy negroes." Thus has the meek and learned Prelate, who so lately represented at Bologna the sovereignty of the Chief Pastor, given place to the slave-dealer, the man of forbidding manners and cruel habits. "I think I see him," says the same writer, " stripped of his embroidered robes, arrayed in the white costume of the remote Islands, and with cudgel in hand, driving, as of old, his wretched negroes. O, Bologna ! Bologna ! learned and noble city ! what hast thou done to provoke the wrath of Heaven, that thou shouldst be thus bent low beneath the degrading yoke of an ignorant and cruel despotism !"—(*Apud Courrier du Canada*.)

And you, constitutionalists of Italy, what have you done that you should be thus reduced to vent in empty words your indignation and your sorrow? How long,

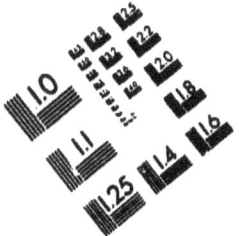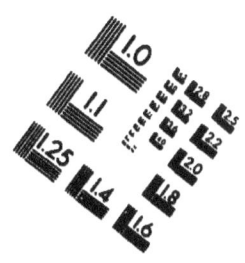

IMAGE EVALUATION
TEST TARGET (MT-3)

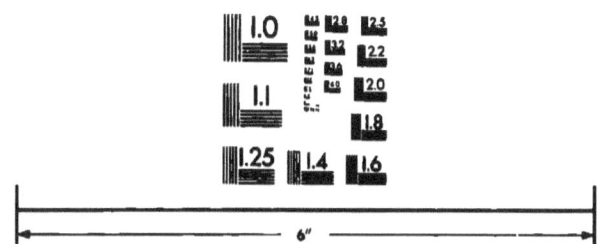

Photographic
Sciences
Corporation

23 WEST MAIN STREET
WEBSTER, N.Y. 14580
(716) 872-4503

O Italian people! intellectual and powerful as you are, how long will you allow to reign over you, this red republic and its *justice* ?

The systematic injustice of the party—now provisionally only, it must be hoped—in power is already producing its fruit. No real, honest election to any office is possible. The unfortunate inhabitants must vote as the powers that be direct them. Whether there be question of choosing a representative or a municipal magistrate, the suffrages are taken at the point of the bayonet. This reign of terror has not yet been sufficiently powerful to do more than cause about one-third of the populations of the alienated Papal territory to concur, or rather, to make a shew of concurring, in sending representatives to the Legislative Assembly. Meanwhile the Assembly is constituted; and whatever abuses it may establish, whatever crimes it may perpetrate, must be charged to its own account, not to the people, whom it by no means represents. Its forced loans, not only shock the sense of justice, so deeply rooted in the popular mind, but cause the greatest discontent, and put an end to trade and businesss of every kind. This is calculated to drive capital from the cities, together with all other sources of prosperity. We learn from authentic documents that it has already done so, and that among the operative and commercial classes, in consequence, the greatest distress prevails. We are informed, at the same time,—talent and merit being placed in abeyance,—that persons of the lowest condition, as devoid of knowledge as of character, are promoted to offices of trust.* This may be necessary to keep the slave-driving Governor in countenance; but it is just, only, according to Red Republican views of justice.

THE SPIRIT OF THE AGE—III., HUMANITY.

If this age justly claims superiority, it is chiefly on the ground of its greater humanity. In Pagan times, everything conspired to render men cruel and ferocious. Religion and social usages tended alike to maintain the reign of cruelty and

---

* An inauspicious sign of the times. The Alcoran, which contains many valuable maxims of worldly wisdom, says, " that one of the signs of the end of the world will be, the advancement of persons of low condition to the highest dignities."

barbarism. And those peoples became the greatest and most powerful in the end, who were characterized not by superior learning and refinement, but by their pre-eminence in sternness and ferocity. Thus did Pagan Rome, celebrated by her bards as " *Roma ferox*," the people of hard, cruel, and unbending mind, whom no considerations of humanity could ever for a moment stay in their career of conquest, obtain dominion over all the nations of the world? Nor with th. attainment of her ends did the rigid character of ancient Rome pass away. She reached at the same time the height of her ambition and the extreme of cruelty. Not only is this manifest in her relations with vanquished states, whose kings she dragged in all the humiliation of defeat at the chariot wheels of the savage warriors, whom she deified, but more still in her inhuman treatment of the Christian people. With an instinctive hatred of that religion which by meekness and self-sacrifice was destined so soon to triumph over her ferocity, she exhausts her ingenuity in devising new tortures for such of her children as, untrue to her traditions of war and blood and superstition, renounce her false gods and embrace the Christian faith. Rome is yet in all the pride and glory of Empire, when the Religion she laboured so anxiously and so mercilessly to destroy ascends her capitol and displays on her imperial crown its imperishable emblem. And now begins the mighty war which throughout all time will not cease to rage—the war of meekness against cruelty—of the mild and humanizing influence of the Cross against the unbending sternness of worldly power—of that new civilization which shall encourage science, foster art, and promote by a thousand means the happiness of mankind,—against the untamed despotism which knows no other law than that of strength overwhelming weakness. Important conquests are now gradually achieved. Whole peoples come under the mild sway of the Heavenly influence. But never at any one time has it been given to all the populations of the world to enjoy this reign of peace. It gains ground, nevertheless, and every day obtains new victories. What progress do we not behold at length in our favoured age! Nations that only half a century ago yielded r~t to Pagan Rome, in their thirst for unlawful conquest, and bore in their national character the same mark of barbarism —a stern, cruel and unrelenting mind, now, as if moved by some overpowering influence, assume an entirely new mode of being. War there is still, and rumour of war. But, hard and savage as it ever must be, war, even, puts on a new face. It is no longer the war of Pagan days, inspired, fostered, and sustained by mutual hate. It is the work of sad necessity— deplorable, melancholy work, which all men regret, mourn over, and endeavour to bring to an end. Are its terrors let loose upon a people, they are confined to the hour of deadly strife, almost to the comparatively narrow limits of the battlefield. There, even, war is not what it was wont to be. Just as in the days of glorious chivalry among a few peoples, so now, in all civilized nations, it respects its victims. It will not trample on the fallen. The brave soldier who has been first in the field of battle, to lay low his country's foes, beholding only in the vanquished and prostrate enemy, his fellow-beings in distress, hastens to bind up their wounds, dispel their fears, and give comfort to their sorrow.

Instances might be adduced, indeed, when, at moments of extreme excitement, the spirit of revenge has blazed forth in all its hideous forms ; but, such occurrences, unusual as they are, only bring into stronger relief that humanity which, it must be acknowledged, is a feature of the age, as general as it is remarkable. And it remains an uncontroverted fact that war, even, in obedience to the spirit of the time, has changed its character. Whatever may be, in regard to such an alternative, at certain times, the position of Governments, the people are ever ready to make sacrifices—to cast into the scales their treasures, and forfeit, if need be, not only their property, but their life also—everything, except national honour, rather than engage in deadly strife. Such was the disposition of the British people when on the eve of the terrible conflict with Russia. Nor do they resolve on war until every resource of diplomacy has been exhausted. And, when state-craft can do no more, and the nation has made up its mind, an influential association makes a final effort in the cause of peace; but in vain: the demon of discord rules. The mighty potentate—the man of a by-gone age, whose views of aggrandizement had made war inevitable—is withdrawn from the scene, and the man of the time succeeds.* This pacific Emperor, brave as he is generous, weeps over the ruin war has made. He stays its cruel arm; and mankind hail with delight the new reign, the reign of progress and of peace.

Nor are other nations of a warlike mind, although possessing, as of old, all the qualities that purchase victory in the battle field. Of this no better proof could be adduced than the noble protest of the Representatives of the French, when their Emperor, erewhile, decided on hostilities with Austria. No doubt there was much in the character of that invasion of the States of Italy, that was not acceptable to a chivalrous and Christian people. But how much of their opposition, and to their credit, it was as great as could be made in the face of Imperial power, may we not ascribe to the growing dislike to strife and bloodshed, which so decidedly characterizes the civilization of the age?

In the administration of justice, also, there is more humanity than in by-gone times. Who would think it reasonable now-a-days that petty faults should be visited with the same chastisements, as great and destructive crimes? And yet, in former ages, it was the received practice in many states to punish with the severest penalties known to human laws, the most inconsiderable violations of property. A very opposite spirit now prevails. With the greatest reluctance only will a jury convict of murder even, lest capital punishment might ensue. And is it not a very general opinion that there should be no such punishment? And is it not the practice of the most enlightened governments, to have recourse to it only rarely, and when there is question of the worst and most execrable crimes?

---

* Recent correspondence has given rise to doubts whether Alexander of Russia will realize, especially in regard of Poland, the high promise with which his reign so auspiciously began. In the meantime, may it still be hoped, that Alexander II. will continue to be a second Alexander. His illustrious Predecessor was sometimes, in opposition to his own sounder views, under the necessity of sacrificing to popular prejudice. Such policy might be carried too far, and retard, if not finally prevent, many proposed improvements.

With regard to political offences, what a change!—Anciently, it may be said, for such crimes there was no forgiveness. The axe, the gibbet, the rack, and the faggot were in daily requisition. Temporary exile, fines, and limited terms of imprisonment, are the severest penalties that in most countries are now inflicted on offenders against the State. If among any people a more rigid policy is at any time followed, it meets with universal reprobation, whilst it frustrates the very end it has in view.

If in any one thing more than another the superior humanity of the age be manifest, it is in the conduct of civilized nations towards slavery. With a few exceptions that can never be sufficiently regretted, they all look upon it as a blot, wherever it exists, that cannot be too speedily wiped out. Long after slavery has fled from her shores, the British nation beholds it with pain in her colonial empire. She resolves that it shall cease, and there ensues a stupendous sacrifice of treasure, together with the temporary ruin of rich colonies. But the slave is at liberty, and the nation is satisfied.

It is no slight indication of the improved feeling of the time that the great peoples all concur in discouraging slavery wherever it is found, and in setting their bann on the cruel and infamous practice of trading in slaves.

One powerful people whilst claiming to be the most free, if not the most enlightened, of any in the world, still countenance and uphold the detested slave system. Amongst them, even, a sounder public opinion and a feeling more in harmony with the humane spirit of the age, are beginning to prevail. May such sentiments increase! May they every day gain strength, until by opinion, and opinion alone, the foul stain be blotted out!

THE PAPAL GOVERNMENT EMINENTLY CHARACTERIZED BY ITS HUMANITY.

The height of reasonable men's ambition is undoubtedly a government conformable to the spirit of the age. None will deny that this age is characterized by a greater degree of humanity than was generally known at any former epoch. If this be so, and I think it has been satisfactorily shewn, the Government of the Roman Pontiffs has more than an ordinary claim on the attention of statesmen and politicians. We have only to consider what a state of barbarism the world was reduced to, in order to understand how opportunely the benevolent rule of the Popes came to the relief of mankind. To such lengths had the selfishness of Pagan governments been carried, that no considerations of mercy and humanity could divert them from purposes and enterprises, however wicked, that were calculated to extend their power, increase their wealth, or in any way promote their material well-being. For this end were whole Provinces and Kingdoms mercilessly sacrificed. The most vexatious systems of taxation were resorted to, and unfeelingly put in practice. No office, no place, no dignity, was sacred in the estimation of the people— who believed that they were made to rule, and who, cost what it would, were resolved to rule. That admirably framed material form on which the Divinity has stamped the impress of mind—even the eternal mind, inspired them with no respect. Nor did they reverence the temple of God itself,—that Holiest of all Holy places, at the portals of which the conquerors of a former age had stood awe-struck and trembling. The very amusements of the people of those times were barbarous and cruel. What more savage than the gladiatorial fights in which they took such delight? Nor was it enough in order to satisfy the depraved appetite of a blood-thirsty populace, that men should contend with men in deadly strife, the trained pugilist, the wrestler, the gladiator must prove his skill, his strength, and his contempt of death, in the unequal contest with more deadly foes, and when the mortal blow is struck a shout of triumph resounds through the crowded amphitheatre. No matter though the victor be an infuriated lion, or a famished tiger. The awful death agony of the strong man struck down in his strength, awakens no kindred feeling, no sympathetic emotion, no salutary thought.

In the midst of these horrors, arises the new power. It is, at first, resisted, as every other power had been. Frequently, even, it is brought, in appearance, at least, to the lowest ebb. The starved tigers, that shall next arrive from the African desert, will devour its last remnant. But, it is not to be thus put down. It will yet live, and ere many days, will shut the tiger's mouth, bid the roaring of the lion cease, and the still more savage cry of "the christians to the lions," that has so long resounded in the thoroughfares of Heathen Rome. To the Romans of old, the shedding of blood was a pastime. The life of man was of no value in their sight. That of an Emperor, however, they held to be of some consequence, and, in order to save it, any number of unimportant lives might laudably be sacrificed. Hence, it was, that when Constantine was ill of leprosy, and in imminent danger, it was recommended that he should have recourse to a bath of human blood,—even the blood of infants. The victims are already selected, when a vision appals and warns the heathen potentate. He seeks the presence of Pope Sylvester, whom the dread of Roman cruelty has driven to the mountains. The holy Pontiff pronounces impious, as it is inhuman, the remedy of blood. "Let the soul first be cleansed," said he, "in the baptismal font, and your leprosy will need no other healing." The Emperor obeys,—becomes a Christian, and, together with the regenerating water, receives his first great lesson of Christian teaching,—that, to shed innocent blood, is a violation of the laws of God and nature. Nor is this lesson to be soon forgot. The mighty Monarch, to whom, through the medium of the Apostolic Pontiffs, it has been given, as a revelation from on High, will bear well in mind, a doctrine, so completely in accordance with unvitiated reason, and will moreover, cause it to be universally respected. Thus is the Roman Empire, by the ministry of its first Christian Sovereign, and through the influence of the Chief Pastor, already divested of half its barbarism. So charmed are mankind with this new and better statesmanship, that, ere many more years have passed away, they will have no other ruler than the Pontiff. In vain does he repel the honor. With all its burthens, he must bear it. The Emperors, themselves, concur with the rest of men in giving up the Government of Rome to its Bishops, whose office will henceforth be twofold. Even, as to the Imperial dignity, had been added the honors of the chief sacerdotal function, so to the office of High Priest, does the christian Pontiff add the cares of temporal Sovereignty. Not, however, without reluctance, does he accept, if he can be said to have accepted, as yet, the new charge, as in compliance with the people's wish, no less than by the Imperial act, he continues to fulfill its duties, he protests that he is only in the place of another power, and in the name of the Emperor, he dispenses justice to Rome and the subject Provinces. That the Chief Pastor, so early as the days of Constantine, no longer compelled by savage persecution to look for safety in the wilderness or the catacombs of Rome, really governed the Western empire—is beyond dispute. It matters not, it does not in the least diminish the reality of this dominion, that the Cæsars still bore their high title, and were acknowledged, as well by the people, as by the Pontiff. Weary of the cares of empire, they beheld without jealousy the sceptre they had wielded, with such power and terror, transferred at length to less terrible but more vigorous hands. Urged by such considerations, the magnanimous Constantine, confiding in the superior wisdom of Pontifical rule, withdrew to the new city he had built, his own Constantinople, and was content to reign over the Eastern portion of the vast Roman world.*

Thus, with a most humane and humanizing act did the temporal rule of the Popes commence. The like humanity has never failed to wait upon its progress. It has never ceased to be the distinguishing characteristic, the chief glory of its long career.

How often do we not behold the Pontifical authority and influence saving Rome, Italy, the whole Western empire from the tyranny of Barbarians who, availing themselves of the absence of the emperors, endeavored one after another to establish their power at Rome. The Heruli, under Odoacer, succeeded in overthrowing the empire of the West. But it is not given to them, to displace the Roman Pontiff who moderates the fury of these savage hordes, and causes justice and humanity to be still respected. The Goths succeed the Heruli, and the Lombards the Goths. But whilst all these

* Vide APPENDIX.

warlike nations, in their turn, become masters of Italy ; to none of them is it permitted, to hold permanent dominion. They are driven to Milan, to Pavia, to Ravenna, and are made to respect the *donation* of sovereignty over Rome and the surrounding countries, made by the first Christian Emperor to the Roman Pontiff. This was, indeed, a victory—a victory in the cause of peace, in the cause of mankind. The power that achieved it was more than that of arms ; it was the power of the unseen but mighty hand, which was slowly but surely and irresistibly accomplishing the greatest of revolutions, changing, remodelling all things, renewing the face of the earth, creating in the moral order a new world. With Italy must the work begin. There, in the very centre of civilization, had barbarism taken up its abode. It is contended with, and it is tamed. Its innumerable errors—its sins against human policy as well as against the laws of nature and of God —are held up and exposed as in the light of the noon-day sun. Its cruelties at first are mitigated ; finally done away with; and its crimes chastised.

Ere all this was brought to pass, what evils was not Italy a prey to whilst yet prevailed the rule of those rude and discordant tribes, if rule that could be called, which was spoliation and anarchy rather than government, to what a mel ncholy state was not the conquered territory reduced. No order, no peace, no progress, no prosperity. It was as a sad chamber of horrors—dark, dismal and repulsive.

"The state of those beautiful countries," writes de Maistre, "cannot be described, and still excites pity as we peruse their history. Laid waste by the barbarians, abandoned by its sovereigns, Italy no longer knew to whom it belonged, and its people were reduced to despair. In the midst of these calamities, the Popes were *the only refuge of the unfortunate*, and without desiring it, by the force of circumstances alone, were substituted for the Emperor, and all eyes were fixed upon them. Italians, Heruli, Lombards, French, were all agreed in this respect."

Need it be added that the government which could thus command the submission, the affection, the reverence of so many warrior peoples, must have been characterized not only by its superior wisdom, but also by that humanity, the absence of which, above all other things, had made every other government impossible. It is the victory of peace over war, the triumph of christian love over the fierce and contending passions of a barbarous age and a crumbling empire.

THE TEMPORAL POWER ORIGINATING IN THE WISDOM AND HUMANITY OF THE PAPAL RULERS—OPINION OF THE CELEBRATED WRITER BALMES.

"Such have been the outcries raised against the colossal power, against this usurpation of rights, that we might suppose the Popes to have been a succession of deep conspirators, who, by their intrigues and artifices, aimed at nothing short of universal monarchy. As our opponents plume themselves on their spirit of observation and historical analysis, I felt it necessary to observe *that the temporal power of the Popes was strengthened and extended* at a time when no other power was as yet really constituted. To call that power usurpation, therefore, is not merely an inaccuracy; it is an anachronism. In the general confusion brought upon all European society by the irruptions of the barbarians, in that strange medley of races, laws, manners and traditions, there remained only one solid foundation for the structure of the edifice of civilization and refinement—only one luminous body to shine upon the chaos, only one element capable of giving life to the germ of regeneration that lay buried in bloodstained ruins. Christianity predominant over and annihilating the remains of other religions, arose, in this age of desolation, like a solitary column in the centre of a ruined city, or like a bright beacon amid darkness.

Barbarians, and proud of their triumphs as they were, the conquering people bowed their head beneath the Pastoral staff that governs the flock of Jesus Christ. The spiritual pastors, a body of men quite new to these barbarians, and speaking a lofty and divine language, obtained over the chiefs of the ferocious hordes from the North a complete and permanent ascendancy, which the course of ages could not destroy. Such was the foundation of the temporal power in the Church; and it will be easily conceived that as the Pope towered above all the other pastors in the ecclesiastical edifice, like a superb cupola over the other parts of a magnificent temple, his temporal power must have risen far higher than that of ordinary Bishops; and must also have had a deeper, more solid, and more lasting foundation. All the principles of legislation, all the foundations of society, all the elements of intellectual culture, all that remained of the arts and sciences, all was in the hands of religion; and all very naturally sought protection from the Pontifical throne,—the only power acting with concert, order and regularity, and the only one that offered any guarantee for stability and perseverance. Wars succeeded to wars, convulsions to convulsions, the forms of society were continually changing; but the one great, general and dominant fact, the stability and influence of religion, remained still the same; and it is ridiculous in any man to declaim against a phenomenon so natural, so inevitable, and above all, so advantageous, designating it "a succession of usurpations of temporal power."

ENQUIRY CONTINUED—THE PAPAL GOVERNMENT ESSENTIALLY HUMANE.

In none of those things in which it is in the power of governments to exercise influences beneficial to the cause of humanity, has the government of the Popes ever shewn itself inferior to the best systems of human policy. On the contrary, it has not only equalled but surpassed them all. Its adversaries, even, acknowledge that none of them are at least so worthy of attention, And that Protestant writer spoke truly who said "There is not, and there never was on this earth, a work of human policy so well deserving of examination." As far as the Papacy is a work of human policy—a temporal government—we find, on enquiring into its merits, that on the ground of humanity alone no other system can at all compare with it. It is of the very nature of the Pontifical power to be able to exercise the functions of government with more humanity than other governments. Its spiritual and sacred character can never be separated from its temporal attributes, and hence, it must always be capable of maintaining order, and administering justice with less severity, although not less successfully, than any other government whatever. Its temporal subjects being unable to abstract the idea of the spiritual from that of the temporal rule, will pay to the latter in part that reverence which, strictly speaking, is due only to the former. Thus, without the terrors of power, does the Pontifical government accomplish the work of power, attracting, as it is so well entitled to do, by its twofold character, that affection, that confidence, that obedience, which all the punishments that merely civil governments are wont to have recourse to never can command. It will easily be shewn that this is no vain theory, but that the idea of the two-fold character of the Papal rule has enabled it to govern with more mildness, and, at the same time, with more advantage to society than any other authority in the world. 1st. It has been more humane in the exercise of its functions as regards the maintaining of peace and order.— 2nd. It has been more moderate and merciful, although not less just, in the administration of justice. 3rd. On the few occasions in which it has reluctantly engaged in war, it has shewn more consideration for human life, more of the spirit of peace and forgiveness, whilst revenge has been wholly unknown to it. 4th. Not only has it encouraged learning and the fine arts, with all their civilizing influences, but more than any other government, it has always promoted education in all orders of society, and that at times when to educate certain classes of the people was, in many great nations, considered worse than useless. 5th. And whilst, as yet, the unfortunate were held to be as accursed beings by the mass of mankind, the government of the Popes cherished the poor and the lowly, establishing every day new institutions for their relief, and doing more from its own limited resources for the encouragement of industry and every useful art by which misery could be obviated or relieved, and the condition of its victims improved, than most other nations with larger means at their disposal, ever thought of undertaking.

HUMANITY OF THE PONTIFICAL GOVERNMENT IN THE PUNISHMENT OF POLITICAL OFFENCES.

The demands of humanity as regards offenders against the

State are at length recognized by the great civilized nations. But this recognition is of very modern date, and it may well be doubted whether it would stand the test of any serious ordeal. The comparative weakness of all merely civil governments drives them to extremes. In moments of great peril they take counsel with fear, and resort to cruelty. If great powers of late, and it is only of late, have acted with magnanimity and shewn mercy, it was only when their power was not really threatened, and when the spirit of the age required some degree of homage at their hands. But the Papal government has not been wont to act like one seized with panic. From the first moment it held civil rule in the world it has been consistently humane. In vain shall we search in the long history of its dominion for the record of any act of cruelty it has deemed it necessary to perform against a State offender. But say its enemies, it has other and more efficacious modes of punishment. We grant them that it has. Its spiritual thunder is still formidable. But at the same time, we claim for the Papal rule a source of excellence and efficiency which no other government can pretend to. This may be the reason why it ought to be dispensed with. Nations that would now do away with all punishments, and rule only by kindness, would be satisfied with the precedents they find in the past history of the Popedom, They are too enlightened to require the model it offers to them in the present age. But let us not mistake it, it is not, it cannot be a model government. It is now, as it has been in all time past, unique. Other states may behold it, may admire it, may study its ways and learn wisdom ; nay, and as far as their position will admit of it, meekness and clemency, too. But there will always be this difference ;—whilst they, by the power of the sword, enforce reluctant obedience, willing homage will be rendered to the Popes.— Whilst purely civil rulers will quell rebellions by their victorious arms, or be overwhelmed by the tide of successful insurrection, he whose sceptre is the Pastoral staff, pressed by the temporary disaffection of his people, and involved in a labyrinth of difficulties, no mortal eye can see the clue to, will to a certain extent, withdraw from the struggle, and to all appearance vanquished, will take refuge in his spiritual dignity. But soon the season of storms and overloaded skies will pass away, and the Sovereign Pontiff and Pontiff Sovereign will be enabled as if by some unseen but irresistible power, to resume the exalted place which, even from the beginning of civilization, Divine Providence appears to have irrevocably assigned to him. More than once have such events been witnessed. But, by what scenes of chastisement were they followed? What scaffolds were seen, spreading terror and creating slaves? What patriot or rebel blood was made to flow, staining the earth and crying to Heaven for vengeance?

If to this great rule some exceptions may be discovered in the ample page of Papal history, they are only such as doubly confirm it. What if at a time there should arise a Pope who, in extreme circumstances, has recourse to the sword with which he is entrusted. However decidedly such views may show the qualities of an individual Pontiff, they alter not the character of the Papacy. And who will say that such a Pontiff goes beyond his rights? Is he not a temporal Prince? And to what prince do we deny the privilege of defending not only his person, but his throne? Generally, as we have seen, the Prince Pontiff finds means of guarding his sceptre, more in harmony with his sacred and greater office. But who shall condemn that Julius, who though a most pious Bishop, believed that he held not the sword in vain, and used it so far as to bring to obedience some rebel cities? This once effected, the "ord gives place to the Shepherd's Crook, and the vigorous hand that has been put forth to quell rebellion, is now raised only to invoke benedictions on a repentant people. The poetry of his time and country has done justice to the character of this excellent Pope. He was far in advance of the age in which he lived, whether as regards the greatness of his views or the singular humanity by which his policy was distinguished.

"Scarcely," says the poet,—and he only celebrates the facts of history,—"is war declared when you are victorious ; but you are as ready to pardon as to conquer. Three things are as one to you—battle, victory, and forgiveness. One day brought us war; the morrow, its termination; and your anger outlived not the hour of strife. The name of Julius bears in it something Divine, and leaves us in doubt whether valor or clemency predominate."*

The very fact that the conduct of a Pope who could have recourse to the civil sword even to remedy intolerable evils, requires to be justified in the eyes of mankind, proves beyond question, that there is inseparably connected with the princely power of the Sovereign Pontiff, a moral influence which has quelled more rebellions, established peace more generally at various epochs, and done more in every way for the cause of humanity, than could have been accomplished by all the arms of all the conquerors whose frequent victories have filled the world with their fame.

HUMANITY OF THE POPES IN THE ADMINISTRATION OF JUSTICE.

When we hear the oft repeated cry for reform; when we read the volumes of abuse a corrupt press unceasingly pours forth against every branch of administration in the States of the Pope, and that especially which is not the least important —the dispensing of justice—parties unaccustomed to inquire for themselves, and who derive all their information from those poisoned sources, that are termed as if in derision, "the best possible public instructors," can scarcely resist the belief that there are no regular tribunals at Rome, and that justice even, sacred justice, depends entirely on the arbitrary will of one man. Far, however, is this from being the case. There is no state where there are more wisely constituted tribunals. Everything connected with the administration of justice comes under their cognizance. And where men of the highest merit fill the judgment seat, whether they be laymen or ecclesiastics, there is every guarantee for sound decision. Men of character, of position, and dignity, they are above corruption, and decide according to their conviction—according to justice. The prerogative of mercy, as in all civilized countries, lies with the

---

* CASSANOVA—*apud De Maistre on the Pope, p. 148, English Edition.*
—DOLMAN, London,

Chief of the State. And if in the few* criminal cases that occur, the holy Pontiff inclines rather to pardon than to condemn, is humanity the loser by his clemency? Ask the philosophy of the age, and it will answer most emphatically, No. It would rather there were no such punishments as those which, from their terrible and revolting character, the Pope almost always remits. With philosophy this doctrine is but of yesterday. Its practice by the Popes is as ancient as the Papacy. Now that the lesson has been taught, and, if splendid declamations prove anything, learned too, the Pope is of no more use. He has intoned his last anthem. The nineteenth century takes it up, and will prolong the strain, as if it were all its own, till the end of ages.

Nor does it derogate from the purity of the tribunals of the Papal States, that they inquire and decide according to the Canon Law. Human ingenuity has not yet discovered anything superior to this law. It is still interwoven with the best institutions of great and highly civilized countries that have long been separated from the See of Rome. "Those who refuse to do justice to the Canon Law," says the most learned Count de Maistre, "have never read it. This code has given a form to our judicial proceedings, and corrected or abolished numerous subtleties of the Roman law, which were not suited to us, if ever they were good. The Canon law was preserved in Germany, notwithstanding all the efforts of Luther, by the Protestant Doctors, who taught it, eulogized it, and even expounded it. In the thirteenth century it had been solemnly approved by a decree of the Diet of the Empire, promulgated under Frederick II., an honor never conferred upon the Roman law."†

But what shall be said in defence of those Popes who in the middle ages, so recently as the fourteenth century, actually *excommunicated* criminals? What could humanity gain by such unwonted legislation? No doubt it was unusual—it

---

* This fact is stated on good authority: "More murders are committed in England and Ireland in the course of a few months, than throughout the whole of Italy in as many years."
—*Lady Morgan's Italy*, London, 1821.

† *De Maistre on the Pope*, page 221, English Ed., London.—DOLMAN.

was now that the crimes of men should be so dealt with. But what was there in the Papacy or in the Religion which it promulgated, that was not new? It was an ever-living contradiction of everything it found in the benighted world. Its canons took the place of the old Roman laws, even as its truth and purity replaced the errors and the corruption of Paganism. Its corrective discipline and its anathemas were substituted for those awful punishments which the philosophers of our age hesitate not to stigmatize as *judicial murders*. And yet it was not an enlightened system. It only tended to perpetuate ignorance and barbarism! Consider the crimes which it anathematized, and then say whether this extraordinary jurisprudence of the Popes contained anything that was the growth of ignorance—anything that could foster barbarous and cruel usages. In the police regulations of that celebrated Bull, "in Cœnâ Domini," there is on the contrary much that was calculated to correct the barbarism and chastise the crimes of a rude age. This Bull, in all the matters to which it refers, constituted the public law of Europe during several centuries. How fortunate would it not be for the men of this age, if mere anathemas could drive pirates and wreckers from the seas, robbers and murderers from the highways! The ignorance, even, which has pronounced it "*a shameful document that could not be quoted*," would rejoice, if, indeed, the philosophy of the time were capable of any real and unfeigned emotion, on finding in its provisions, in such pacific means alone, a remedy rather than a punishment of crime. For my part, I can discover in it nothing shameful. There is no mention in it of racks, thumb-screws, or torture of any kind. And to shew that it may be quoted, I shall even present you with some of the more prominent crimes which it denounces as deserving of excommunication. No man of reflection will fail to recognize in the Chief of the great Catholic world, a right which is every day exercised by the most obscure and inconsiderable sects—the right to cut off from his society the perpetrators of crimes such as those enumerated in the Bull:

The Pope excommunicates,—

Art. 3—All pirates ranging the seas without letters of marque

Art. 4.—Every man who shall dare to steal anything from a shipwrecked vessel.

Art. 5.—All who shall establish in their lands new taxes, or shall take it upon them to increase those already existing, except in cases provided for by the law, or in the event of obtaining the express permission of the Holy See.

Art. 6.—The falsifiers of Apostolic Letters.

Art. 7.—All who shall furnish arms or munitions of war of any kind to Turks, Saracens, or heretics.*

Art. 8.—All who intercept provisions of any kind whatsoever on their way to Rome, for the use of the Pope.

Art. 9.—Those who shall kill, mutilate, rob, or imprison persons on their way to the Pope, or returning from him.

Art. 10.—Those who shall treat as above described, pilgrims whom devotion induces to visit Rome.

Art. 11.—Those who should be guilty of the like acts of violence towards Cardinals, Patriarchs, Archbishops, Bishops, and Legates of the Holy See.

Art. 12.—Those who strike, rob, or maltreat any person on account of causes he is pursuing at the Court of Rome.

Art. 20.—Those who usurp the countries or territories under the sovereignty of the Pope.

It is not our object here to inquire how conducive it was to the peace of the world, that many precious rights should have been secured and rendered sacred in the eyes of mankind by the publication of a Papal Bull, rather than by war and bloodshed. Later, when excommunication was not so much dreaded, such valuable privileges could only be extorted from despotic rulers, and not without torrents of blood.

Let it suffice to observe that it was infinitely more humane to suppress crime by penalties, which, however severe during the time of their infliction, were removed as soon as the culprit returned to duty and atoned to society for his misdeeds. It may well be doubted whether all the "judicial murders" it would have been necessary in the absence of these penalties

---

* Catholics are agreed—and the Popes never held any other view—that *heretics* are such, and such only, as *wilfully* and *obstinately* reject the Church. Such persons obviously excommunicate themselves.—When in arms against the Church, as they often were, it could not but be deemed unlawful to assist them.

to commit, would have produced equally great results. If we live in better days, and scarcely ever read of a common robbery on the highways of Europe, far less of such crimes as doing violence to cardinals, legates, ambassadors, or other public functionaries when on their way to the Pope or any other Sovereign, we owe it chiefly to the necessity there was for stigmatizing such iniquities by the censures of the Church.

HUMANITY OF THE PAPAL RULE.—WAR.

During the long period the Popes have borne sway, they have never ceased to act on the principle, that there ought to be no war between Christians. On inquiring into their history, it will be found that, notwithstanding the difficulty to which it may have subjected them, the danger to which it may have exposed them, they have never failed to maintain as far as circumstances would permit, a position of dignified neutrality. This policy was never more manifest than when the Sovereign Pontiff, urged by the greatest conqueror of modern times to make war on Great Britain, nobly declared *"that all Christians being his children, he could have no enemies among them."* We shall understand the value of this declaration when we call to mind that at the time it was made almost the whole of Europe lay helpless at the conqueror's feet. It would be difficult to discover any leaning on the part of Rome, towards the cause of that conqueror. It is just then a Napoleonic idea, and no more, that the Popes, though tolerably impartial, rather inclined to the stronger side. The venerable Pontiff was not ignorant of the penalty he incurred by refusing to pronounce against the British people. And it is well known that it was beyond the power of this people, notwithstanding their most laudable endeavours, to rescue him from the galling captivity to which he was reduced. Meanwhile, the hour of retribution was at hand. The ancient arm of the Pontiff was put forth in his defence. The real though unseen power that gave him victory of old over the proud barbarian, who, arrayed in all the panoply of destructive war, already thundered at the gates of Rome, intervened once more, and the haughty Emperor, hitherto great and unconquered, who had laughed to scorn the moral weapons of the Holy Pontiff, is crushed beneath its blows. "What means the Pope by his excommunication? Does he think it will make the arms fall from the hands of my soldiers?" The Russian winter made reply, as it tore the dread implements of war from the firm grasp of his strongest warriors, and left them a prey to the enemy he had so deeply wronged.

Nor was it on this memorable occasion only, that the Popes fought their battles with the arms of peace. It has in all ages been their custom. What although one or two in so great a number, (there have been two hundred and fifty-five Popes in regular succession,) should have met war with war's own weapons! This would not alter the character of the Papacy. This would not rob it of the praise of having been always eminently pacific and humane. In looking into the long history of Rome's temporal sovereignty, I meet with only one instance of a Pope who actually waged war. And what were the wars of Julius II.? Merely affairs of internal police. His direct and prompt interference in these matters, although it may have derogated somewhat from the sacred dignity of the Pontiff, was peculiarly serviceable to the cause of humanity. The Venetians enter the Papal territory in the capacity of robbers, and as robbers they are punished by the Pope. They seize and unjustly keep possession of some of the Pontifical towns, and for once Rome's material thunders are levelled against offenders. In this I, for my part, can see no injustice, no inhumanity. It is only to be desired that all robbers met with the like treatment. One can almost see vinegar and gall oozing from the starched visage of Abbe Feller, as he exclaims: "Julius allowed the sublime of his position to escape him. He saw not what his wise successors now see so well, that the Roman Pontiff is the common Father, and that he ought to be the arbiter of peace, not a kindler of war." We have yet to learn, for there are some things that cannot be learned from M. Feller's dictionary, that even Julius II was a "kindler of war." That he found it necessary to quell rebellion in some portions of his states, is no proof that he enkindled war. Nor is the allegation proved by the fact that he obliged certain rebellious cities to surrender. This only shows that he made use of the temporal sword with which he was entrusted, for a purpose that no statesman, no moralist, will pretend to condemn.

The painful events here alluded to, only tended to show forth in stronger and brighter relief the Pontifical character of this Pontiff Prince. In his time the age of letters, of refinement, of superior humanity, was at its commencement. The glorious day of Leo X. was even then dawning. And yet, what was the conduct of all merely temporal princes in circumstances similar to those in which the part borne by Julius is so mercilessly criticised? Invariably did they avail themselves of their privilege. It belonged to kings to punish rebels. And accordingly a rebellious city, when conquered, had little mercy to look for at their hands. Even the best of monarchs would have considered it a breach of duty to forgive. Their enemies they might pardon, but their rebel subjects never. In cases of suppressed rebellion, it was a custom never to be departed from to put all the ringleaders to death. No dignity, no virtue, no merit could rescue from this cruel sentence. How pleasing is it not, to turn from the consideration of such cruelties, and the stern sovereignties which required them to the contemplation of the Pope's temporal rule;—that rule which, softened and humanized as it necessarily is, by its union with the mild authority of the Pontiff, is merciful even in the vigorous hands of a Julius. It is necessary, he conceives, for the integrity of his states, the peace and the happiness of his people, that rebellion should be vanquished. But he has only pardon for the rebels. Here "the sublime of his position" is recovered. What, indeed, could be more grand, than to behold a sovereign, at a time when humanity was so little understood, especially by Princes, dispensing mercy with as liberal measure, as others were wont to inflict justice! The rebel city of Mirandola is no sooner brought to obedience, than he no longer has an enemy within its walls. Well might the poet say that he was "as ready to pardon as to conquer," and "that his anger outlived not the hour of strife." To grant amnesties is now the rule. But lest the men of this age should think that they have discovered humanity, even as they have invented steam-engines and the amazing telegraph, it is but proper they should be told who first gave the lesson.

It would be difficult, indeed, to find just ground for asserting that the Popes have enkindled the flames of war. Their enemies can have no better reason for making the assertion than the desire to lessen the Pontifical character, by representing it as being allied, more or less, with the ferocious mind which thirsts after war and blood. But, as has been observed, one Pope is not all the Popes. One Pope does not constitute the Papacy. If even the one Pope who engaged in war was wholly guiltless of war's cruelties, and shewed his dislike to the sad game by a most speedy termination of hostilities; if this same Pope was never known to stir up strife, nor to perform any act nor utter any speech that could be considered a provocation to war, what becomes of the hostile accusation? The chiefs of all other dynasties have been warlike princes.— That some of them have been pacific by no means disproves this assertion. So neither is it reasonable to maintain that the Papacy has been a ceaseless cause of wars because that one Pontiff found it necessary for the pacification of his States to put forth the arm of his temporal power. "If it be observed," writes that learned statesman, M. de Maistre, "in regard to war in particular, that they (the Popes) have been engaged in it less than other princes, *that they have carried it on with more humanity, that they have never sought it nor provoked it*, and that from the time when princes, by a sort of tacit convention, which ought not to be overlooked, appear to have agreed to recognize the neutrality of the Popes, we no longer find the latter mixed up with political intrigues or warlike operations; it is impossible not to acknowledge that even in civil affairs they have always maintained that superiority which men have a right to expect from their religious character."

THE SPIRIT OF THE AGE.—EDUCATION.—THE ARTS AND SCIENCES ENCOURAGED BY THE POPES.—THE POOR AS WELL AS THE HIGHER CLASSES EDUCATED BY THEIR CARE.—REMARKABLE TESTIMONY OF MR. LAING AND BARON GERAMB.

There never was a time when greater zeal was shown, or

more general efforts made in the cause of education. Educate, instruct, enlighten. Such is now the device of every civilised people. You cannot more grievously insult a nation than by asserting that it is well pleased to remain in ignorance, and takes no pains to educate its children. And yet, amc vhat people can such views as these lay claim to antiquity. he learning and civilization of ancient Rome once swept away, ignorance everywhere prevailed, and to such an extent that men knew not that they were ignorant. The new civilization had already done battle for many centuries with the barbarism it found in possession of the world, when, even in the higher orders of society, it was still the privilege of rank to be ignorant. Kings and great lords were above learning, as they were by their rank above the rest of men. And, simply because they were potent personages, they claimed exemption from the task of learning to read and write. That expiring barbarism should have clung to ignorance, as its last hope, need not astonish us. But it is, indeed, surprising that the Christian Church, and, above all, the Popes, should have been accused of fostering ignorance, and even of exerting their great influence to retard the work of education, the march of intellect, the development of the human mind.*

If such were the case, how strangely have the Popes misunderstood their true interests! Who does not know how favourable knowledge is to the religion of which they are the chiefs? From its first appearance in the world science has been a devout worshipper at its shrine. No sooner is it announced than men versed in all the learning of their time make haste to pay it homage and proclaim its truth to mankind. A generation has not yet passed away when not a few among the votaries of science become not only its ardent admirers, but its most fervent disciples. Who was that Paul whom "zeal consumed?" Undoubtedly, a man possessed of great knowledge. That he was so his very enemies bore witness when they declared that "much learning had made him mad." All were "mad," in the estimation of the vulgar, who in those days embraced the religion of the cross. No reputation of learning could save them

---

*Vide Appendix.

from this stigma. And yet the learned, in defiance of the scoff of ignorance, press around its banner. The physician, Luke, the statesman of Athens, Dionysius, are followed by many highly educated men, whose minds were already prepared and adapted by science for the reception of that truth which contains within itself the knowledge of all things, whether of this world or of that which is to come.

It would be an error to suppose that true science could be opposed to revealed truth. All false systems of religion in past times have invariably fallen before the light of science. Such men as Socrates and Plato necessarily rejected the vulgar superstitions of their age. They held up the lamp of science to expose them, and false religion, panic-struck, put Socrates to death. Without farther discussion, therefore, it may be considered as proved, for all history is the witness, that whatever is false, whether in Religion, in philosophy, or in politics, must abhor the presence of true science. No false system has been able, hitherto, to pass through this ordeal. In modern times only the sects that have accused the Popes of fostering ignorance have shewn an instinctive dread of knowledge. Some of them will not allow that men of any learning should be ministers of religion. The more powerful, as, for instance, the great Anglican sect, have actually forbidden the diffusion of letters. During the palmy days of this sect in Ireland it was penal to teach even the alphabet. Any priest or schoolmaster who dared so to teach was treated pretty much in the same way as Socrates was by the mob, or if you will, the people of Athens. In England, even, knowledge was, as regarded the great body of the people, proscribed by this puissant sect. It was the idea of the time, and the true religion was not at hand to correct the error, that it was unsuitable to educate the lower classes. They remained in ignorance, therefore, whilst science kept its court in the two great universities of the land. It could not long shed its light there in vain. It delights to be the hand-maid of the true religion. Whilst, therefore, all erroneous systems necessarily grow dim and vanish in its presence, that religion which alone claims to be the one true revelation from on high, only shines brighter in the light which true science throws around it. And thus it has appeared in the eyes of many of the most learned men of those celebrated universities in which the lamp of science had never ceased to burn, altho' that of true faith had, in an evil hour, been utterly extinguished.

The religion of the Popes, it need not be further insisted on, has no reason to dread knowledge.* It can only gain by its diffusion. It is well known that in Western Europe, where letters have been more cultivated, chiefly under the auspices of the Roman Pontiffs, the Catholic religion has been maintained in its purity. Why should this religion, then, or its Bishops, be the enemies of science? They have never been so. And one cannot but marvel at the simplicity of those good Protestant people who really believe that the Popes have made it their study to check the growth of knowledge, and to throw impediments in the way of intellectual development.— The Bishops of Rome have uniformly encouraged all liberal studies, and have themselves frequently been distinguished by their profound investigations of the secrets of nature; and that at all times alike,—as well when science was held in honor as when men of great learning were looked upon as worse than mad, and even dreaded and shunned as magicians, necromancers, and ominous persons having relations with the evil spirit. Who could have been more eminent for science,—who by his great attainments could have been more in advance of his age than the illustrious Pope Sylvester,—that holy Pontiff, who was the minister of Divine mercy in bringing into the one fold the Emperors of the mighty Roman world, who linked together, in his own person, the two great eras of the Church's life, coming forth, the successor of the martyr Popes of three centuries, and the first of a long line of sovereign Pontiffs, from his mountain lurking place, and from the catacombs of Rome, to proclaim, in the light of day, that truth of which he was as well the divinely constituted guardian as the most eloquent Apostle?

It is not disputed that the Popes have in all ages of their

---

* Mr. Laing, an eminent Scottish Presbyterian writer, says:—"The Popish clergy have, in reality, less to lose by the progress of education than our own Scotch clergy."—*Notes of a traveller.*
"Education is not only *not repressed*, but is *encouraged in the Popish Church, and is a mighty instrument in its hands, and ably used.*" *Idem*

long history, adorned their high station by great talents and acquirements. But, say their enemies, these treasures of genius and knowledge they have reserved for themselves. They have kept their light under a bushel. In respect of learning, what has humanity, what has civilization to thank them for?

It is indeed true, that letters were for a long time the exclusive possession of the Popes and of the Clergy. But this by no means shows that they took no pains to disseminate knowledge—to instruct mankind. In their endeavours to enlighten the world, they met with formidable opposition. Custom, opinion, prejudice,—every thing was against them. War and pleasure engaged, in turns, the time and the thoughts of men. They could not afford to be idle. And the noble leisure of learning was in their estimation, idleness. With exceptions sufficiently numerous to show that the clerical order had no wish to make a monopoly of knowledge, the study of letters, the pursuit of science, was left almost entirely to the care of the clergy. Meanwhile religion, which was gaining ground so rapidly, could not be diffused among men, and deeply rooted in their minds, without communicating along with its more precious spiritual gifts, some portion of the outward garb in which it necessarily clothed itself, and without which it was impossible that it should reach the mind. It was not indeed a matter of absolute necessity that the apostles of the new law, should be endowed with eloquence; and yet how often were they not so? How often from the days of St. Paul, who although he professed not to have come on his mission to mankind, "with the persuasive words of human wisdom," was nevertheless in an eminent degree, possessed of that powerful eloquence which moves the soul to its depths; have there not been accomplished orators in the church? and whilst, like St. Paul announcing truth to Governor Felix and King Agrippa, they preached with more than the power of human language, to a rude and unbelieving world, they could not fail to impart some idea of that more refined and noble literature which arose, so early, together with the sublime religion of which it is designed to be the handmaid.

The preachers of christianity, as they conversed with men,

not only taught them religion, but in like manner also, "the humanities" "humaniores litteras." But, as this was only an incidental teaching, and of incalculable less importance than that to which it ministered, public schools and universities were founded, in which all branches of letters and of science were taught, not only to those who were destined to hold the sacred office of the priesthood, and to fulfil the high duties of apostolic teachers, but to all who chose to come to quench their thirst for knowledge at these great, and pure, and never failing fountains. As time advanced these temples of learning were more and more frequented, and from their ever open portals, was constantly pouring forth a stream of truth, which, in due time, renewed the face of the world, causing the stern and unconquered warrior even to sigh for the happy time, when he too could share the repose, the elegance and the honors of a learned life.

It would be little to the purpose to enumerate here the noble universities the Popes have caused to be founded throughout christian Europe. The number merely of universities in any country, is no test of its facilities for acquiring knowledge. It would be rash, for instance, to assert that there exist for the class of persons who study at college, greater opportunities of learning in Scotland, which for many centuries has possessed five universities, than in England, which, until a recent period, enjoyed only two. Oxford and Cambridge in England consist of so many colleges, all richly endowed,—their endowments rating from the days of Papal ascendancy,—that it would be difficult to decide whether these two seats of learning be not equal ⁊ several others of less extent. It is of more importance to observe, that of almost all these celebrated British universities, the Popes have been the chief founders. Glasgow, Aberdeen, St. Andrew's, and in part Edinburgh, owe their academic honors to their fostering care. The most Catholic Empire of Austria has no fewer than nine universities,—Vienna, Prague, Pesth, Padua, Pavia, Lemberg, Gratz, Innspruck, and Olmutz. In these seats of learning, four hundred and nineteen Professors hold chairs and give lessons to sixteen thousand students. Was there ever a country in which literature and science were so flourishing as in Poland, whilst that unhappy land remained, as yet, in full communion with the Pope? The state of College or University education in all Catholic nations, evinces the like zeal for the diffusion of knowledge, on the part of the Popes and the people who respect their authority. This educational policy, if policy it may be called, of the Papacy, is, as may be supposed, still more efficiently carried out, in those countries over which the Popes hold temporal sway. In Rome, accordingly, and in all parts of the States of the Church, there exists the greatest facility for attaining proficiency in the higher departments of study. If on due enquiry, we find also that the common people there are equally well cared for, we shall in this, surely, behold a reason why that temporal rule should be continued, which tends so powerfully to humanize and to improve, than that it should be compelled to give place to a new order of things, of which in modern times the world has had no experience save in the sad and disastrous, but happily short days, of the first French revolution and reign of terror. Under such a regime every humanizing influence would be exceedingly diminished, perhaps entirely done away with, in order that mankind might in time become adapted to the new state of things,—fitted, as only rude, stern, and illiterate men can be, for the works and the wars of an anti-social faction,—a faction whose hand would be against every man, whilst every man's hand, by a forced and cruel reciprocity, would necessarily be against them.

But, is it true, that the more humble class of people, under the direct civil sway of the Popes, are so carefully educated? I shall not merely assert that they are, but will show from the writings of distinguished authors, both Catholic and Protestant, that there is no nation in the world in which the blessings of education are more generally and more abundantly dispensed.

If it were, indeed, a system with the clergy of the Catholic Church to keep, or to endeavour to keep the people in ignorance, the chief of the clergy would unquestionably be at the head of the great conspiracy. And bearing part in such widespread iniquity, he would assuredly be unfit to hold the civil government of any civilized people. Classic Rome and learned

Bologna could ill bear the rule of a man who considered it his duty to patronize ignorance and to head a conspiracy against intellectual development. But, so far is there from being any such conspiracy, that even as the Papal church provides for the education of the more influential classes of society, so does she also, as far as she is able to accomplish so great a task, break the bread of knowledge to the still more numerous class, who, although individually the world regards them not, are of equally great value in her sight. "This opinion of our churchmen, (that the Catholic clergy keep the people in ignorance,) seems," says the learned Presbyterian, Mr. Laing, "more orthodox than charitable, or correct. The Popish clergy have, in reality, less to lose by the progress of education than our own Scotch clergy. In Catholic Germany, in France, Italy, and even Spain, the education of the common people, in reading, writing, arithmetic, music, manners and morals, is at least, as generally diffused, and as faithfully promoted by the clerical body, as in Scotland. It is by their own advance, and not by keeping back the advance of the people, that the Popish priests of the present day, seek to keep ahead of the intellectual progress of the community. Education is, in reality, not only not repressed, but is encouraged in the Popish church, and is a mighty instrument in its hands, and ably used. In every street in Rome, for instance, there are, at short distances, public primary schools for the education of the children of the lower and middle classes. Rome, with a population of 158,678 souls, has 372 public primary schools, with 482 teachers, and 14,099 children attending them. Has Edinburgh so many public schools for the instruction of those classes? I doubt it. Berlin, with a population double that of Rome, has only 264 schools. Rome has also her university, with an average attendance of 660 students. And the Papal States, with a population of two and a half millions, (now, 1860, more than three millions,) contain seven universities. Prussia, with a population of fourteen millions, has only seven. The statistical fact that Rome has above a hundred schools more than Berlin, for a population little more than half that of Berlin, puts to flight a world of humbug. Is it asked what is taught to the people of Rome by all these schools? Precisely what is taught at Berlin,—reading, writing, arithmetic, geography, languages, religious doctrine of some sort."—(*Notes of a traveller by Mr. Laing.*)

In the face of these facts, it is still maintained that, even as regards education, the Government of the Pope is behind the age. But they who never cease to represent that it is so, would, no doubt, tell the same tale of Berlin too, if they could hope thereby to overthrow the reigning power, and establish in its place that model of all Governments,—the communist utopia.

The learned and pious Baron Géramb, having alluded to the higher schools of Rome, proceeds to say: "There are here various secondary establishments where select masters teach the elements of literature. The poor have schools where they can send their children, so that the father of a family who leaves his offspring to remain in ignorance is more culpable in Rome than elsewhere. The number of free schools is almost infinite, and the proselytism for instruction is become one of the characteristics, not merely of the higher orders, but of all pious people. I repeat it then, my dear friend, and that with a deep conviction of its truth, that Rome is the seat of science as well as of faith. Religion, guided by the Holy Spirit, who is a spirit of light, opens here its sources for both sexes, for all ages and for all conditions. It combats ignorance and refutes errors; and, although calumniated, it labours not less to form Doctors and literati, than Apostles and Confessors."—(*Baron Géramb's journey to Rome, Letter XXV.*)

It is one of the chief glories of christian Rome, that she educates her poor,—those humble members of the community whom, because they were unfortunate, Pagan Rome held in contempt. But this care of the holy city and her government for misfortune, which she studies to console and to elevate, as well by the light of knowledge as by the more immediate blessings of religion, does not divert her attention from the cultivation of science and the fine arts. It was the sublime mission of the Popes to christianize and civilize the world. Without instruction this mighty work could not have been accomplished. But let us hear once more an important witness discoursing on the learning of Italy :

"As it was naturally impossible," writes Baron Géramb, "to civilize men without instructing them, the city which was chosen to be the centre of christianity, was also made the depository of human learning. If, then, amidst the darkness of ignorance, Italy preserved the sacred light of science,—if she emitted a bright and steady flame ; if finally, she brought forth new master-pieces of religious art, it is to religion, it is to the Sovereign Pontiffs, that she owes this glory. The writers who distinguished themselves first after the revival of learning, were Dante, Petrarch, and Boccacio. These gifted men made their fellow-citizens sensible of the value of the master-pieces left them by the age of Augustus ; and while they created a taste for Roman literature, they excited a curiosity for that of Greece, which was its source. Thus the love of learning was already diffused in Italy, at the commencement of the fifteenth century, before Constantinople was taken ; when its learned men, affrighted by the desolation of that city, took refuge in the West. Many of those fugitives came to Rome, and enriched her with the literary treasures they had snatched from the ruin of their country.

"Much time was, however, still required to release the human mind from the shackles wherewith ages of ignorance had bound it. First efforts are not always successful. But the day which began to dawn, shed a clearer and more diffused light, and finally shone out, with meridian splendour, at the commencement of the sixteenth century, under the Pontificate of Leo X.

"This Pope, of the illustrious house of the Medici, was only thirty six years of age, when raised to the chair of Peter. Confided from his infancy to the care of the most able masters of the time, he had enriched his mind with varied science. His court was the most brilliant in Europe. Science and art were his guests, and true merit was sure to find there a fluttering reception, and enjoy consideration, honor and reward. The *literati* were the Pope's friends. He lived with them on terms of familiarity. His liberality animated their labours, which he appreciated with the judgment of an enlightened connoisseur. This love of the fine arts, these favors conferred on those who cultivated them, merited for him the honor of giving his name to the age in which he lived,—an honor which, among the crowd of Sovereigns that have reigned, three only enjoy with him, Alexander, Augustus, and Louis XIV.

"Most of the successors of Leo have been animated by the same spirit. If it be true, that to honor talent, is the best means of exciting it, we owe to them a number of great men, who were the lights of their age, and the benefactors of the human race. Where do we find a Prince who recompensed learning with more munificence than Clement VIII., who raised Baronius, Bellarmin, D'Ossat and DuPerron to the Cardinalship, and decreed the honors of a triumph to Tasso !

* * * * * * * * *

"I do not hesitate to add that all the arts and sciences, all branches of human knowledge are cultivated here, (at Rome,) and that many authors who, in modern times have acquired celebrity in other countries, owe most of their glory to the great men whom Italy produced, in the ages which have preceded ours.

"The ancient Romans believing themselves destined to achieve the conquest of the world, loved nothing but arms and combats. Things are now changed, and the modern Romans confine all their ambition to cultivate the arts their ancestors neglected. They surpass all other people in this respect, and Rome is still the Queen of nations. But it is no longer by arms,—it is by intelligence that she extends her Empire and governs the universe."—(*Baron Géramb's journey to Rome, Letter XII.*

WISDOM AND HUMANITY OF THE PAPAL GOVERNMENT, AS
MANIFESTED BY ITS NUMEROUS INSTITUTIONS FOR
THE RELIEF OF HUMAN MISERY.

The temporal rule of the Popes is distinguished above all other Governments, by its benevolence. It would be difficult to point out the State, where more abundantly than in the States of the Church, provision is made for suffering humanity, as well through the patronage and encouragement, as by the immediate action of the Government. In this we cannot fail to recognize the great advantage the civil power derives from its alliance, in the person of the Pope, with that authority which is essentially beneficent. The enemies of the Papacy never grow weary in asserting that its spiritual character is lessened in public estimation, and really deteriorated by its connection with an order of things which concerns only the affairs of this world. I shall not pause to show that no such result can be dreaded, and that the temporal, as far as regards the high character of the spiritual power, only serves to show forth its excellence, in some degree, even as the magnificence and splendour of the material universe is necessary for the manifestation of the still greater lustre and glory of the invisible world. I would rather call on those who behold, or pretend to behold, in the Pope's temporal sovereignty, a source of weakness to that great Pastorship which is above all earthly things, to consider, in how many ways temporal rule is improved, modified and adapted to the real wants of mankind, by its intimate relation with an institution which has been raised up by the hand of Heaven itself, for the sublime purpose of regenerating, remodelling, creating anew, and exalting the whole human race. The age desires improvement, progress, perfection. How, if not through so excellent a medium, are those noble ends to be attained? If in by-gone days this institution, for which we claim heavenly origin, was equal to the stupendous work of bringing into subjection to the laws of right, of reason, and religion, a barbarous and degraded world, why should it be incapable to-day of affording aid in promoting peace and order, together with individual well-being, national prosperity and happiness, in one small section of the great christian community? That it does so, and to such an extent as to put to shame all Governments that are not animated by the like spirit, the consideration of those benevolent institutions alone, which the civil rule emulous of its example and guided by its inspirations, has been able either to originate, to encourage, or to sustain, would more than suffice to demonstrate.

These Institutions may be classed under the following heads:
1. Institutions for the sick, lunatic, and convalescent.

Of these, eight are public hospitals: 1st. One for men suffering from fevers, scorbutic and chronic disorders. This Hospital has 1,616 beds, and receives annually 11,903 patients. It possesses 35,000 crowns of private revenue, and receives annually from the State, 36,000 crowns. 2nd. The second is for women suffering from fevers, scorbutic, chronic, and consumptive diseases. It receives annually 2,528 persons, and has an allowance from the State of 11,400, and 17,600 crowns of private revenue. 3rd. The third is for both sexes; wounds, ulcers, and other surgical cases. It accommodates yearly 1,625 individuals. In addition to its private income of 13,240 crowns, it is allowed by Government 16,760 crowns. 4th. The fourth is for both sexes; wounds and fractures. It receives annually 826 persons. Its private revenue amounts to 8,350 crowns, and the State allows it 3,750. 5th. The fifth, for lying in women, receives 170 persons annually. Its revenue is 1,800 crowns of private property, and 690 from the State. 6th. The sixth for both sexes; leprosy and other cutaneous diseases, receives annually 349 persons. It has 2,600 crowns of private income, and 10,000 crowns from the State. 7th. The seventh, for insane persons of both sexes, has 420 beds, a private income of 5,000 crowns, and 10,000 from Government. 8th. The eighth is for pilgrims and convalescent of both sexes. The annual number of convalescent amounts to 8,390. Its private revenue is 15,600, and the Sate allows it 2,400. The number of pilgrims it entertains, in ordinary years, is 400, and in the year of Jubilee, one hundred thousand.

Almost all these hospitals have been either founded or considerably augmented by the Popes.

The first, " S. Spirito in Sassia," was founded by Innocent III. in 1198, and increased by Sixtus IV. 1471; by Benedict XIV. 1751; and by Pius VI. 1790.

The second, " S. Salvatore," founded by Card. Gio. Colonia, 1216, was augmented by Alexander VII.

The third, " St. Giacomo Augusta," founded by Card. Gine. Colonna, 1338, was increased by Card. Salviati, 1600, and Pius VII. 1815.

The fourth, " Sto. Maria della consolazzione," founded under

Calintus III. 1455, was augmented by Duke Valentino and Card. Corza, 1660.

The fifth, "S. Rocco," was founded by the company of S. Rocco, 1500, and afterwards increased by Cardinal Salviati, 1600; and Mr. Riminaldi, 1776.

The sixth, " S. Gallicano," founded by Benedict XIII. 1725, was augmented by Benedict XIV. 1754, and Leo XII. 1825.

The seventh. "Ste. Maria della pieta," founded by Fernando Ruiz, Diego, and Angelo Bruno, 1548, was increased by Benedict XIII. 1726, and Leo XII. 1825.

The eighth, "S. S. Trinità," founded by St. Philip Neri, 1548, was increased by Paul IV. and Clement XII.

THERE ARE, IN ADDITION TO THESE, MANY NATIONAL AND PRIVATE HOSPITALS,

For men's medical diseases; for sick apothecaries; for sick bakers; for pilgrims and sick persons from Lombardy; for pilgrims and sick persons from Poland; for sick Florentines; for sick persons from Lucca; for sick, and pilgrim Germans; for sick, and pilgrim Portuguese; for sick people from Bergamo; for sick persons of both sexes; for chronic invalids of both sexes. These two last are not properly hospitals, but provision for attending the sick at their own homes. The former, Limosineria Apostolica, was founded so early as the seventh century, by Pope Conon, (687) and afterwards increased by Innocent XII. The State affords it, in addition to its private resources, an annual income of 7,000 crowns.

The latter founded by Signor Baccari, a missionary of the congregation of St. Vincent of Paul, was afterwards increased by several Parish Priests. It enjoys a grant from the State of 648 crowns. The excellent Sisters of Charity, in connection with this institution, minister to the sick at their homes.

Here, also, may be mentioned the Arch-Confraternity dell' Orazione e morte, founded in 1551, for the interment of those found dead in the Campagna, and for the relief of their suffering souls.

II. In the second place, may be enumerated those institutions at Rome, for foundlings, orphans, old men, female penitents, and widows, which owe their existence either to the patronage and encouragement, or to the direct agency of the Papal Government. Of these there are six for old men, and orphans of both sexes. The first, for foundlings of both sexes, has 2,073 inmates, and an income from its foundation of 50,000 crowns. The second, for orphan boys, has an income from its foundation of 14,500 crowns, and maintains thirty-eight orphans. The third, "Ospizio Apostolico di St. Michele," for orphans, and invalids of both sexes, founded by Sixtus V., and afterwards increased by Innocent XII., 1693; Clement XI., 1708; and Pius VI., 1790; receives 570 inmates, on its foundation, which amounts to 50,000 crowns per annum, and 140 more persons who pay board. The fourth, "Ospizio di Tata Giovanni," founded by Giovanni Borgi, 1784, was augmented by Pius VI. and Pius VII. It receives one hundred foundling boys on its income,—1,600 crowns arising from its foundation, and 2,760 crowns granted by the Government,—and twelve more children for whom payment is made. The fifth, "Casa D'Industria del' Can. Manfredi," receives orphan boys, only. The sixth, "Ospizio de St. Maria Degli Angeli," founded by Pius VII. 1815, and increased by Leo XII. 1824, and Gregory XVI. 1835, maintains 900 poor people of both sexes, on its foundation of 4,000, and a public grant of 35,000 crowns.

There are two houses of refuge for poor persons at night. One of these receives 224 men; the other 30 women.

The city of Rome possesses no fewer than twelve asylums for female orphans. 1st, For female Neophytes. 2nd, For poor orphan girls of good families. 3rd, and 4th, For orphan girls. 5th, For orphan girls of good families. 6th, For adult orphan girls. 7th, and 8th, For orphan girls. 9th, For orphan girls, children of State Officers. 10th, For orphan girls. 11th, For female foundlings. 12th, For poor and virtuous young females. 13th, For young females who pay a small pension. The incomes of some of these truly philanthropic institutions, arising from their foundations, amounts to as much as 2,000, 2,500, and 4,000 crowns, whilst they are at the same time, liberally endowed by the Government; the grant to some of them being 4,512 crowns annually.

There is also a house of refuge for poor widows.

Misfortune, arising from culpable conduct, is not denied compassion and relief, and Rome contains three asylums for female penitents. 1st. " Retiro della Croce," founded by Maria Teresa Sebastiani,1793,and increased by Pius VII.1804,receives young females, twenty in number, who leave the hospital of St. James. Its foundation is 360 crowns, and the Government allows it 1,200 yearly. 2nd. " Rifugio di S. Maria in Trastevere," has a foundation of 200 crowns, and 800 from the Government. It receives 14 inmates,—women who leave St. Michael's prison. 3rd. " Rifugio della Lauretana," founded by Teresa Doria Pamfili, 1825, with a foundation of 1,000 crowns, maintains fourteen inmates,—women who leave the hospital of St. James. It will be seen, from the number of inmates mentioned here, that persons requiring the shelter of the three last named Institutions, are not very numerous at Rome.

Besides these hospitals and establishments for the relief of sickness and misfortune, there are many excellent eleemosynary institutions in the Papal city. A brief and descriptive catalogue of them will show, that whilst they relieve want, they fail not, at the same time, to encourage industry. These institutions are not so numerous, or of such a character, as to show that poverty prevails more, or even so much, at Rome, as in most other great cities. One thing, however, they prove; and it is highly creditable to the Pontifical Government, as well as to the christian spirit of the Roman people, namely, that whilst existing poverty meets with compassion and relief, still greater pains are bestowed in preventing an evil, which, in almost all countries, is the source of so many other evils. Of the twenty-six eleemosynary institutions of Rome, enumerated in the admirable work of Baron Géramb, thirteen are destined to afford dowries to young women in humble circumstances, thus paving the way to industry, prosperity, and happiness; for numerous families who, without this aid, might never be able to surmount the difficulties incident to their condition. There are three which provide for the gratuitous defence of poor suitors. Two give aid to reduced respectable families. One assists poor and industrious persons; another, young and virtuous females. Three only give alms to the indigent; one of these also grants loans to encourage industry, whilst relieving want. Two, one of which,—the Sagro Monte di Pieta,—is on an extensive scale, directly tend to promote industry and trade. This last named institution dates from the time of Leo X., who granted a charter in its favor. It has often, since that time, been the object of the benefactions and the Governmental care of the Popes. Pius VII. in particular, who is no less celebrated for his sublime resignation under misfortune, than for the wisdom and benevolence of his rule, showed great favor to this institution, and studied to increase its means and extend its usefulness. It has not been always equally prosperous. During the wars of the great Revolution, it could not fail to share in the disasters of the times. But having recovered from the shock of evils, by which greater and less perishable establishments were shaken, it now affords important aid to the least favored class of society, preventing poverty, and lessening the temptations to idleness, by encouraging enterprise. Its revenue, amounting to 32,000 crowns, is derived from private property. There are 100 persons employed in its administration. Two hundred thousand individuals annually receive from its funds pecuniary assistance, on account of which they pay a small rate of interest, and give a pledge as security for repayment.

The poor of Rome are munificently relieved by the committee of public works. In almost all countries there is a numerous class whose poverty arises from the impossibility of finding remunerative occupation. Such persons meet with adequate relief at Rome; and this relief is not doled out to them as alms, but paid to them as wages for the work which they perform. This work is highly advantageous to society. It increases the public weal, by the improvement of waste lands, by repairing and making roads, by renewing and adorning places of general resort, as well as those public edifices, the loss of which from neglect would be a subject of universal regret. By such means poverty is not so much relieved as obviated, and that degradation which it is so much the fashion in certain countries, and among certain classes of people,—not the most enlightened it must be well understood,—to accuse the Popes and their Government, of inflicting, in order that a blind despotism may be the better maintained, is completely prevented. And not only this, but the objects of this enlightened, and most considerate charity, instead of being treated as paupers, shut up in workhouses, or imprisoned as vagrants, are placed in a position of comfort, as well as of perfect freedom, and instead of being crushed and branded for life, are enabled to attain to independence, and to whatever grade, in the social scale, their activity and abilities may fit them for. The " Committee of Public Works" owes its origin to the Popes. By them also it has been fostered and increased. In the time of Leo XII., every labourer employed under this committee received eleven pence daily, besides bread. On occasion of the great festivals their pay was doubled, and in addition to it they received some meat, and a certain quantity of cloth. To these works Pius VIII. set apart 500 Roman crowns, weekly. This sum was considerably increased by Gregory XVI., the glory of whose Pontificate could only have been surpassed by the difficulties with which he had to contend. There is now at the disposal of the committee an annual revenue of 33,293 crowns.

There is no charity so laudable as that which takes pains to discover, in their obscurity, the real and proper objects of its care, and bears unostentatiously to their homes its opportune assistance. By this better system, more than by any mode of relief that has yet been devised, the cause of true benevolence is efficaciously served. The ties of domestic affection which extreme poverty so often rudely dissevers, are more closely knit; a feeling of thankfulness, together with a sense of happiness, pervades whole families that under other circumstances might have remained desolate, whilst one of the members, perhaps, would have been, in some measure, relieved by the receipt of an alms grudgingly bestowed, or by imprisonment in a work-house, and the cruel separation from all whom he held dear. From the earliest times of the Papacy poverty has found, under its auspices, this kindly and considerate attention. In order to facilitate this labour of love, as early as the seventh century, Pope Conon appointed an almoner whose charge it should be to assist indigent families, either by paying to them a fixed pension, or by carrying aid to them at their homes. This office has been continued, and is at present entrusted to a

Prelate who is a member of the Household of the Pope. The funds for this charity, derived from the Government and other sources, amount to 22,800 crowns yearly. Whilst nothing can surpass the philanthropy of this institution, its admirable economy is also deserving of attention. Here is no list of needy officials through whose hands the funds of charity must pass before they reach their object, and whose salaries must, to a certain extent diminish, whilst their want of care, their mismanagement, or their indifference to the poor, may completely mar the purposes of benevolence and christian love. A Prelate, whose very calling is charity, who is independent of all profits and per centages, is selected by the Holy Father for so responsible an office, not only on account of his upright and irreproachable character, but because, by his care and tender regard for the suffering and the lowly, he appeared to be called to the work of ministering to the poor. The example of the Popes, in this respect, has not been without its influence. Hence, the office of almoner in more than one of the most important European Sovereignties. The example of that great Institution,—the Papacy,—has not yet, however, been so generally followed as to render it no longer necessary, as a guide and an influence in the world.

One of the greatest of the unostentatious charities of Rome, which do not, by great publicity, require that modest indigence should pay for the aid which they afford, owes its establishment, in great measure, to the co-operation of Father James Laynez, the second general of the Jesuits. The object of the founders, who were guided by the advice and encouragement of this illustrious Father, was to provide for the relief of that class of unfortunate persons who suffer less from the wants of the present moment, than from the recollection of bygone happiness. This institution still continues, sustained by the same fervent and enlightened zeal to which it owed its foundation, and by the same delicate and sublime feeling which first inspired it.

Another institution, the *Divina Pieta*, having the same objects in view, was founded by a venerable Priest, John Stanchi of Castel-Nuovo, in 1679. One of the regulations, in the highest degree creditable to the founders, is as follows: "No member shall be required to give an account of the money confided to him for distribution; the names of the persons relieved are to remain concealed, and never to be registered." When it is remembered that this precaution was prompted solely by the most delicate consideration for the feelings of the parties who might become the objects of the charity, we behold in this institution no ordinary philanthropy, but the genuine spirit of christian love. It enjoys a revenue from private property of 4,000 crowns.

We have seen that the public charities of Rome tend to encourage industry, as well as to relieve want. By the same good spirit also are private individuals actuated. The wealthy Marquis and Marchioness of Carpegna practised such economy in their household, lived so penuriously, that public opinion pronounced them misers. They were spending, meanwhile, the income arising from their princely fortune, in giving relief to their indigent fellow-countrymen. Death at length removed the veil which concealed their good deeds from observation. By their last will, it appeared, " they made donations of all their property in favor of disabled old men, destitute widows, orphans, the blind and the lame, or those parents whose exertions would not be sufficient to supply the wants of their families. They desired, moreover, and this cannot be too well remarked, *that their liberality should tend to the encouragement of virtue, and ordered that their alms should be given only to those who would labour according to their ability.* They were not to be imparted to the vicious, but to those who had the fear of God, who complied with their religious duties, who gave a christian education to their children, and taught them the catechism."—(*Baron Géramb.*)

The Cardinal Odescalchi, a holy Prelate of our times, was appointed by the Testators, the Executor of these excellent bequests. To the good Cardinal, whose chief happiness it had been so long to distribute alms from his own resources, this administration of charity was indeed a labour of love.

But it would be an endless task merely to enumerate all the benevolent institutions of christian and Papal Rome. Without therefore dwelling longer on this interesting theme, I shall ask with Baron Géramb, and without fear of contradiction, " If, in proportion to its population, there be a city in the world where the poor, the aged, the orphan, the unprotected female, and the prisoner, find so many asylums and resources? Do you think that your philanthropists, with all their fine theories, would ever realize results equally satisfactory? "I have seen much of the world, but I have not seen anything equal to it elsewhere; and this character alone would suffice, in my judgment, to merit for Rome, the glorious name of "Holy City" and "Capital of Christianity!" * * * * France, you will, perhaps, tell me, possesses many charitable institutions. I know it, and I am unwilling to detract from this portion of its glory. But as I belong not to either country, and, therefore, am not liable to the suspicion of partiality, I may be allowed to say, that Rome has the advantage of France, in the number of asylums she opens for suffering humanity; by the sacrifices she has made to establish and endow them, by the zeal with which they are administered, and the privations which the Romans impose on themselves to enable them to maintain them."

THE SPIRIT OF THE AGE.—LIBERALITY.

In all ages of the world, tyranny has been held in abhorrence. Nor can the present age be said to excel those which have preceded, in its superior hatred of oppression. Nevertheless, it is an eminently liberal age. And, not so much is its liberality shown by the zeal of the people, subject to authority, for liberal institutions,—zeal which, in every period of the world's existence, has risen even to enthusiasm; but more, much more, in the inclination now so prevalent amongst those who hold rule, to extend the liberties of the peoples governed,—to liberalize,—to constitutionalize their governments. There are not wanting those who hold the opinion, that this change in the minds of kings, is a direct result of the great commotions by which Europe was convulsed towards the end of last century. But whence, will these profound thinkers be pleased to inform us, whence came the ideas which influenced the world so powerfully before these commotions were dreamt of, and which, carried to excess, produced the most terrible of all revolutions? They could not be both cause and effect,—the consequence, as well as the principle, of that most extraordinary course of action, by which were brought about so many changes in the moral and social world. They were either the one or the other. They were the cause undoubtedly, and they sprang from the purest source. How they were deteriorated, and how they came to result in so much that was evil, let those men tell, who abusing the great ideas bequeathed to them by their forefathers, hurried into every excess. All that is aimed at here, is to show that these ideas were not altogether new, even so early as the commencement of this enlightened age, and that if in earlier times the people loved liberty, there were kings ar ⅃ mighty potentates also who were capable of appreciating, and who did appreciate the noble aspirations of the subject nations. If history does not wholly deceive us, they were kings who, in modern Europe, first introduced liberal institutions and promoted legislation that was wholly in accordance with the utmost degree of national liberty. Such among the Saxons were Alfred the Great, and Edward the Confessor. When under a new and less patriotic dynasty, popular rights were not respected, the people desired no higher boon than the restoration of the wise laws and constitutions of these paternal Sovereigns.— A not unsatisfactory proof that this early constitution was in harmony with the wishes of the people, and being so, afforded the greatest possible measure of liberty; for we are not to suppose that the people of those times were less capable of appreciating free institutions, or less anxious to enjoy them, than the men of our own day. Nor must we believe that liberty was beyond their reach, the stern usages of feudalism becoming more and more rigid, as we recede into the past. This was far from being the case. In the times alluded to, the feudal mode of social being, if it may be so expressed, existed not, as yet, certainly not, as it is now understood, and as it prevailed in England after the removal of the Saxon dynasties. Anterior to that event kingly government in that country was rather patriarchal than despotic, whilst among the celtic races, when Druidism receded before the advancing light of the Christian faith, the Patriarchal rule alone remained in vigor.

The present age boasts not a monopoly of liberality; it is nevertheless eminently liberal. When was there a period when, as at the commencement of the nineteenth century, all the kings of the civilized world combined in support of liberty? This great idea they conceived at a time when their power was consolidated by victory,—by victory over the fell tyranny that had sprung from the inordinate pursuit of liberty. Gregory XVI. yet reigned, that Gregory whom pretended liberals have so nefariously calumniated as the enemy of every thing free and generous, when the Sovereigns of Europe resolved to meet the wishes of the populations and constitutionalize their Governments. A king, to whom history will yet do justice, Louis XVI. of France, had laboured to extend the rights and privileges of his people. A wisely framed constitution would have been the result. A constitutional monarchy would have been engrafted on that kingly power of France which never had been a despotism; feudalism would have been corrected, the civil and political rights of the people more fully recognized; such institutions established, as would have secured for many ages to come, the highest degree of rational liberty. But, by unheard of revolutionary excess, all these wise and noble schemes were marred, and the cause of constitutions ruined. Louis of France perished in the wreck of that liberty—he was so anxious to establish. But his example was not without its beneficial influence. Kings and Statesmen, instructed by the lessons of the past, entered on a career of reform. The Pontiff ruler blessed their work, and encouraged them to proceed. Nor did he himself shrink from so great a task. Gregory XVI., of immortal memory, led the way. Pius IX. followed in his track, but with bolder and more rapid steps. His labours, as we have seen, ended in temporary discomfiture. But they were not on that account less meritorious—less worthy of the enlightened Statesman and the liberal Pontiff. The other Sovereigns of Italy, not excepting the late king of Naples, had commenced the work of reform, were actually transforming themselves into constitutional rulers, when the same cause,—revolutionary excess,—which marred the plans of Pius IX., stopped these monarchs mid way in their liberal career, and compelled them to wrap themselves up anew in the mantle of their absolutism. That this was not an unqualified despotism, without any safeguards for the privileges and liberties of the people, it is not the object of this discourse to show.

Looking towards other portions of the civilized world, we find mighty potentates engaged in the work of reform. The king of Prussia addressed his beloved Berliners, and promised them a constitution. But either he or they, or all of them together, were not as yet fitted for, or were not deserving of the advantages of free and constitutional Government. Belgium has its constitution, and a king who understands it. France, when it could no longer possess its constitutional monarchy, established for itself a republic. Russia, pervaded by the spirit of liberality, is reforming herself, the Autocrat leading the march in the great onslaught on serfdom,—the first formidable impediment to constitutional Government that must needs be swept away. The Sublime Porte, even, unmindful of the Koran, and neglecting the long cherished traditions of the Caliphate, is endeavouring to liberalize the institutions of the once great Mohammedan Empire. It may be said, indeed, that this is the only course by which he can hope to save, for a time, the crumbling Empire of the Crescent; that he must now court the favor of the great christian powers by adopting, as far as is, as yet, possible, the manners and customs of christian civilization. From whatever cause he may have been induced to pursue the liberal policy which has hitherto marked his reign, it is beyond doubt that he is the first of a long line of Rulers, the most absolute the world has ever known, who has dared to change or modify the immutable laws and customs of "the Prophet." But such is the spirit of the time. Kings, Emperors, and Sultans, all must be borne away from the time-hallowed current of their ways, by the powerful and irresistible tide of public opinion.

Another characteristic of the age is the liberality with which, throughout the whole civilized world, men are accustomed to treat the political, and even the religious opinions of those who, in such matters, are opposed to them.

In countries where representative government has been long established, this milder trait of modern civilization is more decided. In Great Britain the conservative no longer looks down upon the reformer as holding opinions that are subversive of social order. And although Whigs and Tories cannot yet agree—in politics, they have no objections to meet and take counsel together, when there is question of any important work for the public good, or any charity for the benefit of the poor. In the great senate of the British nation, even, where every matter of national importance is seriously, and often warmly discussed, the opinions of opposite parties are alluded to with respect, and at the close of the most keenly contested questions, or even in the midst of the most animated debate, members of all shades of opinion, hurry away together from the parliament halls to enjoy, in common, the amusements of Derby day. In other nations the same spirit more or less prevails. Everywhere it is to be found in proportion to the national measure of social and political progress.

It need hardly be observed that however steadfastly people adhere now-à-days to their religious principles, difference of opinion in religion, is not, except indeed among the uneducated and ill-informed, held to be a ground of exclusion from the social circle. The Pope receives with his accustomed urbanity and kindness, the Protestant, as well as the Catholic visitor; whilst the Catholic guest or Ambassador is treated with the same courtesy and consideration as other distinguished personages, at the Court of that Sovereign who is the head of the greatest Protestant establishment. Authority, itself, with all its necessary sternness, in all save one or two remote nations, has the same laws for men of all shades of religious belief. A Protestant monarch is the popular ruler of Catholic Belgium. Prussia, in as far as it is a Catholic country, is similarly circumstanced, and as regards the person of the Monarch, to the satisfaction of all parties. The Catholic governments of Europe, not excepting that of Austria, not only mete out justice with an equal hand, to the dissenters from the national religion, but even provide for their religious well-being.

Nor must we forget, for it is no inconsiderable proof of the superior liberality of the age, that this century has beheld the obliteration from the British statute book, of degrading penal-laws which held in bondage and disgrace one-third of the British people; and that in France, it has seen the downfall of the scoffing philosophy of Voltaire, which had grown tired at length in labouring to laugh down a religion which, as the experience of past centuries had well shown, the sharpest weapons of ridicule could not even wound.

THE PAPACY ESSENTIALLY LIBERAL.

In defending the temporal sovereignty of the Pope, it is of the highest importance to show that the spiritual power with which it is allied, and by which it cannot fail to be influenced, is not that stern despotism over the minds of men which its enemies unceasingly represent it to be. If we consider only how the Papacy is constituted, we shall at once see that it cannot be otherwise than liberal. It is in fact, a model constitutional government. As there is no system of rule or constitution in the world that has endured so long, so is there none that can claim to be so perfect. Many governments have followed in its track, and have copied and appropriated what appeared to them good in its constitution, but none have, as yet, surpassed, or even equalled it in excellence. An institution that was not in every way admirably adapted to the wants of mankind,—that was not, by its organization and its teaching, calculated to meet the real wishes and aspirations of the human mind, could not, as it has done, have existed and flourished throughout so many centuries without any diminution of its original power. The enemies of the Papacy, even, acknowledge that in this age of liberality, this nineteenth century, it exhibits, not as yet, "any sign which indicates that the term of its long dominion is approaching. It saw the commencement of all the governments, and all the ecclesiastical establishments, that now exist in the world; and we feel no assurance that it is not destined to see the end of them all. It was great and respected before the Saxon had set foot in Britain,—before the Frank had passed the Rhine,—

when Grecian eloquence still flourished at Antioch,—when idols ... e still worshipped in the temple of Mecca, and, it may still exist, in undiminished vigor, when some traveller from New Zealand, shall, in the midst of a vast solitude, take his stand on a broken arch of London Bridge, to sketch the ruins of St. Paul's."

Second only to the protection of Divine Providence, was the excellence of the church's constitution, in securing to it that vitality and permanency which can never fail to be a subject of astonishment. In an order of things, in every way so admirable, there could not have been any narrowness of view, anything mean, and petty, and illiberal. Such things were repugnant to the genius of the Papacy. This great institution contained within itself all the strength and authority of a strong and well consolidated monarchy, together with all the liberal elements and the vigorous mind of a republic. From the very beginning its Sovereign has been elective. Moreover, he has always been the elect of the elect. The body from whom he is chosen consists of members selected from amongst the higher dignitaries of the church, not only, on account of their superior abilities and greater learning, but more still in consideration of the high character which eminent virtue confers. His reign is more limited than that of hereditary monarchs. Years and experience have matured his mind before he is called to the cares of Government. Greater authority is vested in his person than in that of any other Sovereign; and yet no Sovereign avails himself more of the knowledge and the counsel of other men. His counsellors are the most eminent representatives of the Christian church, and he never decides without consulting them. His enemies have never done descanting on his despotism, and there is no ruler less despotic. By the very nature of his office, it is impossible that he should be a despot. On the contrary, there is no Sovereign so constitutional, for he governs according to established and well known laws. Without him, in all probability, no liberal government would ever have existed. His mild but firm rule supplanted the incorrigible despotism of ancient Rome, and paved the way for the well regulated monarchies and republics of modern Europe. Without him, what would these governments have been? If, indeed, they had ever come into being, independently of the reconstituting influence of the Papacy, they would have been nothing better than rigid types of kingly rule on the one hand, and on the other, of fierce, untamed, and untamable democracies.

When, accordingly, there was question of reorganizing society, after the effete despotism of Rome had passed away, men found in the Papacy, a mode of government, than which nothing more excellent could be devised. "The christian councils," says a distinguished Protestant writer, "were the first examples of representative assemblies. There, were united the whole Roman world. There, a Priesthood which embraced the civilized earth, assembled by means of delegates, to deliberate on the affairs of the universal church. When Europe revived, it adopted the same model. Every nation by degrees borrowed the customs of the church,—then the sole repository of the traditions of civilization. It was the clergy who instructed them in the admirable system which flourished in the Councils of Nice, Sardis, and Byzantium, centuries before it was heard of in the Western world, and which did not rise in the "woods of Germany," but in the Catacombs of Rome during the sufferings of the primitive christians."*

If remote peoples who, on the dissolution of the Roman Empire, experienced the necessity of establishing for themselves regular governments, could find no better model than the great spiritual polity of the Papal church, it cannot be supposed that that temporal Sovereignty, which was as the earthly inheritance Divine Providence had assigned to the Popes, remained unmodified by its close proximity to the more important government, whose care is the spiritual well-being of the whole human race. Nor has it been at any time denied the aid of this better influence. It has experienced it in greater measure, and profited by it more abundantly than any other social organization in the world The Papacy has never ceased to be the soul and life of the

---

*Sir Archibald Alison.—History of Europe, Volume II.

earthly rule that has subsisted so long in conjunction with it. Hence it is not difficult to account for the wisdom, the goodness, the most kindly consideration for the shortcomings of humanity, and to say all, in one word, the liberality by which the temporal Sovereignty of the Popes has ever been distinguished.

The church of which the Papacy is the chief organ and the head, is divinely appointed to bear witness, throughout all time, to certain truths, which it is of the highest importance for mankind to know and believe. She can neither add to these truths, nor diminish them; neither can she interpret them in one way to-day, and in another way to-morrow. She is the witness of what has been committed to her keeping. And that she will always be a faithful witness, the word that deceives not, is her guarantee. But beyond the range of revealed truth, to which the church can never cease to bear testimony, there is a wide field of enquiry. And so long as the sacred deposit is not touched, the utmost freedom of discussion may rightfully prevail. Why should charity between disputants be so urgently recommended, nay, enjoined, if no disputation were permitted? In regard to manifestly essential points of Revelation, the belief of christians must necessarily be one. *In necessariis unitas.* But in those things that are not clearly a portion of that truth to which the church bears unerring testimony, opinion is at liberty. *In dubiis libertas.* Who shall say, that there is not thus presented to the human mind, with the full sanction of that authority which is accused of wishing to enchain it, a field of investigation sufficiently extensive for the exercise of all its faculties? Nowhere has this most liberal doctrine been better understood than at Rome. Opinion, persecuted in other lands, has ever found refuge there. Even when it goes beyond its proper sphere, it meets with consideration. It is informed, and if possible rectified, but never harshly dealt with. The great maxim is ever kept in mind—"*In omnibus charitas.*" Contrasts with other institutions, highly favorable to the Papacy, might here be established. Discarding many fabulous and exploded accounts of imaginary persecutions, a few well authenticated facts might be produced which would exhibit, in no amiable light, the heads and founders of opposing systems. Usurpations are necessarily tyrannical. They are often cruel. Since Geneva, herself, now deplores the errors of her Calvin, it were unnecessary here, to bring into parallel, his cruelty, on the one hand, and on the other, the moderation, the kindness, even, of a tribunal of the Papal church, which, whilst it declared to be contrary to the testimony of all ages, the doctrines, it spared the person of the unfortunate man, who afterwards became the victim of the stern heresiarch.

But had not Rome its Inquisition? In the interest of humanity, we rejoice that it had. In scarcely any other state was there ever a religious institution that was not more or less perverted to worldly ends. The Papal Inquisition was never thus tainted. Without stain, itself, it was able to correct whatever there was of evil in similar institutions elsewhere. If in Spain the Inquisition, which was in that country more, much more, a political than a religious tribunal, at any time used undue severity, Rome was, by universal consent, entitled to apply the remedy; and in the fulfilment of this duty, the Papal Inquisition never failed. In Spain, an illustrious Archbishop incurs the displeasure of his Sovereign. The Inquisition,—more a royal than an ecclesiastical institution,—is made the instrument of persecution. But in those days of Spanish domination, power and glory, it says not a little for the superior influence of Rome, its superior enlightenment, its superior justice, that Carranza could carry his appeal before its high tribunal, could be heard, without molestation, from his all but omnipotent Sovereign, and hear the strictly impartial sentence, which, whilst it noted some verbal errors in his most learned and energetic writings, elicited from him an explanation, which raises him to the proud position of an eminent champion of the great christian church.

But that must have been a terrible instrument of persecution which caused so much annoyance to so eminent and so good a man. This is not the place for a history of the Spanish Inquisition. Let it suffice to say, that this tribunal was erected by the Sovereigns of Spain,—Ferdinand and

Isabella,—as a defence against the Jews and the Moors. The former had become odious in Spain, not only because of their hatred to the christian faith, but on account also of their usury and extortion. They were the sole money lenders of the country, in an age when regular banking was unknown. The power they thus acquired had become dangerous to the state, and the government for its own protection, was obliged to legislate against them. It was a common practice with them, the better to mask their designs, to declare themselves christians. Some, no doubt, were sincere in conforming to the christian creed. It was to test their sincerity that the Inquisition was established. Many Jews were glad to embrace the religion of the ruling power, provided that they could still follow, in secret, the practices of their ancient faith. The Inquisition rendered this extremely difficult—almost impossible.

The Moors, after the conquest of Granada, were, in regard of the victorious Spaniards, in the same position as the Jews. Dissimulation and hypocrisy were often had recourse to. But all danger to the state, from their pretended christianity, would, it was conceived, be obviated by the searching tribunal of the Inquisition. Thus did the Sovereigns who had been so successful in war, and had raised their country to the pinnacle of grandeur and renown, hope to prevent the return of Moorish and infidel rule, as well as Jewish monopoly and usurpation. In this they completely succeeded. If, on the contrary, they had allowed Jewish and Moorish influence to increase, until the necessity for a renewal of hostilities had arisen, and if new victories had crowned their arms, this age, which now only carps at their persecuting spirit, would celebrate in fine writings and eloquent orations their warlike fame.

As Ferdinand and Isabella had erected the tribunal in question, for the purpose of destroying Jewish and Moorish ascendency in their dominions, so did Philip II., not unmindful of the policy of his predecessors, employ this mighty engine against the nascent protestantism of his time. By the Inquisition, more perhaps than by any other means, did he succeed in excluding from his territories this modern philosophy which was, at that time, not only heresy in the church, but also rebellion against the state. In the low countries it triumphed over his arms, which so many victories had crowned. In Spain it quailed and fell before the Inquisition. This may well account for the violent writing so frequently indulged in by protestant authors. If they would only confine themselves to facts, we might, perhaps, discover grounds for sharing in their indignation. But this would only be the spirit of the age in which we live, waging war against the genius of a long departed era.

The Spanish Inquisition was, indeed, a terrible institution. The Protestantism of the sixteenth century was more terrible still. The Protestantism of to-day, is all sweetness, all compassion, all philanthropy. Its tender sympathy with the unfortunate race of Israel, can only be equalled by its fellow-feeling with the good people of the Turkish empire and their reforming Sultan. The dreadful inquisition of Spain pursued and punished Jews, who professed christianity, and practiced Judaism; Moors, who publicly renounced their infidelity, and followed in secret, the superstition of their Prophet. Protestantism, whilst yet in its primitive excellence, before it had degenerated into the mild and inoffensive philosophy which men are so anxious now to consider it, was intolerant alike of all Jews. Hear its chief teacher, the Prophet, the very Mahomet of its creed. "Their synagogues ought to be destroyed, their houses pulled down, their prayer-books, the Talmud, and even the books of the Old Testament, to be taken from them; their Rabbis ought to be forbidden to teach, and be compelled to gain their livelihood by hard labour." Such was the teaching of Luther, as related by Seckendorf, one of his apologists. Protestants who read this, will remember, when meditating on the severities of the Spanish Inquisition, that, not indeed, in the time of the more humane protestantism of this age, but in the palmy days of grand Inquisitors,—THERE WAS A PROTESTANT TORQUEMADA.

The conduct of the Spaniards towards Jewish converts who relapsed into Judaism, rigid though it was, contrasts favorably with the barbarity of the early Protestants towards all Jews whomsoever. The severity of Spain, was no doubt, dictated by the policy of the time which beheld imminent danger to the state, in the numbers, the wealth, the influence and the hostile mind of the Jewish people. It was reported moreover, and generally believed in Spain, that the obnoxious race were guilty of many crimes against the christian population, such as poisoning, sacrilege, conspiracy. They went so far, it was believed, as to crucify christian children, and, the more to show their contempt for religion, they perpetrated these atrocities on occasion of the greatest of the christian festivities. A Spanish knight, of the family of Guzman, actually beheld a child crucified in the house of a Jew, when the christians were celebrating the Eucharistic sacrifice. No wonder if the resentment of the people was enkindled. The very thought of such atrocities causes, at this length of time, a thrill of horror, and we cease to be astonished at Spanish cruelty, and can marvel only that the Spaniards and their Sovereigns should have been able to restrict themselves to the punishment of convicted hypocrites and apostates.

If we look now to Rome, we shall find that there, instead of vengeance and indignation, there prevailed the true spirit of the Gospel. This was well understood, and especially by all who were in dread of being pursued by the Spanish Inquisition. Such persons fled, if it were possible, to Rome. Many availed themselves of the right of appeal to the Holy See. And the Papacy, as it had power, never failed to enforce this right. During the first fifty years of the existence of the Inquisition, innumerable cases were summoned from Spain to Rome; and in every case the condition of the accused was ameliorated. The Roman tribunal, under the mild influence of the Papacy, always inclining to the side of mercy and indulgence. It was the constant study of the Popes to restrict the Inquisition—to cause it to respect the laws of justice and humanity. On this account they had to contend with the most powerful monarchs. The Catholic Sovereigns anxious that all cases coming under the cognizance of the Inquisition, should be finally decided in Spain, urgently requested that the Holy Father should name a judge of appeal in that country. To this he consented; and the first of these Judges was the Archbishop of Seville. A great number of appeals from the Spaniards of Seville were still, however, carried to Rome. In a bull of 2nd August, 1483, the Pope formally alluded to these appeals which were made by the appellants on account of the danger they incurred of being arrested by having recourse to the Archbishop of Seville. Some of those who thus appealed to the justice of the Holy Father, had already, the Bull stated, received the absolution of the Apostolic penitentiary, and others were about to receive it. The Pope complained, moreover, that indulgences granted to divers accused persons, had not been sufficiently respected at Seville. He then proceeded to admonish, in a manner worthy of the chief Pastor, the illustrious Sovereigns, Ferdinand and Isabella, observing to them, among other things, that mercy towards the guilty was more pleasing to God than the severity which it was desired to use. He urged, as an example to them, the good Shepherd who follows the sheep that has gone astray, and concluded by exhorting them to treat with mildness those who voluntarily confessed their faults, and by desiring that they should be permitted to reside at Seville, or any other place they might choose, and that they should be allowed to enjoy their property as if they had not been guilty of the crime of heresy. The Pope, who addressed these sublime lessons to the most powerful monarchs of the time, was in advance of his age, no doubt, and in diametrical opposition to it. But he was not in advance of the Papacy, nor at variance with its teaching. The enlightenment, the humanity, the philanthropy of the nineteenth century, one would say, had shed their radiance upon him. But no. It was the genius of the Papacy;—that spirit of knowledge and christian love which was the same yesterday, as it is to-day, the same in the first, and second, and third centuries, when it preached justice and benevolence to the persecuting Cæsars, as in the fifteenth, when correcting the perverse mind of the time, it preached clemency to kings, and mutual charity to christian peoples; and, as when now, in the nineteenth, the tide of public opinion no longer flow-ing in opposition to it, but rather pretending to guide it, and bear it along in its mighty current, it proclaims aloud that unchanging truth, of which it is the faithful depository,—that justice and that humanity of which it is now, as it has ever been, the unerring witness—the perfect model.

The model, undoubtedly; for have not its deeds been always in accordance with its words of peace and love and pardon? In Spain, at the close of the 15th century, when popular indignation ran high against the Jewish race, instances occured, although not so frequently as has been alleged, of extreme sentences having been put in execution on the persons of Jewish converts who had returned to Judaism, or who practiced it in secret. But Rome was never doomed to witness such awful scenes. It would, indeed, have been a profanation of the Holy City. "It is a remarkable thing," says the most learned Spanish writer, Balmes, "that the Roman Inquisition was never known to pronounce the execution of capital punishment, although the Apostolic See was occupied during that time by Popes of extreme rigor and severity in all that relates to the civil administration. We find in all parts of Europe scaffolds prepared to punish crimes against religion. Scenes which sadden the soul were every where witnessed. Rome is an exception to the rule; Rome, which it has been attempted to represent as a monster of intolerance and cruelty. It is true that the Popes have not preached, like Protestants, universal toleration; but facts show the difference between the Popes and the Protestants. The Popes, armed with a tribunal of intolerance, have not spilled a drop of blood; Protestants and Philosophers have shed torrents. What advantage is it to the victim to hear his executioners proclaim toleration? It is adding the bitterness of sarcasm to his punishment. The conduct of Rome in the use she made of the Inquisition, is the best apology of Catholicity against those who attempt to stigmatize her as barbarous and sanguinary. In truth, what is there in common between catholicity and the excessive severity employed in this place or that, in the extraordinary situation in which many rival races were placed, in the presence of danger which menaced one of them, or in the interest which the kings had in maintaining the tranquility of their states, and securing their conquests from all danger? I will not enter into a detailed examination of the conduct of the Spanish Inquisition with respect to Judaizing christians; and I am far from thinking that the rigor which it employed against them, was preferable to the mildness recommended and displayed by the Popes. What I wish to show here is, that rigor was the result of extraordinary circumstances,—the effect of the national spirit, and of the severity of customs in Europe at that time. Catholicity cannot be reproached with excesses committed for these different reasons. Still more, if we pay attention to the spirit which prevails in all the instructions of the Popes relating to the Inquisition; if we observe their manifest inclination to range themselves on the side of mildness, and to suppress the marks of ignominy with which the guilty, as well as their families, were stigmatized, we have a right to suppose that if the Popes had not feared to displease the kings too much, and to excite divisions which might have been fatal, their measures would have been carried still further."—(*Balmes' Protestantism and Catholicity in their effects on the civilization of Europe.*)

The Moors, a savage African race, had maintained a terrible war against the christian monarchy of Spain, for the long period of eight centuries. They were conquered at last. But their hatred to their ancient enemies, whom they had defied so long, was not extinguished. They could not be reconciled to their defeat. A proud and warlike nation, they could but ill brook the state of subjection and humiliation to which the fortune of arms had reduced them. But they found it expedient to temporize,—they disguised their wrath and their resentment. Many of them even assumed the mask of the profession of christianity. Their hypocrisy must be unveiled. And the conquering people directed against all who were of Moorish blood, whether Moors, or Mooriscoes, the terrors of the Inquisition. The more humane spirit of the nineteenth century exclaims against such cruelty, even as it has protested against the savage and useless massacres, which were lately had recourse to, by one of the highly civilized nations of modern Europe, against a race who stood in regard to them, as nearly as possible, in the same position as did the Moorish people in relation to the Spaniards after the conquest of Granada. It cannot even be supposed that the Hindoo tribes were animated with such deep-rooted hatred to the nation that had governed them, during a comparatively short time, as that which eight centuries of barbarous war had implanted in every Moorish bosom. The Spanish people were deeply exasperated against the vanquished nation. The results of this deplorable feeling were the severities of the Inquisition. Our age condemns such things. But it cannot boast that this superior wisdom is peculiar to the present time, or that a special revelation has at length been made of the great lessons of humanity. In favor of the vanquished, but still dreaded and hated Moors, the Papacy was heard to urge the dictates of humanity, when no other voice could be raised in their support. In the fifteenth century it was not the custom or the fashion anywhere to advocate mercy towards Pagan offenders, or to maintain that relations of peace and amity, might safely be held with Jews and Infidels. Nevertheless the Roman Pontiff, although with as little hope perhaps of being heard as he is now when proclaiming truths that do not happen to be in harmony with the ephemeral notions of the time, exhorted, in truly christian language, the Sovereigns and the people of Spain, to refrain from measures of severity against the unfortunate Moors. *The ignorance of these races, the Pope insisted, was one of the principal causes of their faults and errors. The first thing to be done, in order to render their conversion solid and sincere, was to endeavour to enlighten their minds with sound doctrine.*

LIBERALITY OF THE PAPACY FURTHER CONSIDERED.—POLITICAL INSTITUTIONS.

No regular Government the world has yet seen was ever condemned by the Church on account of its particular form. No doubt the Papacy has had, and still has its predilections. And it would be unreasonable to suppose that an institution which has itself been raised up for the greater good of mankind, should treat with the same favor every possible system of human polity;—that it should have the same praises for the monarchy that is irresponsible and without check, and which may at any moment degenerate into absolutism and tyranny, as for that which is surrounded by every safeguard nations can desire; that it should smile upon and bless, not only the republic that is firmly founded upon wisely conceived views of political liberty, and provides with the same care for the rights, the privileges, and the happiness of every member of the community, but also that which has its origin in an excess of selfishness, and which, proclaiming aloud unbounded liberty and the universal rights of man, endeavours only to make the masses captive for the benefit of a few. Tyranny alone excepted, there is nothing in human Governments repugnant to the mind of the Papacy. But tyranny from whatever source it may flow, whether it be the tyranny of kings or of mobs, it holds in abhorrence. Autocrats, who, laying aside all salutary and constitutional restraint, became tyrants, have been known to incur the displeasure of the Papacy and have quailed before its power—the power of reason, of justice, of humanity, of liberty. Republics, degenerating into the worst of tyrannies, have alike fallen under its withering frown. The despotic rulers of ancient Rome, abusing their authority, sank into insignificance before the advancing influence of the Popes. The monarchies of modern Europe, fostered by the Papacy, have risen at certain epochs to the height of grandeur and of glory. It was only in contending with this power, by setting reason at defiance in violating the constitutions by which they existed that they lost ground, or even perished utterly. Why were they so favored? Not more surely because they were monarchies, than because they were constitutional monarchies. The despotism of ancient Rome proved its ruin. The constitutionalism of modern Europe, so dear to christianity, to the church, and to the Popes, preserved civilization and maintained the social state throughout ages of barbarism, of civil strife and political turmoil. Absolutism could not have lived amid so many perils. The christian monarchies not only existed, but progressed and flourished, shaking off by degrees the dust and the dross they had borne away with them from the wreck of the ancient heathen-frame work. To say that the Popes cherished these noble monarchies, is to say that they loved republics too. For what were these monarchies, if not republics, having a hereditary, sometimes an elective chief? Nor was the form of a republic odious to the Roman Pontiffs. Such systems of government have existed for ages, and still exist, within the immediate range of their mighty influence.

It would be difficult to call to mind any monarchy which arose under the auspices of the christian church,—and such are all the monarchies of modern Europe—that was not eminently constitutional. Monarchs endeavoured, not unfrequently, to extend unduly their prerogatives. But their tendencies to absolutism were invariably met by resistance that they were seldom able to overcome. And when every other barrier against oppression was broken down, that afforded by the Papacy remained—"confronting in the middle ages tyrants and hostile kings with the same spirit with which it confronted Attila." In the days of its prolonged ascendency it was the surest safe-guard of the people's rights —the recognized and constitutional bulwark of liberty.

But is it not said that the Popes encourage despotism, by maintaining the Divine right of Kings? On this important matter the Roman Pontiffs have never held, have never preached, have never acted upon any other doctrine than that which the church has invariably taught. This doctrine, as laid down in the sacred Scriptures and in the writings of the most eminent Theologians, it will not be out of place now to consider. It is somewhat different from what separated churches hold, and have at certain epochs loudly preached. The despotism of the Papacy too, has, at more than one period, been their favorite theme. They boasted at the same time their own superior liberality, whilst they were in reality less liberal than the Popes.

"There is no power that does not come from God."—(*St. Paul to the Romans.*)—This looks like Divine right undoubtedly. The Divine right of Power, but not of Princes. Society, like the family, consists of members that are mutually dependent, and must necessarily have numerous relations. As in families, there must be order and authority to watch over their preservation; as this authority is founded upon, arises out of essential family relations,—is established by nature,—in other words, is of Divine appointment; so in society which is an aggregation of families, there must be authority to watch over its manifold relations. This authority,—the civil power,—originates in the very nature of society. It is essential to it. Order, upon which society depends, could not exist without it. Power, then, is founded in nature, proved by reason, sanctioned by revelation. Hear Str. John Chrysostom in a homily on the epistle to the Romans: "There is no power that does not come from God." What do you say? Is every Prince then, appointed by God? I do not say that, for I do not speak of any Prince in particular, but of the thing itself, that is, of the power itself. I affirm that the existence of principalities is the work of the Divine Wisdom, and that to it it is owing that all things are not given up to blind chance. Therefore it is that the Apostle does not say, that there is no Prince who does not come from God; but he says, speaking of the thing in itself, "There is no power which does not come from God."

The idea of Catholics, therefore, in regard of Divine right, is by no means what the revilers of the church ascribe to them. Instead of imagining that each King or Prince holds his throne for himself and his family by letters patent, as it were, from heaven, we only recognize a principle which was held sacred by the legislators and statesmen of antiquity, which is agreeable to sound philosophy and in harmony with the events of history. We have seen, moreover, that this doctrine is inculcated in the Scriptures, and enforced by the early Fathers of the Church.

We find it also in the writings of the most eminent Theologians of more recent times. St. Thomas, of Aquin, has written voluminously on the origin of civil power. A short quotation may suffice to show what view of this important question was entertained by this most learned Doctor, whose works have been held to be of the greatest authority.

in all schools of Theology, for the last six hundred years. "Iu natural things it was necessary that inferior things should be brought into their respective operations, by the natural virtue which God has given to superior things. In the same way also, it is necessary that in human things those which are superior should urge on the inferior, by the force of authority ordained by God. To move by means of the reason and the will, is to command; and, as by virtue of the natural order instituted by God, inferior things in nature are necessarily subject to the motion of superior things, so also in human things, those which are inferior ought by natural and Divine right, to obey those which are superior."

"To obey a superior is a duty conformable to the Divine order communicated to things." In answer to the question, whether christians are obliged to obey the secular powers, St. Thomas says: "The faith of Christ is the principle and the cause of Justice, according to what is said in the epistle to the Romans, chap. III. 'The Justice of God by the faith of Jesus Christ.' Thus, the faith of Christ does not take away the law of Justice, but rather confirms it. The law wills that inferiors should obey their superiors; for without that human society could not be preserved; and thus the faith of Christ does not exempt the faithful from the obligation of obeying the secular powers." Thus is it obvious that this great Doctor, the Angel of the schools, whilst adhering to a dogma, clearly laid down in the sacred volume, considers the Divine law as a confirmation and sanction of the natural and human law.

From the earliest ages until now, all Theologians have taught that civil power—public authority—comes from God. St. Augustin in almost all the forty-five books of the "City of God" bears witness to, and proves the soundness of this teaching.

All Doctors are agreed that this doctrine is founded on Scripture. "By me Kings reign"—"By me Princes rule," says the Divine wisdom in the book of Proverbs. The Prophet Daniel, in denouncing the wrath of Heaven against an unfaithful king, declared that his punishment should last

7

until he knew "that the most High ruleth over the kingdom of men, and giveth it to whomsoever he will."

Cardinal Bellarmin commenting on the above and similar passages of the inspired writings, concludes, that civil power comes from God, and explains in what sense *it must be understood* that it does so. "In the first place political power, considered in general and without descending in particular to monarchy, aristocracy, or democracy, emanates immediately from God alone; for, being necessarily annexed to the nature of man, it proceeds from him who has made that nature. Besides that power is by natural law, since it does not depend upon men's consent, since they must have a government, whether they wish it or not, under pain of desiring the destruction of the human race, which is against the inclination of nature. It is thus that the law of nature is Divine law, and government is introduced by Divine law; and it is particularly this which the Apostle seems to have had in view when he says to the Romans, chap. XIII. 'He who resists authority, resists the ordinance of God.'"

Some philosophers of the last century had made the ingenious discovery, that all government is the result of human convention. Certain heretics have held and taught the equally dangerous and destructive doctrine, that by their christian liberty men were emancipated from the controul of all authority, thus condemning civil power as an evil,— and, indeed, "making liberty a cloak for malice."

Man was created to live in society. The Author of his being has not left him, the sport of blind chance, as to the means by which he shall fulfil this high condition of his existence. He has given to man social rights. He has imposed on him the d ty of preserving these rights. He has made government a law of his nature; and, in imposing on him the obligation of obedience, he has only charged him with the duty of self preservation. This may be servitude. In the estimation of the Atheist philosopher, and the intractable heresiarch it is so; but we shall continue to prefer it to the only other possible state of existence—that, which, casting man beyond the pale of civilization, dooms him to

ver the kingdom
ll."

ove and similar
that civil power
e *it must* be un-
political power,
ing in particular
anates immedi-
y annexed to the
has made that
aw, since it does
ey must have a
t, under pain of
which is against
ie law of nature
by Divine law;
seems to have
ap. XIII. 'He
of God.'"

had made the
is the result of
held and taught
ne, that by their
om the controul
er as an evil,—
alice."

Author of his
ance, as to the
condition of his
ights. He has
ese rights. He
nd, in imposing
ily charged him
y be servitude,
and the intrac-
nue to prefer it
e—that, which,
dooms him to

roam the uncultivated forest, like the wild beast, or the scarcely less wild Barbarian.

Civil power is from God. Let us now see how, according to Cardinal Bellarmin, and with him, generally, the Theologians of the Catholic church, it pleases the Divine Being to communicate this power to those who represent and exercise it for the benefit of mankind. "In the second place, observe, that this power resides, *immediately*, as in its subject, in all the multitude, for it is by Divine right. The Divine right has not given this power to any man in particular, for it has given it to the multitude; besides the positive law being taken away, there is no reason why one should rule rather than another among a great number of equal men; therefore power belongs to the whole multitude. In fine, society should be in a perfect state; it should have the power of self-preservation, and, consequently, that of chastising the disturbers of the peace."

To the superficial reader, this passage will seem to be in contradiction with what the learned Divine had already stated. He had just said that all power is from God; and now he makes it reside immediately in the multitude. The eminent Spanish writer,—Balmes,—will unveil, if indeed, it requires to be unveiled, the meaning of Cardinal Bellarmin. "His doctrine may be conveyed in this form: Suppose a number of men without any positive law; there is then no reason why any one of them should have a right to rule the rest. Nevertheless, this law exists, nature itself indicates its necessity, God ordains a Government; therefore, there exists among this number of men, the legitimate power of instituting one. To explain more clearly the ideas of this illustrious Theologian, let us suppose that a considerable number of families, perfectly equal among themselves and absolutely independent of each other, were thrown by a tempest on a desert island. The vessel being destroyed, they have no hope either of returning home or of pursuing their journey. All communication with the rest of mankind is become impossible. We ask whether these families could live without government? No. Has any one among them a right of governing the rest? clearly not. Can any individual among them pretend to such a right? certainly not. Have they a right to appoint the government of which they stand in need? certainly they have. Therefore, in this multitude, represented by the fathers of families, or in some other way, resides the civil power, together with the right of transmitting it to one or more persons, according as they shall judge proper. It is difficult to make any valid objection to the doctrine, placed in this point of view. That this is the real meaning of Bellarmin's words, is clearly shown by the observations which follow: "In the third place, observe, that the multitude transfers this power to one person, or more, by natural right; for the republic not being able to exercise it by itself, is obliged to communicate it to one, or to a limited number; and it is thus that the power of Princes, considered in general, is by natural and Divine law; and the whole human race, if assembled together, could not establish the contrary, viz: that Princes or Governors did not exist."

The church has been loudly accused of favoring servitude, of encouraging despotism. But her Theologians concurring in their interpretation of the written word, as to the origin of civil power, agree also in allowing to society, the full right to choose that form of government which they may conceive to be the best adapted to their wants. All forms of government are reconcilable with the fundamental principles which we have just considered. And although learned Theologians may have their predilections, as to the systems of polity that are best calculated to secure permanently the peace and prosperity of the community, there is nothing in their teaching that can be construed as hostile to, or incompatible with liberty. But let this be still more clearly understood; and so let us hear Bellarmin once more. "Observe, in the fourth place, that particular forms of government are, by the law of nations, and not by Divine law, since it depends upon the consent of the multitude, to place over themselves a King, Consuls, or other Magistrates, as is clear; and for a legitimate reason, they can change Royalty into Aristocracy, or into Democracy, or *vice versa*, as it was done in Rome.

"Observe, in the fifth place, that it follows from what we have said, that this power, in particular, comes from God, but by means of the counsel and election of man, like all other things which belong to the law of nations; for the law of nations is, as it were, a conclusion drawn from the natural law by human reasoning. Thence follows a twofold difference betwen the political and the ecclesiastical power: first, difference with regard to the subject, since political power is in the multitude, and ecclesiastical, in a man, *immediately*, as in its subject; second, difference with respect to the cause, since political power, considered generally, is by Divine law, and in particular, by the law of nations, while the ecclesiastical power is, in every way, by Divine law, and emanates immediately from God."

When Theologians say that "it depends on the consent of the multitude, to place over themselves a King, Consuls, or Magistrates;" and that "for a legitimate reason, they can change Royalty into Aristocracy, or into Democracy, or *vice versa;*" we must beware of falling into the mistake, that their teaching tends to justify capricious changes in forms of civil rule, or that "the multitude," to whom they ascribe so much power, is,—in any section or class, however numerous and influential,—not the whole community itself. Thus, in Great Britain, for instance, nothing could be more erroneous than to suppose that any portion of the nation, although claiming to be "the people," could reasonably demand, without the concurrence of the rest, a change in the existing form of the government. The "religious" section of the community alone would not be entitled to obtain such a constitution as they would consider more favorable to their 'views' than the actual state of things. The commercial classes would not have the right to require such alterations in the government, as they might think would be more conducive to industrial success. The Aristocracy would have no right to insist upon any new, and, in their idea, better form of polity, which would have more consideration for their interests and privileges. Nor would the classes who are commonly called *the people*, be justified, according to what all the great Theologians have invariably taught, in endeavouring to bring about radical changes in the British Constitution, however conducive they might conceive that such changes would be to their own interests, without the consent and concurrence of all the other classes of the community. It follows, hower, as a necessary corollary of Theologic teaching, founded as it is upon the Word which is incapable of erring, that the entire community—Sovereign, Lords, and Commons—are competent to resolve themselves, in the event of the existing state of things becoming intolerably oppressive, into an oligarchy, a republic with universal suffrage for its basis, or a pure and unmitigated despotism. This they are free to do. But they are not at liberty to dispense with all government. They are by nature so constituted as to be necessarily subject to civil rule of some kind. God has made it essential to them,—an indispensable condition of their existence,—their existence in the social state, their existence as a people, and as a nation.

Much more, surely, is the community entitled to select a form of civil rule when there exists no government at all; either in the case where, as in new communities, it has not as yet been established; or where, by great political convulsions, or other means, it has been done away with.

Hence the great nation of the French, if so recent an example may be adduced, only exercised a right,—an undoubted right, when, being without government, after the failure and the fall of many systems of civil rule, they chose for themselves the most despotic form of polity it is possible to conceive. Nor does it in the least weaken or invalidate the title on which they acted, that it pleased them, in the exercise of the Divine right, of which, by circumstances and the designs of Providence, it became necessary that they should avail themselves, to select for their Monarch the very man who had been mainly instrumental in overthrowing the more liberal and democratic form of government, which they themselves had only a short time before established. They were free to choose. God, whilst he has made authority necessary for men and has accorded to them the privilege of choosing the form of rule under which they shall live, has by no means assured them that they will always wisely use this privilege. Without allusion to the French, or to any nation in particular, it may be truly said that, that kind of Legislature which is best adapted to a people, whether on account of their demerits or their deserts, whether for the purpose of rewarding them with prosperity, or of punishing them with political difficulties and national disaster, generally becomes prevalent.

ORIGIN OF CIVIL POWER.—DOCTRINE OF A LEARNED JESUIT AND OTHER EMINENT DIVINES.

It ought to suffice that a Theologian so intimately connected with the Court of Rome, as the illustrious Cardinal Bellarmin, has been quoted in support of the most liberal and true doctrine in regard to the origin of civil power. This very learned Doctor was not only held in great estimation in his own time at Rome, where he enjoyed the favor and the friendship of the most distinguished men of the time but throughout the whole christian world, and is even now looked upon as one of the ablest theological writers in the Catholic church. His opinions are of the greatest weight in all schools of Theology. That such a man should have written and taught, as we have seen, on the Divine origin of Government, is no slight vindication of the Papacy against those revilers who cease not to represent it, as beyond measure, hostile to every liberal doctrine as well as to every liberal institution.

But the learned Bellarmin does not stand alone. Theologians of no less celebrity than himself, defend the same doctrine. As we consider their opinions, it will appear that it is not Rome, or her Doctors, who hold extreme views as to the Divine right of Kings, but they who have credit for being more liberal, although on what ground we know not, unless it be their habitual opposition to every thing that emanates from the Holy See.

The renowned Suarez, a Spaniard and a member of the Order of Jesuits, not only teaches, but, at the same time, bears witness that it is the common teaching of the Divines of the Catholic church, "that God, inasmuch as he is the author of nature, gives the power; so that men are, so to speak, the matter and subject capable of this power; while God gives the form, by giving the power."—(*De ligibus, lib. III., c. 3.*)

As to the way in which power is communicated, Suarez holds exactly the same opinion as the Doctors already quoted. "It follows," he says, "from principles he has just laid down, that the civil power, wherever it is found in a man or a Prince, has emanated according to usual and legitimate law, from the people and the community, either directly or remotely, and that it cannot otherwise be justly possessed."—(*Ibib, c. 4.*)

So decidedly was the learned Suarez opposed to the doctrine that royal power proceeds *directly* from God, that he wrote a book in vindication of his opinion, and in reply to a work by "the most serene James, King of England," in which the extreme view of the Divine right of Kings was vigorously upheld. In this work, according to Suarez, "the most serene King not only gives a new and singular opinion, but also acrimoniously attacks Cardinal Bellarmin for having affirmed that Kings have not received authority *immediately* from God, like the Popes. He himself (the King) affirms, that Kings hold their power, not from the people, but *immediately* from God: and he attempts to support his opinion by arguments and examples, the value of which I shall examine in the next chapter."

As our only object here, is to show what opinions are held by learned Divines, and not to enter into a formal discussion, the following short quotation from Suarez will suffice: "Although *this controversy does not immediately concern the dogmas of Faith, for we have nothing in reference to it, either in the Scriptures or the Fathers,* it may nevertheless be well to discuss and explain it carefully; 1st, because it might possibly lead to error in other dogmas; 2nd, because the above opinion of the King, as he maintains and explains it, is new, singular, and apparently invented to exalt the temporal, at the expense of the spiritual power; and 3rd, because we consider the opinion of the illustrious Bellarmin, *ancient, received, true, and necessary.*"

At all periods the same doctrine has been taught, and not

by Jesuit Divines only, but by all theologians alike. It has been preached under monarchies the most absolute, and without danger to the throne, no less than in well ordered republics, where the people could be reminded of their inherent right, without any fear of trouble to the State. Cardinal Gotti, in the early part of the last century, spoke of it as an opinion that had been long received and established. Hermanu Busenbaum, and Liguorio clearly express this opinion: "It is certain that the power of making laws exists among men, but as far as civil laws are concerned, this power belongs naturally to no individual. It belongs to the community, who transfer it to one or to more, that by them the community itself may be governed."

In the *compendium Salmaticense*,—which serves as a text-book to the Professors of ethics in the schools and universities of Spain,—"It is universally admitted that Princes receive this power (the civil legislative power) from God; but at the same time it is maintained with more truth, that that they do not receive it *directly*, but *through the medium* of the people's consent; for all men are naturally equal, and there is no natural distinction of superiority or inferiority. Since nature has not given to any individual, power over another, God has conferred this power upon the community; which, as it may think it more proper to be ruled by one, or by many appointed persons, transfers it to one, or to many, that by them it may be ruled; according to St. Thomas Aquinas. From this natural principle arises the variety in the forms of civil government; * * *

Princes, therefore, receive from God the power of commanding; for, supposing the election made by the whole State, God confers upon the Prince, the power which was vested in the community. Hence it follows that the Prince rules and governs, in the name of God, and whoever resists him, resists the ordinance of God, according to the words of the Apostle."

Billuart, a French Divine, who wrote in the early half of last century, when monarchical ideas were highly prevalent in France, inculcates the same opinions.

Father Daniel Concina, a Roman writer, who flourished

about the middle of last century, expresses with no less concision, than perspicuity, the important opinion, of which there is question. Having shown how it is to be understood, that civil power comes from God, he writes as follows: "It is evident, therefore, that the power existing in the Prince, the King, or in many persons, whether nobles or plebeians, emanates from the community itself, directly, or indirectly; for if it came immediately from God, it would be manifested to us in a particular manner, as in the instances of Saul and David, who were chosen by God. We consider, therefore, erroneous, the doctrine, that God communicates this power immediately and directly upon the King, the Prince, or any other head of supreme government whatsoever, to the exclusion of the tacit, or expressed consent of the public. This discussion, it is true, is one of words rather than of things, for this power comes from God, the author of nature, inasmuch as he has ordained and appointed, that the public, itself, shall confer, upon one or more, the power of supreme government, for the preservation and defence of society. The nomination of the person or persons appointed to command, being once made, their power is said to come from God, because society itself is bound by natural and Divine right, to obey him who commands. In fact, it is the will of God that society should be governed, whether by one individual, or by several. In this manner the several opinions of Theologians are reconciled with each other, and the oracles of Scripture appear in their true sense: 'He that resisteth power, resisteth the ordinance of God.' 'There is no power but from God.' 'Be subject, therefore, to every human creature, for God's sake, whether to the King, &c.'"

This recognition of Divine power in the affairs of mankind, does not, by any means, do away with the various *media* of human acts and institutions, through which civil authority is at first communicated and afterwards exercised.

On the two points contained in the question of Divine right,—the origin of civil power, and the mode in which it is communicated,—the learned Spanish writer, Bolmes, discourses in the following eloquent manner:

"The former point—the origin of civil power—is a question of doctrine. No Catholic can entertain any doubt upon it. The second is open to discussion; and various opinions may be formed upon it without interfering with faith. With regard to Divine right, considered in itself, true philosophy agrees with catholicity. In fact, if civil power comes not from God, to what source can we trace its origin? Upon what solid principle can we support it? If the man who exercises it does not rest upon God, the legitimacy of his power, no title will avail him to uphold his right. It will be radically and irretrievably null. On the contrary, supposing authority to come from God, our duty to submit to it becomes evident, and our dignity is not the least hurt by the submission; but, in the other supposition, we see only force, craft, tyranny, but no reason or justice; perhaps a necessity for submission, but no obligation. By what title does any man pretend to command us? Because he is possessed of superior intellect? Who had the right of adjudging to him the palm? Besides this superiority does not constitute a right; in some instances its direction might be useful to us, but it will not be obligatory. Is it because he is stronger than we? In that case the elephant ought to be the king of the entire world. Is it because he is more wealthy than we? Reason and justice exist not in metal. The rich man is born naked, and his riches will not descend with him into the tomb. Upon earth, they have enabled him to acquire power; but they do not confer upon him any right to exercise it over others. Shall it consist in certain faculties conferred on him by others? Who has constituted other men our proxies? Where is their consent? Who has collected their votes? or how can either we or they flatter ourselves that we possess faculties equal to the exercise of civil power? and, if we do not possess them, how can we delegate them?"

WHETHER IN ANY CASE ESTABLISHED POWER CAN BE CONSCIENTIOUSLY RESISTED.

Protestant and philosophical writers admit, indeed, "that the principle of religious royalty is elevated; moral and salutary; but that it is difficult to combine with it the rights of liberty and political guarantees."—(*Guziot, Lecture IX.*)

Nothing in this wold can be more elevated, or more moral, or more salutary, or more calculated to secure permanently the peace and well-being of society, than the royalty which the learned statesman thus highly compliments. But history shows, at the same time, that it has proved a better safeguard to liberty—than any system of civil rule by which it was preceded. The truth is, that before this christian royalty was established, mankind had exhausted their ingenuity in devising forms of government, under which society should not only enjoy peace and order, but also liberty. The true principles of government were forgotten or neglected; and, hence, neither royalty, nor republicanism was found adequate to the end in view. Christianity appears. It not only blesses, but instructs the power by which the world must be ruled. It says not that this or that form shall be preferred. But it insists that under all forms, the duties of power shall be fulfilled. It says not only that kings must understand these duties, but that they must also be the study of all who hold rule among men: "All ye who judge (govern) the world, receive instruction." *Erudimini qui judicatis terram.*" Does royalty forget this precept? Does a king, elated by the success of his arms and the greatness of the people over whom he reigns, pretend that all power centres in his person? He is at once corrected. Religion, although every other influence, whether moral or material, may have been subdued, raises her voice in the cause of justice and humanity. "The kingdom is not made for the king, but the king for the kingdom. For God has constituted kings to rule and govern, and to secure to every one the possession of his rights; such is the aim of their institution; but if kings, turning things to their own profit, should act otherwise, they are no longer kings, but tyrants."—(*St. Thomas de rege. Princ., c. II.*) In such doctrine as this, there is surely nothing adverse to liberty. It is "elevated," it is "moral," it is "salutary;" but it is not irreconcilable with a due measure of human freedom. It combines admirably with "the rights of liberty," and it would be difficult to imagine any surer "political guarantee." Hear this doctrine still more plainly unfolded: "Kings, Princes, Magistrates," writes the venerable Palafox, "all jurisdiction is ordained by God for the preservation of his people, not for their destruction; for defence, not for offence; for man's right, and not for his injury. They who maintain that kings can do as they please, and who establish their power upon their will, open the way to tyranny. Those who maintain that kings have power to do as they ought, and what is necessary for the preservation of their subjects and their crown, for the exaltation of faith and religion, for the just and right administration of justice, the preservation of peace, and the support of just war, for the due and becoming *éclat* of regal dignity, the honorable maintenance of their houses and families; speak the truth without flattery, throw open the gates to justice, and, to magnanimous and royal virtues."—(*Palafox apud Balmes*, cap. 53.)

Even in France, at the time of its greatest despotism, these doctrines were fearlessly preached. Louis XIV. was not an absolute monarch. He only imagined he was, when he said that "he was the state." (*L'état c'est moi.*) He only desired to be so, when he expressed to Marshal d'Estrées, his envy of the Persian Shah. He contrived, nevertheless, to forget, sometimes, that he was a christian, that is, a constitutional king. Refusing to accept the *elevating*, the *moral*, the *salutary* teaching of the Papacy and of the Catholic church, he acted on occasions, with extraordinary harshness towards portions of his subjects, failing to remember that all were alike his people and the objects of his royal solicitude. But of this enough. Let us only insist that it was not in obedience to the lessons of Massillon and Bourdalone, and Bossuet and Fenelon, that Louis XIV. oppressed and impoverished his kingdom, by aggressive and extravagant wars,—or that he banished the poor Hugonots.

Catholicity instructs kings and all magistrates whatsoever, that they, as well as other men, have duties to fulfil. It requires that the people, subject to their authority, should obey them. Without obedience to civil rule, there could be no social order. In regard to this important matter, the Papal church might be favorably contrasted with all separated sects. Doctrinally, they all hold that rebellion is justifiable. Many of them, whatever their teaching may be, are content to practice inert and servile submission. These are the extremes. Wisdom disowns them. So does the well informed Catholic. But may not circumstances occur, in which resistance, according to Catholic teaching, would not only be allowable, but even expedient and laudable? Undoubtedly. But how rare must not such circumstances be! Tyranny might be carried to such an extent, as, from its excesses, to render opposition lawful, whilst on other grounds it would be highly inexpedient, and consequently criminal, inasmuch as it might occasion bloodshed and incalculably great national calamity, without any commensurate result. In other words, circumstances might arise in which it would be lawful to oppose, I do not say, the legitimate civil power, but that established government which, from the complete neglect of its duties, and by violating every law of justice and humanity, had degenerated into an intolerable tyranny, and so ceased to be lawful authority.

On this most important subject, it is fitting that we should hear a very learned Theologian and eloquent orator, Father Ventura, the fellow student and friend of the reigning Pope, in his own incomparable style, will now instruct us, in the first place, as to what, according to Christian principles, must be avoided.

"We must bear in mind, that foreign to, and beyond the pale of Catholic doctrines, there are to be found two distinct and mutually antagonistic systems, by means of which men seek a solace or a remedy for tyranny and oppression. One is submission to them with stupid apathy,—the other, their repulsion by physical force. The former bends to them like a slave,—the latter rises up against them like a rebel. The one is called "*passive obedience,*" the other "*active resistance.*" The former is the system of Mahommedan fatalism and infidelity; the latter, that of heretical rationalism. But, oh! how much more disastrous are such remedial means than the evils they pretend to cure!

"The system of *passive obedience*, or the inert resignation to all that which power may please to do with a people, consigns to the caprice of a tyrant, not only the property, the honor, and the life of the subject, but still more, his understanding, his heart, his conscience, his thoughts, his reason, his will—all—the entire of that which makes man worthy of the name of man. It degrades man into a brute, which is utterly and completely at the discretion of him who is its owner. It leaves to man nothing of humanity except the form; and even in that form, is not long to be found revealed the Divine origin of man, and his innate dignity.

"The system of *active resistance*, or of sedition, whether it be adverse or triumphant, is ever fatal. If triumphant, it merely makes a change of persons, and leaves unchanged the circumstances, and untouched the state of things, against which it was directed. The same parts are represented by different individuals; but, the tragedy is still enacted, and precisely in the same manner in which it had been previously performed. The slave plays the tyrant, and he who had been the tyrant, wears the garb and clanks the chains of the slave; and all goes on as before, to its sad and fitting catastrophe. The sovereignty of all is the slavery of all, for the profit of a few. And if at any subsequent period the movement brings forth any advantage, such an event never occurs until a long period has elapsed, and until those who created the movement have paid for it with their lives, and until the traces of those passions which produced its triumph have been obliterated.

"But woe! woe! to a people if their attempt at resistance has failed. The wounded pride of tyranny is no longer to be kept within any bounds. That which it did from caprice, it then believes that it is bound, as a matter of duty, to perpetrate. Before, it oppressed because oppression was an instinct of its nature; and afterwards it oppresses because oppression is regarded as the necessary means of its own conservation. Distrust changes to hatred, and hatred lashes itself into fury. Judicial forms are no longer attended to. Every thought is punished as an offence, and every word condemned as if it were sedition. Talent, wealth, virtue, are converted into crimes, and suspicion the sole—the sufficient ground for condemnation. Fetters are made more heavy, chains are added to chains, to bind the limbs of freemen, whilst sycophants become more shumeless, courtiers more vile, executioners more cruel, despotism more atrocious, and persecution more inhuman."

The orator now contrasts with these two systems, two courses of action that are admirably in harmony with the sublime teaching of christianity, and which the soundest human policy cannot at the same time fail to sanction.

"Between these two systems which, by opposite paths, lead generally to the same end—the ruin and slavery of the people—stands the system of Catholic christianity; which, condeming rebellions a. *v* *nults*, teaches us to oppose to oppression, and especial: eligious oppression, no other species of resistance, but those of *passive resistance* and *active obedience*.

"*Passive resistance*, when the subject refuses to obey the commands of man, in matters which would be to the prejudice of the duties of conscience, or in opposition to the laws of God: but *passively*, that is, suffering (and without having recourse to Physical force) those pains and penalties which are an honor to Him, when endured for the confession of His Faith. For our Lord Jesus Christ has said, that "all," even those who resist religious oppression, "that take up the sword, shall perish by the sword:" *Omnes enim qui acceperint gladium, gladio peribunt;* (Matt. XXVI., 52.) that is to say, that religious persecution should never be combatted by the strength of the body, but by the virtues of the soul; that in a war, which is completely spiritual, we ought never to employ arms that are merely material, and by which, although we may succeed, yet we may also perish; that we should have recourse solely to spiritual and invisible arms, constancy in the faith—meekness—patience —and prayer; arms, of which as the use is noble, so is the success certain. When the maintenance of the true faith is in question, it is easier to overcome and destroy persecution by consenting that our own blood should be shed, than by attempting to shed that of the persecutor. The martyr in his sepulchre is more terrible to the tyrant, than the armed rebel who faces him in the field. He who suffers is stronger than he who resists; he who receives a blow, than him by whom it is inflicted; the christian who succumbs, than the insurgent who conquers. The christian children of Calvary were multiplied by being decimated; they received new vigor and fresh life by dying; they triumphed by being humiliated: '*Quo plures metimur, plures efficimur.*' (Tertullian.) And while they won for themselves, in Heaven, an immortal crown, they assured to their brethren and the church, an invincible strength, and infallible victory on this earth. Ancient christian Rome, and modern Catholic Ireland, constitute the clearest proofs of the truth and the success of this doctrine.

"In prescribing, however, a *passive resistance* to a power oppressive of conscience and of faith, the teaching of Catholicity intimates that there may be an *active obedience.* Whilst it preaches the necessity of *resisting by suffering*, it permits also the practice of *obeying by acting*, for the purpose of escaping from injustice: the meaning of which is, that in condemning rebellion, the Catholic doctrine does not proscribe action—in forbidding violent resistance, it does not prohibit the employment of such means as justice and the laws allow. In requiring the subject to respect the rights of power, it does not require that he should renounce his own.

"The self same St. Paul, who so strenuously inculcates obedience to legitimate powers, as in the order of things established by God himself, did nevertheless, himself appeal to Cæsar, from an inferior tribunal. *Ad Cæsarem appello.* He did not renounce his rights, nor forego his privileges as a Roman citizen, for such he proclaimed himself: *Civis Romanus sum.* Thus, the Catholic system, whilst it exacts resignation in the subjects of a tyrannical government, does not mean that they should renounce the personal attributes of humanity, and that, as soul-less inanimate substances, they should abandon themselves to the sanguinary caprices of tyrants. Coincident with the rational obedience of subjects, it also recommends a national loyalty from them as men: *Rationabile obsequium.* (Rom.) While it assures obedience to power, it does not sanction every species of power as legitimate; but leaves free the course by which the wise, the prudent, and the just can protest against oppression; and thus, it reconciles the dignity of man with social order."*

LIBERTY OF SPEECH.

That in the Papacy, which to so many, appears only to enchain thought and fetter its expression, is in reality, the greatest safeguard of mental freedom, and the best guarantee for liberty of speech. The Papacy abhors coercion. If, therefore, the bounds of reason and of prudence are transgressed, the temporal rule guided by its influence, has recourse rather to remonstrance, to admonition, to instruction, than to the stern appliances of human law. And yet there has been, from time immemorial at Rome, a tribunal which takes cognizance of such public expressions of opinion as are alleged to be in opposition to the teachings of that Divine Religion, to which the Papacy is appointed to bear witness; but who ever heard that any harsh and severe measure was put in execution by the Roman Inquisition? Many things have been written, nevertheless, which were clearly at variance with sound Theology. And has the searching eye of the Inquisition been blind to such things? Or seeing them has it wanted courage to expose and to chastise? By no means. But its punishments have ever been of a widely different nature from those which worldly tribunals are wont to inflict. In matters of opinion, it points out the truth,—it instructs,—it argues and persuades. In questions of faith, it bears witness, and pronounces whether the views that are subjected to its examination be in accordance with Apostolic testimony. True such children of the church—and such of her ministers as oppose her teaching, and obstinately rebel against her Divine authority, by virtue of which she will testify to all christian truths, until the end of ages, must by this same authority be punished. But by what penalties? By stripes, imprisonment, death even? By none of all these. The Inquisition of Rome, although qualified to try every species of crime

---

* The funeral oration on Daniel O'Connell, M.P., delivered in Rome, June 28th and 30th 1847, by the very Rev. Father Ventura.

against religion, has never been known, on any occasion, to inflict the punishment of death. But that dread tribunal surely does punish. Undoubtedly. And he who obstinately persists in giving expression to opinions proved to be ill-founded and erroneous, incurs through its instrumentality, the censures of the church. Only when there is question of those things to which the church and its head on earth, are appointed to bear witness, can such censures be pronounced. In all besides, there prevails the utmost freedom of thought and of discussion. "*In dubiis libertas.*" Where, in what nation, under what form of government does the like measure of liberty obtain? In scarcely any of our modern republics is there any liberty of thought whatever. If any one be inclined to doubt this statement, let him repair to the Southern States of the American union, and express his idea of human liberty, and his detestation of the slave system, he will speedily learn, and perhaps to his cost, how far it is consistent with truth, and how, and in what degree, a most highly lauded republicanism is calculated to secure liberty of speech. We know too, how rudely have been used in the Northern States, men of highly respectable position, who presumed to think differently from the surrounding multitude, on the important subject of education. It is also in remembrance that, under the shadow of the British Constitution, an author of distinction, an English gentleman, who indulged in various moral and theological speculations, that did not happen to be in harmony with the crude ideas of the peasantry around his mansion, was compelled by violence and malicious fire-raising, which left him without a house, to abandon his country. In the British parliament, even, the most free and independent of all representative assemblies, there are limits to the freedom of the tongue. And yet who will say that that honorable house claims dominion over thought, when it sentences a member who has given utterance to indiscreet expressions, to acknowledge the supremacy of the representative body, and beg pardon on his knees? Nor with such atonement for an undue use of that liberty which our free constitution concedes, does the house on every occasion rest satisfied.

None of us have as yet forgot that a very eminent member,* a gentleman no less renowned for dignity of character, than for his ancient and honorable descent, was condemned by this same assembly to the pain of imprisonment in its dungeons, because he was not pleased to understand the precise measure of liberty of speech that even a British subject is privileged to enjoy. And this measure is unquestionably great. But it has its limits. And is it not highly reasonable that he who should endeavor by imprudent, and even criminal expressions of opinion, to sap the foundations of the state, to overthrow the constitution, or insult the representatives of the people, or the person of the sovereign, should be judged and punished? In such a state of things, even if, on occasions, a certain amount of injustice should ensue, there is no British subject who does not rejoice. Must there, then, be one law at London, and another at Rome? This cannot be. It is the one great law to which the immortal Cicero bears witness, and which is every where the same.—"*Non alia Romæ et alia Athenis.*"

But the temporal Government of Rome does not always take example from the moderation of the Spiritual authority. It would be strange if it did not, considering the close alliance. The temporal may be under the necessity of doing in the fulfilment of its functions, or even for its own preservation what the spiritual power would refuse to sanction. We cannot admit any such necessity. It never can be advantageous to any government, to set aside, even for an apparently laudable purpose, the laws of justice and humanity. The Papal Government, nevertheless, did so act not long ago, when there was question of saving its reputation with foreign States. It cruelly banished an unoffending correspondent of an eminent London newspaper, solely on account of his zeal and industry in supplying the news of the day to his employers. If it were so, there could be no question as to the offence against justice and humanity. If on the other hand, the man whom the Romans, through the medium of their Government, expelled from their city, was

* Mr. Smith O'Brien.

inent member,*
f character, than
a condemned by
ment in its dun-
tand the precise
ritish subject is
unquestionably
ighly reasonable
id even criminal-
s of the state, to
presentatives of
hould be judged
ven if, on occa-
sue, there is no
there, then, be
This cannot be.
al Cicero bears
ie.—" *Non alia*

oes not always
itual authority.
g the close alli-
essity of doing
its own preser-
se to sanction.
never can be
le, even for an
e and human-
did. so act not
its reputation
n unoffending
per, solely on
ig the news of
re could be no
humanity. If
s, through the
heir city, was

not an inoffensive character, was not a faithful and truthful correspondent, but a person of more than doubtful reputation, who was more notorious for his crimes, than celebrated for good qualities and noble deeds, and who instead of despatching true accounts of what was passing in Rome and the Roman States, conveyed to the office of the London *Times*, to be thence distributed over the civilized world, the most fictitious narratives, giving them as the true record of passing events, and building upon them the most gross and calumnious misrepresentations, doing every thing, in a word, that he could devise, in order to bring into disrepute the Government of the Pope, and so weaken his temporal authority at a time when it was threatened by powerful States, as well as by great but untoward political influences; if such, indeed, was the man whom Rome cast forth from within her walls, the cause of justice and of humanity was not only not slighted, but eminently served, and wisely promoted. It is not difficult to decide who were the violators in such a case of liberty of speech, whether they who so moderately punished its violation, or he who was guilty of perverting the highest privilege of freedom, to the vile purposes of slander, falsehood and misrepresentation."*

---

* The following letter to the *Weekly Register* will show what sort of person the correspondent in question was:

STAFFORD CLUB, Feby. 15, 1860.

MY DEAR SIR,--I enclose a copy of a note addressed by me last week, to the Editor of the *Times*. I need hardly say I had no answer. The fact is, as you well know, that the *Times'* correspondent at Rome, who was thence summarily dismissed a few days after his arrival, is the notorious Galleaga, whose malachite handed stiletto and its possessor's intention of making the King of Sardinia share the same fate as Count Rossi, the Pope's Minister in 1848, are fresh in the memory of all who followed the course of public events at that time. But of course, we are not surprised to find that the *Times'* "own correspondent" is a well known political assassin. I would only call the attention of some of those good Catholics, who believe in any degree, in that unscrupulous journal's account of the state of things in Rome and Italy, generally, to the fact, that the *Times* had suppressed the "damning" name of their correspondent in Rome, and then launched one of its most ribald tirades of abuse against the Holy Father, and his Government, for the expulsion of their "anonymous" correspondent, as though he had been "warned off," simply as a correspondent of the "leading journal," and not as a notorious political assassin. How long are we to be hoodwinked as a nation by this atrocious and systematic war on a grand scale?

I may add, that, whereas, the *Times* laments its innocent and "highly respectable" correspondent's pecuniary loss. The fact is, that the police offered him an ample compensation for the loss he might sustain by having engaged his apartments for some months. I have addressed

If in a country which has always been eminently Catholic, there has, at all times, prevailed more liberty as regards the exyression of thought than in any other nation, there is no room to doubt as to what is the real spirit of Catholicity as concerns this important matter. But who, out of Spain, will believe that there, more than anywhere else, the people have always enjoyed liberty of speech? Such, however, is the fact. And what renders belief in this respect so difficult with many, is the very thing which made liberty of thought and word so practicable in Spain;—and this is that the people of that country have been always eminently Catholic. The greatest degree, one would say, of freedom of thought is peculiarly the privilege of Catholic peoples. And whilst they enjoy it in greater measure, they use it with more wisdom, and without danger to themselves, to religion, or to the state.

The Spanish monarchy was singularly despotic, especially in the time of King Philip III. But then, even, there prevailed in Spain the most complete liberty of speech. Authors under Philip's reign, instead of extolling absolutism, wrote in support of quite opposite theories, and with a degree of freedom and boldness which would astonish, even in our own times. The book of Father Mariana, *de Rege et Regis Institutione*, which was burned at Paris by the hand of the public executioner, had been published in Spain, as Balmes relates, eleven years before, without the least obstacle to its publication, either on the part of the ecclesiastical or civil authority. It was even at the instigation of D. Garcia de

a similar communication to various papers; you at least, will not decline to insert it. I am, my dear Sir,
Yours very sincerely,
J. L. PATTERSON.
[COPY.]

To the Editor of the Times.

SIR,—Will you oblige your readers by informing us, whether I am right in believing that Signor Gallenga, your Roman correspondent, whose summary ejection from the Papal dominions, you lamented in a recent leading article, is the same Signor Gallenga, who, at the instigation of Mazzini, attempted or undertook to assassinate the King of Sardinia, Charles Albart, in 1848? If, as I have reason to believe, he is the same person; some light is thereby thrown on the proceeding of the Romagna police. Awaiting an early reply,
I am sir,
Your obedient Servant,
JAMES LAIRD PATTERSON, M. A.
Stafford Club, Saville Row, Feby. 9. 1860.

Loaisa, who was tutor to Philip III., and subsequently Archbishop of Toledo, that Mariana undertook the work. It was, moreover, intended for the instruction of the heir apparent. It is impossible to speak with more freedom than it does, of kingly power, to condemn tyranny more strongly, or to proclaim more loudly popular rights. Notwithstanding the very liberal views it inculcates, this work was published at Toledo, in 1599, in the printing office of Pedro Rodrigo, printer to the king, with the approbation of the superiors of religious orders of the greatest eminence—those of the society of Jesus, in particular, under the generalship of Claude Aquaviva. More important still, there was added the royal sanction, and a dedication to the king himself.— Not satisfied with all this, Mariana, on occasion of publishing another work, his Spanish version of the history of Spain, which he also dedicated to Philip III., says, addressing the king: "I last year dedicated to your majesty a work of my own composition, upon the virtues which ought to exist in a good king, my desire being that all princes ould read it carefully and understand it."

If we examine the political opinions of the learned author we shall find that his theory of civil power is as liberal as any modern democrat could desire. In drawing a parallel between the king and the tyrant, he says, without hesitation or ambiguity : "The king exercises with great moderation the power which he has received from his subjects.— Hence, he does not, like the tyrant, oppress his subjects as slaves, but governs them as freemen ; and having received his power from the people, he takes particular care that during his life the people shall voluntarily yield him submission." (Lib i.: cap. 4.)

So wrote monks in Catholic Spain, with the sanction of their superiors ; so wrote the subjects of an absolute monarch in the land of the Inquisition, which was a royal tribunal; and yet, no censure was pronounced, no edict from the crown interdicted the publication of opinions that were so freely expressed. The work of Father Mariana, on the contrary, was honoured with the complete approval of both church and state. Many other writings might be quoted, in which the same liberty of expression is employed, the same liberal opinions inculcated. They all tend to shew how groundless are the fears, and how unfounded the ideas of those who maintain that the Catholic church is hostile to liberty, and has not only not hastened, but retarded the emancipation of mankind from the state of slavery in which she found them.* The truth is that Catholic principles are the best safeguard of liberty, and in those countries is freedom of thought and speech the greatest where these principles are most deeply rooted. Let us now hear how a Spanish writer, who was also a distinguished Catholic divine, accounts for the extraordinary liberty of speech which prevailed in Spain, without the slighest danger to the church or to the state, and under the shadow of the terrible Spanish inquisition.

"How does it happen," enquires Balmes, "that at the end of the sixteenth century the Council of Castile was not alarmed at the bold principles of Mariana, in his book *de Rege et Regis Innstitutione*, whilst those of the Abbe Spedalieri, at the end of the 18th century, were such a terror to it? The reason of this lies not so much in the contents of the works as in the epoch of their publication. The former appeared at a time when the Spanish nation, confirmed in religious and moral principles, might be compared to those robust constitutions capable of bearing food difficult of digestion. The latter was introduced amongst us when the doctrines and deeds of the French revolution were shaking all the thrones of Europe, and when the propagandism of Paris was beginning to pervert us by its emissaries and books.— In a nation in which reason and virtue prevail, in which evil passions are never excited, in which the well-being and prosperity of the country are the only aim of every citizen, the most popular and liberal forms of government may exist without danger. For in such a nation numerous assemblies produce no disorder, merit is not obscured by intrigue, nor are worthless persons raised to the government, and the names of public liberty and felicity do not serve as means to raise the fortunes or satisfy the ambition of individuals. So

* Vide Appendix.

also in a country in which Religion and morality rule in every breast, in which duty is not looked upon as an empty word, in which it is considered really criminal to disturb the tranquility of the state—to revolt against the lawful authorities,—in such a country, I say, it is less dangerous to discuss, with more or less freedom, questions arising from theories on the formation of society, and the origin of the civil power, and to establish principles favorable to popular rights. But when these conditions do not exist it is of little use to proclaim rigorous doctrines. To abstain from pronouncing the name of *people*, as a sacrilegious word, is a useless precaution. How can it be expected that he who respects not Divine majesty should respect human power?"
—*Balmes' civilization*, c. 52.

THE ARGUMENT AGAINST PAPAL RULE, FOUNDED ON THE ALLEGED STATE OF THE POPULAR MIND, CONSIDERED.

It is, no doubt, highly advantageous to the Catholic world that the Pope should be a sovereign prince, and, as such, beyond all danger of coercion by other powers and sovereignties. But are the Catholics throughout the earth, numerous and influential though they be, entitled to require so great a sacrifice on the part of the subjects of the Pontiff as that they, to the prejudice of their own interests, should submit unwillingly to his authority? To this question, to which more importance is ascribed than it deserves, it might be, once for all, replied, that supposing what is alleged to be the case, the subjects of the Pope would not be in a worse position than other peoples. Where is the people that enjoys that government which it would prefer? Or what people can be named that has been able, in all freedom, to choose for itself a government? If we consider the nations of our time, it will be difficult to find even one that has been favored to exercise this privilege, or that does not owe its form of government, and its position in regard to other nations, to events and circumstances over which it had but little or no control. Some peoples by great, and certainly, not always warrantable efforts, have succeeded in destroying the systems of rule which they possessed. But

in how many cases have these been succeeded by the form
of government which it was desired to establish ? And,
supposing that now, in the Papal States, the civil rule that
has subsisted for so many ages, and which has so admirably
shown how well it can be adapted to the wants of a people
at every epoch of their exis'ence, were overthrown, would
the populations be consulted as to the ruler, or form of rule,
under which they should henceforth live ? There is not the
least probability that the real wishes of the communities in
question would be at all considered. Everything as regards
sovereignty and sovereign, form of government and distribution of territory, would be settled according to a *programme* already. decided on. In what respect, then, would
the subjects of the Pope enjoy greater political privileges
than, for instance, the people of Poland, when their national
government was, against their will, and all the opposition
they could make, taken away, and their country partitioned
as suited the convenience of foreign potentates?

But, *Pons non cadit*. It has yet to be shewn that the
people of the Papal States wish to do away with the government under which they and their forefathers have enjoyed so
many blessings, and the surpassing honor of possessing in their
own capital, the metropolis of the Christian world. They
are too happy in being ruled over by the elective monarch
whom they, themselves, have chosen, to desire, in preference to him, the shadow of a king—the satrap of an imperial despot. It was not they who, in a *patriotic endeavor* to
shake off the Pontifical yoke, raised the standard of rebellion in so many cities and provinces of the Papal States.—
This was wholly the work of foreigners. A Bonaparte, attended by a numerous and well disciplined army, ...rdes
Italy. His arms are, to a certain extent, successful. Another
Bonaparte, meanwhile, excites to revolt the Pontifical city
of Perugia. He succeeds in raising a disturbance, which is
speedily settled by a handful of Roman soldiers and the good
and loyal sentiments of the people. In other cities, by the
like instrumentalities, like movements are occasioned. By
the goodwill of the people they are suppressed; and the
Pontifical government, warmly thanks the mayors and mu-

nicipalities of seven or eight cities, for their zeal in putting down the nascent revolution. At Bologna, the capital of the Romagnol or Æmilian provinces, a cousin of the Bonapartes, the Marquis Pepoli, whom the benevolence of the reigning Pontiff had restored to his country, stirs up rebellion, and causes the Pontifical Government to give place to revolutionary rule. Who were the abettors of the ungrateful Pepoli? His associates of the secret societies, others who were foreigners at Bologna, and some malcontents of that city itself. But all these were far from being the Bolognese people—far from being the people of the Bolognese provinces. Without the encouragement of France what could such rebels have effected? And "it is France," the illustrious M. de Montalembert affirms, "that has allowed the temporal power of the Pope to be shaken. This is the fact, which blind men only can deny. France is not engaged alone in this path, but her overwhelming ascendancy places her at the head of the movement, and throws the great and supreme responsibility of it upon her. We know all the legitimate and crushing reproaches that are due to England and Piedmont, but, if France had so willed it, Piedmont would not have dared to undertake anything against the Holy See, and England would have been condemned to her impotent hatred. * * * * * * The Congress of Paris, in 1856, having solemnly declared *that none of the contracting powers had the right of interfering, either collectively or individually, between a sovereign and his subjects*,*—after having proclaimed the principle of the absolute independence of sovereigns in favour of the Turkish Sultan against his Christian subjects, thought itself justified by its protocal of April 8th, and in the absence of any representative of the august accused, in proclaiming that the situation of the Papal States was *abnormal* and *irregular*.— This accusation, developed, aggravated and exaggerated in Parliament and elsewhere, by Lord Palmerston and Count Cavour, was, nevertheless, formally put forward under the presidency, and on the *initiative* of the French minister for

---

* Protocol, March 18th.

foreign affairs. Consequently, France must be held accountable for it to the Church, and to the rest of Europe." The war which "the skilful but guilty perseverance of Piedmontese policy" succeeded in occasioning between France and Austria, facilitated not a little the work of revolution in the States of the Church. In order to dispel the fears that prevailed, the following words were addressed to the Bishops of France by the minister of the Emperor:—"The Prince who restored the Holy Father to his throne in the Vatican wills that the head of the Church should be respected in all his rights as a temporal sovereign." A little later, the Emperor of the French, elated with his military success, issued a proclamation which renewed the apprehensions that had been so happily allayed. "Italians!—Providence sometimes favors nations and individuals by giving them the opportunity of suddenly springing into their full growth. Avail yourselves, then, of the fortune that is offered you! Your desire of independence, so long expressed, so often deceived, will be realized, if you show yourselves worthy of it. Unite, then, for one sole object, the liberation of your country.—Fly to the standards of King Victor Emmanuel, who has already so nobly shewn you the way to honor. Remember that, without discipline there can be no army, and, animated with the sacred fire of patriotism, be soldiers only to-day, and you will be to-morrow free citizens of a great country."

"The Romaguese," continues Montalembert, "took the speaker at his word. Four days after the appearance of this proclamation, they rose against the Papal authority, created a Provisional Government, convoked a sovereign assembly, voted the deposition of the Pope, and the annexation to Piedmont. Finally, seeing their authority remained unpunished, they organized an armed league, officered by Piedmontese, and commanded by Garibaldi,—that Garibaldi, who, having been vanquished by French troops ten years ago, now avails himself of our recent hard-won victories, to boast that he will "soon make an end of clerical despotism."

Three months after the revolution had been established in the Romagna, M. de Montalembert wrote: "The Revolution triumphant, is still asking Europe to sanction its work.

France has to impute to herself all the scandals and all the calamities that will follow. Great nations are responsible not only for what they do, but for what they permit to be done under the shadow of their flag, and by the incitement of their influence. The war which France waged in Italy, has cost the Pope the loss of the third part of his dominions, and the irreparable weakening of his hold on what remains. The eldest daughter of the church will remain accountable for it, before contemporaries, before history, before Europe, and before God. She will not be allowed to wipe her mouth like the adultress in Scripture, '*quæ tergens os suum dicit, non sum operata malum.*'"

Another power which was, in the full sense of the term, *foreign*, in the Roman States, still more directly aided the cause of Revolution. This power was the army of Garibaldi. Consider what troops it was composed of, and say whether it were not wholly alien in the States of the Church. In this motley corps, there were—

    6,750 Piedmontese Volunteers.
    3,240 Lombard   do.
    1,200 Venetians.
    2,150 Neapolitans and Sicilians.
      500 Romans.
    1,200 Hungarians.
      200 French.
       30 English.
      150 Maltese and Ionians.
      260 Greeks.
      450 Poles.
      370 Swiss.
      160 Spaniards, Belgians and Americans.
      800 Austrian deserters and liberated convicts

Could such an army as this, be held to be a representation of the people of the Papal States? One third of it was supplied by two hostile nations, one of which, Piedmont, had actually, by the intrigues of its Government and in pursuance of a policy which an able statesman, a most candid writer, and an honorable man, Count Montalembert, has stigmatized as *criminal*, caused the rebellion in Romagna, and has since earnestly laboured to avail itself of the state of things, by annexing Central Italy to the territories of the

Piedmontese King. It were superfluous to direct attention to the numbers of foreigners from various states. It is however, deserving of remark that the whole population of the Papal States, amounting to 3,000,000, should have shown its alleged sympathy with the "cause of Italy," by sending only 500 men to fight its battles. They did not want courage, as was shown in 1848, when neither the considerate advice and paternal remonstrances of the Holy Father, nor the wise counsel of grave Statesmen and learned Cardinals could moderate the ardour of the Roman youth, believing, as they had been persuaded, that patriotism and duty called them to follow the standard of King Charles Albert. Then, they took up arms, as they conceived, in the cause of Italian liberty. But now, that honorable cause is manifestly in abeyance; and they will not leave their homes and endanger their lives for the phantom of national independence offered them by the revolution.

The French are equally wary. They sympathize with Italy. They fight for their Emperor. But they have no admiration for Piedmontese ambition or that of Murats, and Pepolis, and Bonapartes.

England is more cautious still. However much her demagogues may exert their oratorical powers at home, they carefully avoid perilling either life or limb in the cause of the revolution. A more numerous band of fighting men of English origin, in Garibaldi's ranks, would have shown more sympathy with rebellion in some Italian States, than the proposal made by a right honarble member of the richest peerage in the world, to raise a penny subscription in order to supply the rebels with bayonets and firearms. When we call to mind that this suggestion was made by that very Lordly Peer who was once Governor General of India, we have little difficulty in understanding why his superiors, the members of the East India Company, dismissed him from the high and responsible office with which he had been entrusted.

No nation or community can be fairly represented by a number of its people, insignificantly small, unless, indeed, these few individuals hold commission from their fellow-countrymen. We have not read anywhere that the Garibaldian *army* was thus honored. Social status, character, respectability, may, on occasions, give to individuals the privilege of representing their country. But on these grounds the motley troop of the revolutionary leader possessed no claim. They were men for whom peace and order has no charms. The powerful corrective of military discipline was applied to them in vain. Their insubordination was notorious. To Garibaldi, even, it was intolerable. And this man, daring as he was, withdrew from the command in disgust. He had scarcely retired when many of his men deserted. These, the people refused to recognize, and would not afford them assistance on their journey. Some fifty of them arrived at Placentia, after having been reduced to mendicancy, before they could reach their homes. The Revolutionary Governor, Doctor Fanti, issued an order of the day, requiring that these men, on account of their insubordination and bad conduct, should not be admitted anew into the army of the League. The general in chief also published an order, under date of 26th Nov. 1859, absolutely forbidding to accept any person who had belonged to Garibaldi's force. An army so composed could, by no means, claim to represent the highly refined, intellectual, and moral populations of Italy. Far less did it afford any proof that the people of the Papal States were anxious to forward the work of the Revolution.

The inhabitants of Rome and the Roman States, far from showing any inclination to side with the revolutionary party, never let pass an opportunity of manifesting their satisfaction with the Government of the Pope. His Holiness walks abroad without guards: and although he seeks the most retired places, for the enjoyment of that pedestrian exercise which his health requires, numbers of the people often contrive to throw themselves in his way, in order to testify to him their reverence and affection, as well as to receive his paternal benediction. Whilst taking his walk on Monte Pincio, not long ago, many thousands came around him, declaring, loudly, their unfeigned loyalty. The following day, still greater crowds repaired to the same place; but the Holy Father, with a view to be more retired, had gone in another direction. There has not yet been time to forget, that, when returning last autumn from his Villa at Castel Gandolpho, the road was thronged on both sides, to the distance of four miles from Rome, with citizens who had no other view than to give a cordial and loyal welcome to their Bishop and their Prince. Had ever conqueror of old, such an ovation, such a triumph? On occasion of the recent progress which the Holy Father made through his States, in order to ascertain, by personal observation, what improvements and reforms were required in the different Provinces, he was every where received with the most lively demonstrations of enthusiastic loyalty, reverence and affection. So lately as the 18th of January last, the municipal body, or, as it is called, "the Senate" of Rome, presented to the Sovereign Pontiff as well in their own name, as on behalf of all the people, an address expressive of their filial duty and loyal sentiments. On the following day, January 19, one hundred and thirty-four of the nobility of Rome, who are, in all, one hundred and sixty, approached the person of the Pontiff, in order to present an equally loyal and dutiful address. The sentiments of this address will be best conveyed in its own plain and energetic language,—language which does honor to the Patricians of modern Rome.

"We, the undersigned, deeply grieved by the publication of various libels which emanating from the revolutionary press, tend to make the world believe that the people subject to the authority of your Holiness, are wishing to shake off the yoke, which, as it is reported, has become insufferable, feel necessitated to show fidelity and loyalty to your Holiness, and to make known to the rest of Europe, which, at the present moment, doubts the sincerity of our words, the fidelity of our persons towards your Holiness, by a manifestation of attachment and fidelity towards your person, proceeding from our duty as Catholics, and from our lawful submission as your subjects.

"It is not, however, our intention to vie with the miserable cunning of your enemies,—enemies of the faith,—of that very faith which they profess to venerate. But placed, as it is our fortune, by your side, and seeing the malignity of those who attack you, and the disloyal character of their attacks, we feel bound to gather ourselves at the foot of your twofold throne, with vows for the integrity of your independent Sovereignty; and once more offering you our whole selves, too happy if this manifestation of our fidelity may sweeten the bitterness with which your Holiness is afflicted, and if you are pleased to accept our offerings. Thus may Europe, deceived by so many perverse writings, be thoroughly convinced that if the nobility have hitherto been restrained from the expression of their desires by respect and the fear of throwing any obstacle in the way of a happy solution, so anxiously desired, they have not the less retained them, and expressed them as individuals; and that they, this day, unite to declare them, heartily and sincerely pledging to them before all the world, their honor and their faith.

"Accept, Holy Father, Pontiff, and King, this energetic protest and the unlimited devotedness, which the nobles of Rome offer in reverence to your Sceptre, no less than to your Pastoral staff."—(*In the Weekly Register of Jan.* 28, 1860, *from the Giornale di Roma.*)

Nor is this loyal and truly patriotic feeling confined to Rome. It is general throughout the cities and Provinces of the Papal States. Even at Bologna, where the revolutionary spirit has been most prevalent, scarcely one third of the population could be persuaded, or compelled at the point of the sword, to vote for popular representatives under the new order of things. Scarcely one in fifty could be induced, as Lord Normanby informs us, to declare for the revolutionary Government.

A portion of the periodical press labours to keep these important facts out of view. But they would require better evidence than they have as yet been able to produce, before they succeed in convincing reasonable and reflecting men, that populations blessed with such a high degree of material prosperity as the subjects of the Pope and the other Princes of Italy, are anxious to see radical changes introduced into the governments, under which they are so favored. That they are prosperous, and but slightly taxed, many distinguished travellers bear witness. None will question the

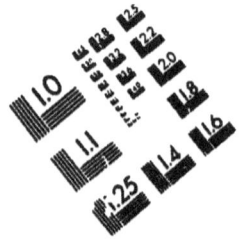

**IMAGE EVALUATION
TEST TARGET (MT-3)**

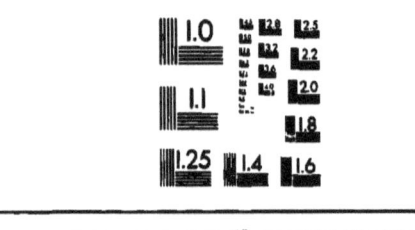

Photographic
Sciences
Corporation

23 WEST MAIN STREET
WEBSTER, N.Y. 14580
(716) 872-4503

evidence of these facts afforded by the Marquis of Normanby and his excellency the Earl of Carlisle. So lately as the month of August last, a distinguished member of the House of Commons—Mr. Hennesey—stated, in that assembly, "that the national prosperity of the States of the Church "and of Austria, had become greater, year after year, than "that of Sardinia, (where a sort of revolutionary constitution "had been established,) and that documents existed in the "Foreign Office, in the shape of reports from our own Con- "suls, which proved it, with respect to commercial interests "in Sardinia. Mr. Erskine, our minister at Turin, in a des- "patch of January 7, 1856, gave a very unfavorable view of "the manufacturing, mining, and agricultural progress of "Sardinia. But from Venetia, Mr. Elliott gave a perfectly "opposite view, showing that great progress was being made "there. The shipping trade of Sardinia with England had "declined 2,000 tons. But the British trade with Ancona "had increased 21,000 tons, and with Venice, 25,000 tons, "in the course of the last two years. He attributed these "results to the increase of taxation in Sardinia, through the "introduction of the constitutional (the *Sardinian* constitu- "tional) system of government, and to the comparatively "easy taxation of Venetia. The increased taxation of Sar- "dinia from 1847 to 1857, was no less than 50,000,000 francs. "With respect to education in the Papal States, he contend- "ed, that it was more diffuse, than it was in this country— "(Great Britain)."

In countries that were so prosperous, every man literally "sitting under his own vine and his own fig tree," it is diffi- cult to believe that there is wide spread discontent, and a general desire for radical changes. To prove that there is so, it would require evidence of no ordinary weight. All testimony that can be relied on, shows a very opposite state of national feeling. In reply to the allegation of Lord John Russell in his memorable Aberdeen speech, "that under their provisional revolutionary governments, the people of central Italy had conducted themselves with perfect order, just as if they had been the citizens of a country that had long enjoyed free institutions;" Lord Normanby says:

"I should like to know where the noble Lord found that
"information. There is not in central Italy, a single gov-
"ernment that has resulted from popular election. They
"were all named by Piedmont—which had, as it were,
"packed the cards. Liberty of speech there was none, nor
"liberty of the press, nor personal liberty.   *   *   *
"The Grand Duchess of Parma was expelled by a Pied-
"montese army, and restored by the spontaneous call of her
"people. She left the country, declaring that she would
"suffer everything sooner than expose her subjects to the
"horrors of civil war.   *   *   *   Numberless atroci-
"ties have been committed under the rule of these govern-
"ments which, according to my noble friend, are so wise
"and orderly. I read to you, the first day of this session,
"the letter of a Tuscan, whose character is irreproachable.
"Since that time I have received from him another letter,
"in which he says: 'You will not be surprised to learn that
"'my letter to you has been the occasion of the coarsest
"'invectives. For what reason I cannot tell, if it was not
"'because it spoke the truth.'

"Here is a second letter, which I received a few days ago
"from an English merchant of the highest standing at Leg-
"horn:' 'No intervention is allowed in Tuscany; and nev-
"'ertheless, my Lord, intervention appears everywhere;
"'even armed and foreign intervention. The Governor
"'General is a Piedmontese; the Minister of War is a Pied-
"'montese; the Commander of the Armed Police is a Pied-
"'montese; the Military Governor of Leghorn is a Pied-
"'montese; the Captain of the Port is a Piedmontese; with-
"'out reckoning a great number of other functionaries of the
"'same nation. This is what I call armed and foreign inter-
"'vention. Let us be disembarrassed of all this; let us be
"'free from the despotic pressure of this government, and
"'the great majority of the country would vote the restora-
"'tion of the House of Lorraine. Almost all the army
"'would be for the Grand Duke, and on this account it is
"'kept at a distance from Tuscany. I can say the same of
"'two-thirds of the national guard. All the great powers
"'have observed strict neutrality here, inasmuch as they

"'have not been present at any ceremony which could be "'looked upon as a recognition of the existing government. "'But since the peace of Villafranca, the English agents have "'taken part in all the ceremonies, in all the balls.' Assur-"edly, thus to recognize such a government, is far from "being faithful to the assurance given last session, by the "noble Lord at the head of the foreign Department. (Cheers)"

Lord Normanby's trustworthy correspondent says, moreover, in the letter referred to, that the Tuscan troops being kept at a distance from Tuscany, the people dread making any demonstration, being well aware that an imprudent word is punished with imprisonment. "At Leghorn, however, some private meetings were held, at which influential persons were present. Public meetings are impossible.—Twenty-three members of the Assembly asked that it should be convened. This was refused them. At the private meeting however, it was decided that Ferdinand IV. should be recalled, on condition of granting a constitution and an amnesty. The people have been dreadfully deceived. All promises have been violated, the price of provisions has risen, the national debt has been enormously increased."

Lord Normanby also laid before the House of Peers the testimony of a distinguished Italian writer, Signor Amperi, whom he describes as a man of high character. This gentleman addresses the governments of Central Italy in the following terms:—

"The false position in which you have placed yourselves has reduced you to the necessity, in times of liberty, as you pretend, but of false liberty, as I conceive, to make falsehood a system of government. Of the promises of Victor Emmanuel that he would sustain before the great powers the vote of the Tuscan Assembly, you have made a formal accepting for himself of this vote, and, in order to deceive the ignorant multitude, you ordered public rejoicings in honour of a fact which you knew to be false. You declared yourselves the ministers of a King who had not appointed you. You administer the government in his name; you give judgments in his name; you plege the public faith of a sovereign who has given you no commission to do any such thing; and, although you forced the Tuscans to acknowledge him for King, you despise his authority to such an extent as to impose upon him the choice of a regent. What right have you to do this, if he be really King, and if he be not, is your right any better founded?"

The Marquis of Normanby laughs to scorn the various attempts that have been made to establish a government in Central Italy against the will of the people. First of all, we have a signor Buoncompagni named Governor General by the King of Sardinia. The Emperor of the French found that the ambitious satrap had exceeded his powers, and Buoncompagni was immediately recalled. The Prince de Carignan was then offered the regency of the proposed kingdom of Central Italy. He thought it prudent to decline. But unwilling wholly to relinquish a cherished object of ambition, he appointed in his place the above named Signor Buoncompagni. What right had he to do so? None whatever. The appointment, as is well known, caused the greatest indignation at Florence, and elicited a protest from the liberal representatives, themselves. Will it be believed, in after times, that the present ministry of Great Britain actually recognized this spurious government, ordering the Queen's representative to pay an official visit to this Signor Buoncompagni? Whilst all Europe held aloof, anxious to avoid wrong and insult to the Italian populations, whence this zeal and haste on the part of the British Cabinet? They had, at first, resolved to be neutral. But there occurs to them the chimerical idea of a great kingdom in Central Italy, and, as Lord Normanby states, in their ignorance they hasten to carry it into effect. * * * "Yes," continued the right honble. lord, when assailed by the laughter of the more ignorant portion of his lordly hearers, "yes, in complete ignorance of the wants, the aspirations and t'e prejudices of the Italian people." * * * *

"It is a painful duty," said the illustrious statesman, in concluding his eloquent appeal to the common sense and honorable feeling of the British peerage, "to have to dispel the illusions of public opinion in regard to Italy. I have endeavored to fulfil this duty by laying before you information that can be relied on; and I have the pleasure to observe that light is now beginning to penetrate the darkness which has hitherto enveloped this question. There is already a greater chance that Italian independence will be established on a more legitimate basis, free from all foreign intervention, and in such a way as to favor the cause of fidelity, of truth, of honor and general order. (Cheers.)"

Let there be no foreign intervention, it is constantly said, and we shall soon see the end of Papal Rule, as well as that of all the other Italian Sovereignties. Such, however, are not the views and sentiments of the Italians themselves. It has been most satisfactorily proved, those people themselves being the witnesses, that such of them as are subjects of the Pope, instead of being discontented and anxious to do away with the existing government, and substitute for it either a republic or a foreign monarch, highly appreciate, and are steadfastly devoted to, the wise and paternal government of their Pontiff Sovereign; while the subjects of the other Princes, as well as the inhabitants of the revolutionized portion of the Papal States, are only prevented by the armed intervention of foreign powers from declaring in favor of their rightful Sovereigns. It is not denied that there are reformers and constitutionalists in those States. But they are not ignorant that all reforms must be the fruit of time and of opinion, and that under the sway of enlightened and benevolent sove. eigns, aided by the learning and counsel of able and conscientious statesmen, such changes in matters of civil polity as are adapted to the wants of the people, will not be delayed beyond the time when circumstances call for and justify their adoption.

Not having been able to discover any traces of the alleged dissatisfaction and desire for radical change, among the populations of the Papal States, any more than among those of the neighbouring principalities there is no need for argument, as regards what it might be necessary to concede to the wishes of so many millions of our fellow beings and fellow christians.

The people of the States of the Church are, however, so much governed by the clergy rather than by competent laymen, that they *ought* to be dissatisfied. They do not themselves think so. They are so far, indeed, from considering discontent a duty, on account of any clerical element in their government, that they generally prefer as civil magistates, Prelates and other clergymen. Count Rayneval, some time ago ambassador from the Emperor of the French to the Court of Rome, says: "*The Provinces administered by laymen, amongst others those of Ferrara and Camerino, are sending deputation upon deputation to the government, for permission to have a Prelate appointed.* The people are not accustomed to lay delegates. *They refuse obedience and respect to these latter. They accuse them of confining their interest to their own families;* and there is nothing, even to their wives, which does not give rise to questions of precedence and etiquette. In a word, the government which, to satisfy this pretended desire of the population to be ruled over by laymen, reserved a certain number of places for them, *finds this disposition opposed by the population themselves.*"

And what should there be in the clerical state to disqualify for civil duties? Is it that the mind grandly developed as it is, by the knowledge proper to that state, is incapable, or less capable than it would otherwise be, of applying to those studies, that are essential to the temporal magistrate? So far is this from being the case, that the largeness of view by which the well educated ecclesiastic is distinguished, peculiarly fits the mind for the profitable consideration of every thing connected with civil government. But this doctrine is best preached by examples. And such are not wanting. Was it narrow and one-sided views, such as some sophists of our age ascribe to the clergy, that produced such eminent statesmen of the clerical order, as Ximenes in Spain, Mazarin and Richelieu in France, Wolsey in England; and so many of the Popes, who have not only been celebrated for ecclesiastical learning, and all the qualities demanded by their sacred character and office, but also by their superior statesmanship?

We have seen at the commencement of this work, with what liberality of view, with what benevolence, with what self-sacrificing devotedness to the people's welfare, the reigning Pope laboured in his capacity of a civil magistrate, when Archbishop of Spoleto and Bishop of Imola. We have seen also how high he stood in popular estimation. It may well be doubted whether any layman in authority was ever so highly considered, and so sincerely beloved. No layman could have applied with the same freedom of mind to public cares. Nor could any with a family, or relatives, dividing his attention and solicitude, as well as claiming a share in his temporal substance, have shown that generosity which often led, not only to the sacrifice of his personal income, but on some occasions even of every thing he possessed. The people could not be blamed for this preference, nor accused of narrowness of view, in considering the Prelates of the Church more fitted by their education and habits of mind, for the important work of civil government, than laymen generally can be, who, however highly educated, can never claim exemption from many of those things by which the mind, if not wholly engrossed, is at least diverted or distracted. It has not, however, been considered advisable, that a great number of the Clergy in the Roman States, should, in addition to the avocations of their sacred office, bear a part in the duties of temporal government. These duties are almost all fulfilled by laymen. Comparatively few ecclesiastics are called to share with them the cares and the toils of State affairs. The following table will show the relative numbers of Lay and Clerical persons, who are charged with the administration of Rome and its Provinces. Whoever reads it, will be forced to acknowledge that the church dreads not to see in her places of authority, the well educated Laity.

MINISTRIES.	PLACES HELD		Annual Salary Recvd.	
	BY ECCLES.	BY LAYMEN.	BY ECCLES.	BY LAYMEN.
Secretariate of State,....	14	18	$100,500	$ 8,340
Ministries—Home, Grace, Justice and Police,	278	3,271	110,205	637,602
Public Instruction,	3	0	1,320	1,824
Finance, ...	7	3,084	10,329	730,268
Commerce, P. Works	1	347	2,400	69,809
Arms, ...		125		51,885
Total ...	303	6,854	$224,755	$1,490,747

[*The Weekly Register*, June, 1859.]

All who are here alluded to as *ecclesiastics*, are not necessarily Priests. Count de Rayneval had occasion to show, "with proofs in his hands, that the half of these supposed Priests were not in orders. * * * The Roman Prelates are not all bound to enter into Holy orders. For the most part they dispense with them. Can we then call by the name of Priests those who have nothing of the Priest but the uniform? Is Count Spada a more zealous or a more skilful administrator now, than, when in the costume of a Priest, he officiated as Minister of War? Do Monsignor Matteuci, (Minister of Police,) Monsignor Mertel, (Minister of the Interior,) Monsignor Berardi, (Substitute of the Secrētary of State,) and so many others, who have liberty to marry to-morrow, constitute a religious caste, sacrificing 'ts own interests to the interests of the country, and would they become, all of a sudden, irreproachable if they were dressed differently? If we examine the share given the Prelates, both Priests and non Priests, in the Roman administration, we shall arrive at some results which it is important to notice. Out of Rome, that is, throughout the whole extent of the Pontifical States, with the exception of the capital,—in the Legations, the Marshes, Umbria and all the Provinces, to the number of eighteen, how many ecclesiastics do you think are employed? Their number does not exceed fifteen,—one for each Province, except three, where there is not one at all. They are delegates, or as we should say, prefects. The councils, the tribunals, and offices of all sorts, are filled with laymen. So that for one ecclesiastic in office, we have in the Roman Provinces one hundred and ninety-five laymen."

RIGHTS OF PEOPLES.—PRETENDED RIGHTS OF FACTIONS AND
INCONSIDERABLE SECTIONS.—OPINION OF "THE TIMES."—
NUMBERS, AND EXTRAORDINARY INCREASE OF CATHO-
LICS.—ENLIGHTENED OPINION AND NOBLE CON-
DUCT OF GREEKS AND PROTESTANTS.

The public opinion of the time, coinciding with the invariable teaching of the church, requires that, generally, the clergy should be exempt from temporal cares, in order the better to apply, with undivided mind, to the more important duties of their sacred office. The government of the chief Pastor, in admirable harmony with these noble and well founded views, has never ceased to set the example, as we have seen, of allowing to devolve on the lay members of the community, the principal burthen of things temporal and material. It agrees, besides, with the philosophy of the time, in all those things wherein it surpasses the wisdom of bygone ages, the nineteenth century in fact, having been disciplined by christian teachings, to better modes of thought —to milder habits—to more humane legislation. That great Institution, therefore, of which the Papal temporality is only the outpost and the earthly bulwark, harmonizing so admirably with the spirit that now pervades society, what party or what influence is there that can justly or consistently call for its abolition? It cannot surely be any number of individuals, or any government professing to hold the ideas, and to be animated by the spirit of the age. There exists indeed a party which holds very decided opinions on the system of rule by which mankind ought to be governed. But the wisdom and humanity of the time repel this faction and their doctrines. The British press, which cannot be accused of any predelection for Papal rule, only gives expression to the general voice of Europe and the civilized world, when it stigmatizes the chief of this party as,

" *An incendiary, whose murderous designs expand in pro-*
"*portion to his own sense of security, and who has no such*
"*regard for the safety of his dupes.*"—(*The Times.*)

Does a monarchy aim at the abolition of the Pope's temporal state? It can only be with a view to its own aggrandizement. For the Papacy has ever been the stay of well ordered monarchies. Is it a republic, or a constitutional power, that would deal the fatal blow, it could only have a sinister end in view; for the Papacy, although it may rather lean to monarchy, looks no less with favor on well regulated republics, and lends them its powerful aid. Does despotism, jealous of all power it is unable to control, seek to lessen the influence of the Roman Pontiff,—to undermine his throne,— its conduct is easily understood. The two powers are essen-

more important
ent of the chief
noble and well
example, as we
members of the
s temporal and
losophy of the
the wisdom of
t, having been
odes of thought
on. That great
porality is only
nizing so admi-
ty, what party
consistently call
umber of indi-
l the ideas, and
re exists indeed
the system of
ned. But the
ction and their
be accused of
pression to the
orld, when it

xpand in pro-
o has no such
mes.)
e Pope's tem-
own aggran-
stay of well
constitutional
d only have a
it may rather
vell regulated
es despotism,
to lessen the
his throne,—
ers are essen-

tially antagonistic. The one, however, anxious to save appearances, is, when circumstances urge, or its policy prescribes, intolerably oppressive. The other, under all circumstances, and in defiance of humany policy, condemns oppression, and in the very face of tyrants, hurls anathemas against tyranny. The former regardless of the improved spirit of the age, makes war on liberty, on justice, on honor, on humanity; the latter, equal to the age, and before the age, leads the van in the great march of human progress, aiding and encouraging every useful effort, guiding and inspiring the toils and meditations of the patriot; not only blessing and consoling the unobtrusive labours of christian love, but opening every day new fields for philanthropic zeal, and promoting well conceived and meritorious plans for the improvement of mankind, and for the continuance of the wished for reign of peace, order, justice and humanity.

Does a family,—does a dynasty seek the ruin of the Papal States,—the mystery may be solved. Ambition has made a new conquest. Its votaries and its slaves must follow in the track it has pointed out. Is new territory within their reach, cost what it will they must grasp the tempting prize. Is more extended influence to be attained, is the new power to be more firmly rooted in the midst of other powers, or above them all, no sacrifice will be spared. Does justice set its bann on certain ambiguous proceedings,—justice is a lion in the path,—it must be battled with, and trampled down. Inordinate ambition holds nothing sacred. Its votaries, once under its control, war with Heaven itself, and they would think little of extinguishing the vital flame,—the vivifying light which Heaven has shed upon the world.

Opposed to such influence, is the still greater influence of the whole civilized earth. Shall it be said that the general interest which this mighty power sustains, has no right against the particular interest of undisciplined ambition? For what besides does the general interest claim support? For no ideal good,—for no untried system,—no newly devised scheme,—no chimera sprung but yesterday from some fevered brain. No such thing as this; but a time hallowed Institution to which humanity has clung for so many cennturies with indestructible affection. Consider it in a merely utilitarian point of view; the experience of ages bears witness to its usefulness. And who dare say, even among those who carp at the usages and discipline of the Papacy, that it has not been in every age a blessing to mankind? From the unworldly nature of its teaching, it may subject some to inconvenience; of others it requires sacrifices; but without offering injustice to any, it never fails to keep in view the general good. The men of short vision and narrow mind will see in all this nothing but evil; just as these same individuals, if, indeed, the pursuit of science had any charms for them, would, in searching the earth for proofs of the genial influences of the sun's rays, discover only parched deserts and burning sands.

The nations are interested in the great Institution. It is their possession. Time has consecrated this right. They are its people. Let them depose it if they will. But until they do so, it must be considered as unassailable.

If the Catholic communities only were its defenders, and alone claimed an interest and a right in its safe and inviolable state, their unanimous voice, now so powerfully raised against the most iniquitous and unprovoked spoliation of which history bears record, possesses an undoubted title to be heard. These children of the Holy Father inhabit every clime. Their numbers are beyond calculation. Their influence, wherever they dwell, is proportionally greater than their numbers. Without delaying to enquire how it is so, let us now consider how numerous are at this day the catholic people, in all those countries and quarters of the globe, whence they are sending forth with such determination of will and purpose, their eloquent and moving, and irresistible appeals in behalf of the rights of the chief Pastor.

According to researches made by learned men, the result of which was given in "*The Scientific Miscellany*" some five and twenty years ago, the number of catholics throughout the world,—in Europe, Asia, Africa, America, and Oceanica, —was 254,655,000.

If we consider how rapidly catholics have increasead during the last quarter of a century, we need have no hesitation n reckoning them, to-day, at 300,000,000.

Whether we take as a test the numbers of the catholic people, as they are now in the great cities, compared with what they were some twenty-five or thirty years ago, or the actual attendance in the churches, on Sundays, we shall find that there is ample ground for believing that the increase has been fully as great, as, without general and exact statistical data, we can suppose it to be.

In the city of Liverpool, in 1831, there were only eleven Priests, five churches, two poor schools, and a catholic population of *thirty thousand*. In 1859, the number of Priests had risen to sixty, of churches to seventeen, of schools to fifteen, and of catholic people, to *one hundred and fifty thousand*. This catholic population contains some who have made fortunes almost colossal, and many who, by honest energy, have achieved a desirable competence. That portion of society which consists of the market dealer, the petty shopkeeper, the skilled artizan, the humble labourer, is in a transition state. The man who but a little while ago was but a rude labourer, now keeps a small and very plain shop. Next year he will improve it, and go on steadily rising. This is beyond question a type of thousands.

The attendance at church on Sundays, in this same city of Liverpool, which is unquestionably one of the greatest strong-holds of the Protestant world, is a no less remarkable proof of the extraordinarily rapid increase of the catholic population. It has been ascertained that the Protestants of Liverpool, of all denominations, with 143 places of worship, show an actual attendance at church on Sunday, of 44,599. The Catholics have only thirteen churches, and their attendance for the whole Sunday, amounts to 44,632. That the numbers of Catholics, attending church on Sundays, should have come within the last few years to equal, and, even, in a certain degree, to surpass that of the numerous and respectable Protestant population of our great cities, is indeed no slight proof that the increased number of Catholics is not over estimated. It is no misrepresentation to speak here of our *cities*, Liverpool being a type of them all. What has been said of it, may also be said, especially as regards the increase of the Cotholic population, of Manchester, Birmingham, Glasgow, Newcastle, and other places of commercial renown. But may there not have been in some countries, a falling off in the Catholic population? In Ireland for instance, during the dreadful days of famine and pestilence, there was a visible lessening in the numbers of the Catholic people. Since that disastrous time, however, they have been steadily on the increase. And whatever loss the sweeping scourges may have caused, is abundantly counterbalanced by the rapid growth of Catholic congregations in the new world. There, they arise together with great cities which already vie with those of Europe, in wealth, splendour and population. If, in these cities, large churches and magnificent Cathedrals are built, it cannot be that there are no people to fill them, no hands to aid in their construction.

Nothing, however, could show so well the augmentation of the church, in our time, as the great number of Dioceses it has been found necessary to erect. It is not yet fourteen years since the accession of the reigning Pope, and he has already, urged by the wants of the daily increasing Catholic world, established no fewer than fifty-six new Dioceses.*

In addition to the great Catholic host, of the numbers, and importance, and influence of which too great an estimate can scarcely be formed, there are some eighty millions of the Greek church who differ so slightly from christians of the Catholic rite and communion. Of these some sixty millions, through the enlightened and magnanimous Emperor, who, if not positively the Ruler, is undoubtedly the most influential Protector of the Russo-Greek church, have protested

* Dr. Cumming.—It is not to be expected that the notorious Dr. Cumming will ever intentionally say anything favourable to the Catholic Church, yet somehow the truth does transpire in some of his outpourings. For instance, in a lecture this month at Brentford, he says:—He would do the priests of the Church of Rome the justice to say that a more earnest, more energetic, a more industrious body, he did not know in any portion of our church; they were labouring incessantly for what they believed to be the truth, and he would that he could say without success, but he was sorry to say, *with great success.* He saw going over to the Church of Rome, a section of the nobility and many ministers of our Church. These were well-instructed, and ought to have known better. In England, account for it as they could, *it had made progress to such an extent during the last 20 years that it had doubled its churches and doubled its priests.* In Scotland, he regretted to find that the Duchess of Buccleuch, the wife of the most popular nobleman there, had become a Roman Catholic, and the Dowager Dutchess of Argyle, a member of his own flock, had also joined that church.—*Weekly Register, 17th March,* 1860.

against the unjustifiable attack which has despoiled the Holy Father of a third part of his States, and threatens to rob him of what remains. The Greek churches, in other parts of the world, are known to entertain sentiments no less friendly to the Patriarch of Western christendom.

But what shall be said of the 48,985,000* Protestant christians, who must surely be taken into account when there is question of what concerns the well-being of the christian church? Do they join in the outcry that has been raised against the "*Pope of Rome,*" by the less informed and low-bred portion of the British press? Far be it from us to think any such thing. Of the contrary line of conduct we possess the most ample proof. The enlightened Protestants of Germany, the children of those people for whom the great Leibnitz wrote, the learned and the high in rank have addressed to the chief Pastor, the expression of their sincere and heartfelt sympathy, no less than their detestation of the perfidious blow that has been aimed against his temporal sovereignty.

Prussia, where the Protestant element predominates, has entered her protest. The Protestant King and Protestant Government have remonstrated, with a determination of purpose, which, to their imperishable honor, history will record. They were even preparing to draw the sword in vindication of violated right and honor, when the Emperor of the French, wearied with blood and *glory*, withdrew from the scenes of carnage he had ordered on the plains of Italy, and for which he alone is responsible to the men of this generation, to posterity, and to God.

The Protestant King of Belgium concurs with his people in their energetic denunciation of the wrong that has been done to the chief and Father of their church.

Illustrious members of the British peerage, although honestly adhering to the Protestant communion, have not hesitated to denounce the Pope's undutiful children and treacherous enemies. They have also exposed the calumnies of

---

* *Scientific Miscellany.*—Vide also in appendix, the opinion of Baron Macaulay.

the infidel press, and laboured to originate throughout the country, a more sound public opinion.

British merchants of high character and status, although Protestants, have dared, whilst by so doing they exposed themselves to the most bitter invective, to write home to their country, from the towns of Italy where they are resident, truthful accounts of the state of affairs, and have shown, on testimony that cannot be called in question, that in central Italy it is not the will of the people, (unless, indeed, an inconsiderable revolutionary faction can be so designated,) nor the vote of the people, that calls for the downfall of the Grand Dukes, and the abolition of the Papal Sovereignty, but Sardinian ambition, Sardinian gold, and Sardinian arms, encouraged and sustained by the power of France, *against the will of France.*

THE END.

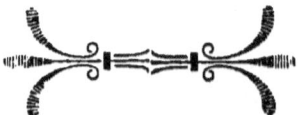

APPENDIX.

[Note—page 80.]

COUNT RAYNEVAL'S REPORT.—REFORM PERSEVERED IN AT ROME AFTER THE EVENTS OF 1848.

As the necessarily narrow limits of this work do not admit of any further details regarding the political history of the Papal States, it may not be out of place here, to insert a summary of that celebrated state-paper, the report of Count Rayneval, French Envoy at Rome, after the restoration of the Pontifical authority, to his Government. It shows that the Holy Father, although at first discomfited by the Revolutionary faction, was far from abandoning his plans of reform and amelioration. He only returned to them with renewed energy when he was restored to his states. The statement of Count Ryneval was never intended for publication, but only for the information of the French Cabinet. It is dated, Rome, May 14th, 1856.

"Pius IX. shows himself full of ardour for reforms. He himself puts his hand to the work. From the very day Pius IX. mounted the throne he has made continuous efforts to sweep away every legitimate cause of complaint against the public administration of affairs.

"Already have civil and criminal cases, as well as a code relating to commerce, all founded on our own, enriched by lessons derived from experience, been promulgated. I have studied these carefully,—they are above criticism. The code des Hypotheques has been examined by French *juris consults*, and has been cited by them, as a model document. Abroad (says this distinguished and able writer), these essential changes that are introduced into the order of things, these incessant efforts of the pontifical government to ameliorate the lot of the populations, have passed unnoticed. People have had ears only for the declamation of the discontented, and for the permanent calumnies of the bad portion of the Piedmontese and Belgian press. This is the source from which public opinion has derived its inspiration. And in spite of well established facts, it is believed in most places, but particularly in England, that the pontifical government has done nothing for its subjects, and has restricted itself to the perpetuation of the errors of another age. I have only yet indicated the ameliorations introduced into the organization of the administration. Above all, let us remember that never has a more exalted spirit of clemency been seen to preside over a restoration. No vengeance has been exercised on those who caused the overthrow of the Pontifical government;—no measures of rigour have been adopted against them,—the Pope has contented himself with depriving them of the power of doing harm by banishing them from the land. In spite of considerable burdens which were occasioned by the revolution, and left as a legacy to the present government—in spite of extraordinary expenses caused by the reorganisation of the army—in spite of numerous contributions towards the encouragement of public works, the state budget, which at the commencement, exhibited a tolerably large *deficit*, has been gradually tending towards equilibrium. I have had the honor, recently, of pointing out to your Excellency, that the deficit of 1857, has been reduced to an insignificant sum, consisting for the most part, of unexpected expenses and of money reserved for the extinction of the debt. The taxes remain still much below the mean rate of the different European states. A Roman pays the state 22 francs annually, 68,000,000 being levied on a population of 3,000,000. A Frenchman pays the French government 45 francs, 1,600,000,000 being levied on a population of 35,000,000. These figures show, demonstratively, that the Pontifical States, with regard to so important a point, must be reckoned amongst the most favored nations. The expenses are regulated on principles of the greatest economy. One fact is sufficient. The civil list, the expenses of the cardinals of the diplomatic corps abroad, the maintenance of pontifical palaces and the museum, cost the state no more than 600,000 crowns (3,200,000 francs). This small sum is the only share of the public revenue, taken by the Papacy, for the support of the pontifical dignity, and for keepihg up the principal establishments of the superior ecclesiastical administration. We might ask those persons, so zealous in hunting down abuses, whether the appropriation of 4,000 crowns, to the wants of the princes of the church, seems to them to bear the impress of a proper economy exercised with respect to the public revenue Agriculture has been equally the object of encouragement, and, also, gardening and the raising of stock. Lastly, a commission, composed of the principal landed proprietors, is now studying the hitherto insoluble question of draining the Campagna of Rome, and filling it with inhabitants. There is, in truth, misery here as elsewhere, but it is infinitely less heavy, than in less favoured climates. Mere necessaries are obtained cheaply. Private charities are numerous and effective. Here, also, the action of the government is perceptible. Important ameliorations have been introduced into the administrarion of hospitals and prisons. Some of these prisons should be visited, that the visitor may admire —the term is not too strong—the persevering charity of the Holy Father. I will not extend this enumeration. What I have said ought to be sufficient to prove that, all the measures adopted by the Pontifical administration, bear marks of wisdom, reason and progress, that they have already produced happy results; in short that there is not a single detail, of interest to the well-being, either moral or material, of the population, which has escaped the attention of the government, or which has not been treated in a favorable manner. In truth, when certain persons say to the Pontifical government, 'form an administration which may have for its aim the good of the people,' the government might reply, 'look at our acts, and condem us if you dare.' The government might ask, 'not only which of its acts is a subject of legitimate blame, but in which of its duties it has failed?' Are we then to be told, that the Pontifical government is a model —that it has no weakness or imperfections? Certainly not; but its weakness and imperfections are of the same kind as are met with in all governments, and even in all men, with very few exceptions. I am perpetually interrogating those who come to me to denounce what they call the abuses of the Papal government. The expression, it must be remembered, is now consecrated, and is above criticism or objection. It is held as Gospel. Now, in what do the abuses consist? I have never yet been able to discover. At least, the facts which go by that name are such, as are, elsewhere, traceable to the imperfection of human nature, and we need not load the government with the direct responsibility of the irregularities committed by some of its subordinate agents. The imperfections of the judiciary system are often cited. I have examined it closely, and have found it impossible to discover any serious cause of complaint. Those who lose their causes complain more loudly, and more continuously, than is the custom in other places, but without any more reason. Most of the important civil cases are decided in the tribunal of the Rota. Now, in spite of the habitual licence of Italian criticism, no one has dared to express a doubt of the profound knowledge and the exalted integrity of the tribunal of the Rota. If the lawyers are incredibly fertile in raising objections and exceptions,—if they lengthen out lawsuits,—to what is this fault to be attributed if not to the peculiarity of the national genius? Lastly, civil law is well administered. I do not know a single sentence the justice of which would not be recognised by the best tribunal in Europe. Criminal justice is administered in a manner equally unassailable. I have watched some trials throughout their whole details; I was obliged to confess that necessary precautions for the verification of facts—all possible guarantees for the free defence of the accused, including the publication of the proceedings, were taken. Much is said of the brigands who, we are told, lay the country desolate. It has fallen to our lot to pass through the country, in all directions, without seeing even the shadow of a robber. It cannot be denied that, from time to time, we hear of a diligence stopped, of a traveller plundered.—Even one accident of this kind is too much, but we must remember that the administration has employed all the means in its power to repress these disorders. Thanks to energetic measures, the brigands have been arrested at all points and punished. When in France, a diligence is stopped; when in going from London to Windsor, a lady of the Queen's palace, is robbed of her luggage and jewels, such incidents pass unnoticed; but when, on an isolated road in the Roman States, the least fact of this nature takes place, the passenger, for a pretext, prints the news in large characters, and cries for vengeance on the government. On the side of Rome, the attacks which have taken place at distant intervals, have never assumed an appearance calculated to excite anxiety. In the Romagna, organised bands have been formed, which taking advantage of the Tuscan frontier, easily escaped pursuit, and were for a time to be dreaded. The government declared unceasing war against them, and after several engagements, in which a certain number of gendarmes were either killed or wounded, these bands have been in a great measure dispersed. The Italians always depend for the completion of their projects on foreign support. If this support were to fail, then they would adopt a proper course much more readily than would be necessary. Meanwhile, in England and Sardinia, the organs of the press should cease to excite the passions, and Catholic powers should continue to give the Holy See evident marks of sympathy. But how can we hope that enemies, animated with such a spirit as influences the opponents of the Holy See, should put a stop to their attacks when they have been made in so remarkable a manner?"

[Note—page 90.]

The following sketch, from the Ottawa *Citizen* of Sept'r 17th, 1859, of lectures delivered in St. Andrew's Catholic Church, Ottawa, by the Rev. Æ. McD. Dawson, Sept., 1859, will shew what the principles, as well as the practice, of the PAPAL CHURCH has always been in regard to SLAVERY and LIBERTY:—

SKETCH OF LECTURE II. AND LECTURE III.

The object of these lectures was to shew how important has been the part borne by the Popes and the Catholic Church in establishing freedom throughout the world. They found the great mass of mankind in a state of slavery. In every nation the number of slaves was incalculably superior to that of freemen. War and other calamitous circumstances were daily adding new victims to captivity. In a few years more not a trace of liberty would have remained, and the wish of the heathen tyrant would have been fulfilled, that the people had but one neck in order that he might the more speedily trample them to destruction.

But degraded and enslaved as the world was, there were great and good and glorious things in store. The new philosophy is proclaimed. Men are no longer to be ruled by the cold and forbidding stoicism which repelled misfortune, and could smile only on those upon whom the world shed its favours. A religion, emanating from the God of love, shall henceforth sway the destinies of mankind. A priesthood, through whose labors this religion shall pervade every land, and exercise its blessed influence over every people, is established forever. True to its sublime vocation, it knows no difficulty, it dreads no danger, it shrinks from no sacrifice, it neglects no duty, however arduous its fulfilment. — Time only will it require for the accomplishment of its lofty purposes. And all time is given to it. "Lo! I am with you always, even till the consummation of the world."

Vain would have been the attempt to change, all at once, the state of society. Nevertheless, "the face of the earth must be renewed;" and there shall be a "new earth" as well as a "new heaven." The fiat is pronounced, and already the great work begins—the changing, the renewing of everything under the sun. For some time, as yet, the slave will be still a slave, but no longer the slave of prechristian times. His condition, wherever the Divine influence prevails, is so modified and improved that his fetters, it may be truly said, have already fallen from his limbs. The master who was wont to hold him as his property, and to exercise over him the most despotic rule, even to the extent of inflicting on him the punishment of death, now treats him as "a most dear brother," beholds in him the image of God, respects and loves him as a member of the same family ransomed by their common Saviour from a captivity more terrible than that of worldly bondage.

As one among many proofs that this great moral revolution was proceeding rapidly from the time that the voice of the Christian Pontiffs was first heard among the nations, it may be called to mind that in modern times, we read not of any such appalling slave rebellions as darken the pages of ancient history. At Rome, Athens, Sparta, and other important places in the Pagan world, the masters, who were as one in ten, lived in perpetual dread of their slaves. War not unfrequently broke out between them, and was waged with worse than barbarian fury. In order to obviate such evils, it was deemed necessary, O strange philosophy! to practice towards slaves the greatest cruelty; "so many slaves, so many enemies," and systematic oppression everywhere prevailed.

In the early ages of the Church, ere yet the influence of Christianity became universally prevalent, there could have been no such provocation to revolt. The slaves of Christian masters were no longer treated as such; whilst those who lived under pagan lords were sustained in their misery by the hope of a happy change in their condition. In the days of absolute heathen rule, of undiminished tyranny, no such change could have been looked for. It is even beyond dispute, that when Christians became numerous and were not confined, as at the beginning they by no means were, to the more humble classes of society, their conduct, in regard to slaves and slavery, became the rule. The Pagans at first wondered,—perhaps admired, but found it in the end more wise, as far as heathen prejudices would permit, to imitate.

Meanwhile, it becomes laudable and worthy of all admiration to enfranchise slaves. In this great work the Church, under the guidance of its High Priest, leads the way, and offers to mankind a bright example.

So early as the Apostolic age, Pope St. Clement writes: "We have known many of ours who have devoted themselves to captivity, in order to ransom their brethren."— *Letter to the Corinthians.*

Neither the Church nor its chief pastors, then, were indifferent as regards the emancipation of slaves, or rather let us say: they were so inflamed with the love of liberty that they could not enjoy this inheritance, of which the world had been robbed, without extending it to other men. Their zeal in the great cause increases from day to day; councils are assembled; means are therein devised for restoring liberty to captives; thence are issued decrees exhorting, recommending, enjoining that slaves shall be ra ned by all lawful means. It is allowed even to devote tl. perty of the Church, and that portion of it, too, which is held most sacred, to the redemption of the enslaved. This laudable practice received the solemn sanction of the Church, and was regulated by its canons. Pope St. Gregory orders "that no one at any time shall venture to disturb either them (slaves ransomed with the money of the Church,) or their heirs (on account of the money paid for their ransom,) seeing *that the sacred canons allow the employment of the goods of the Church for the ransom of captives.*"—*Lib :* 7, *epist.* 14.

Such was, in regard to slaves and their emancipation, the conduct of the Popes. Their teaching was no less favorable to the cause of liberty. "In the beginning nature made all men free," says Pope Gregory I., "and they have only been subjected to the yoke of servitude by the law of nations.— Since, therefore, our Redeemer, by means of his Divine Grace, has broken the bonds of servitude which held us captives, it is a salutary deed to restore to men, by enfranchisement, their native liberty."—*Lib :* 5, *epist :* 72.

Christian communities throughout Europe vie with one another in their zeal for the emancipation of slaves.

Everything, at length, is ready; the fulness of time is come; the harvest of liberty is ripe; the circumstances of the world demand a sweeping and decided measure; the final blow is struck; the greatest of revolutions is accomplished. Pope Alexander III., at the head of a council of the universal Church, (1167) pronounces slavery abolished.

In reflecting on the arduous and prolonged labours of the Church, and the slow and gradual but sure operation of Christian teaching, we must take into account also the magnitude of the evil that had to be struggled against, consider how generally it was diffused, and remember how firmly it had laid its grasp upon the minds of men. We shall then the better understand how it required the unceasing toil of so many ages to achieve so great a victory; we shall know what it cost to purchase freedom; we shall appreciate the triumph won for mankind by the abolition of slavery throughout Christian Europe.

II. EPOCH, COMMENCING WITH THE ABOLITION OF SLAVERY IN EUROPE, BY POPE ALEXANDER III., IN 1167.

Christians had now to dread only the slavery that was beyond their borders, but which ceased not to assail them. The great Mohammedan imposture sends its hordes against the children of the cross. In the dreadful wars they are obliged to wage in self-defence, christians are often carried into captivity. Nor in the heat of battle only does the infidel secure his victim. Even in the intervals of peace, he scruples not to snatch from freedom her noblest votaries. The brave warrior who has spent his best days in doing battle for her cause, is borne away, in a moment of supposed security, to the land of the heathen and the stranger. There, where neither humanity nor liberty are known, he is doomed to wear out his days under the galling yoke of servitude. The merchant, whose spirit of enterprise leads him to throw the ties of commerce around discordant nations, and bind them together in amity, becomes alike the victim of these fell invaders. He is reduced to slavery, and must find in chains the only recompense of his care and toil. Nor is innocence respected. The youthful maiden, while playing with her companions by the sea-shore, and unconscious of danger, is pounced upon by infidel pirates, and is sold remorselessly for a price in the land of exile, of bondage and of infamy.

For such great and intolerable evils, that inexhaustible love which ever animates the church will find a remedy.—And who more than the saints, whose histories adorn her annals, have been impelled by this divine principle to noble deeds?

John de Matha, inspired by that charity which "beareth, believeth, hopeth, endureth all things," devotes to the cause of his captive brethren all that can enrich and adorn the individual man—wealth, nobility of birth, sanctity of life, powerful intellect, boundless zeal. He aspires, he prays, he labors. His efforts are crowned with success. And now is founded, or rather arises in the full development of its existence, *the Institute of the most holg Trinity, for the redemption of captives.* The Sovereign Pontiff, at that time (the 12th century,) so powerful, not only affords to the new order the weight of authoritative sanction, but also confers upon it additional riches, employs in its support his influence with foreign and even infidel potentates; and facilitates, by every means in his power, the great and inappreciable labors of its members, in ransoming those numerous christians who groaned under the yoke of Mohammedan tyranny.

Scarcely has this illustrious friend of oppressed humanity gone to enjoy his reward, when (1218,) there appears another and equally zealous soldier of the cross. Peter Nolasco, whilst meditating on the sorrows of so many christian families, whose members had been carried into exile by ruthless Pagan invaders, and reduced to slavery, is inspired with the sublime idea of devoting his great wealth and still greater mind to the cause of enfranchisement. THE ORDER OF MERCY is founded. The Sovereign Pontiff of that day—Gregory IX—yields not in zeal and munificence to the most humane of his predecessors. And the order, with all the influence which Papal sanction could impart, and all the aid the treasury of the Pontiff could afford, commences its self-sacrificing work. Who shall say how many captives it restored to freedom?—how many children of christian families it was blessed to rescue from the profane grasp of the basest, the most cruel and the most degrading of all tyrannies.

A little later, and the discovery of the new world, whilst it opens new funds of wealth, reveals also new sources of bondage and oppression. Avaricious adventurers, not satisfied with gold and precious stones, nor yet with merchandize more valuable than either, will traffic in the very liberty of the native populations. What a field for the labours of christian love! And it grows not cold at the sight of so much selfishness. Touched with new fire, and as if wings were added to its zeal, it flies to the succor of the distressed. And not without great and comforting success, does it hasten to interpose the ægis of its protection between the oppressor and the oppressed—between the victim of avarice and the rapacious adventurer.

Scarely has the cry of the enslaved reached the shores of

Europe, when the christian Pontiff, moved to sorrow, and filled with indignation, raises his apostolic voice against the new iniquity. A holy Bishop is the bearer of his message of peace and liberty. Although humanity must ever weep over the unfortunate natives of the new world, whom avarice retained within its iron grasp, there is abundant cause to rejoice that so many were rescued—that great and important conquests were achieved for liberty. The Catholic, too, will call to mind, and not without a well founded feeling of pride, that some four hundred years before the statesmen of Europe began to deliberate whether they should interfere in behalf of oppressed humanity, the chief Pastor, in defiance of an empire that boasted itself the most devoted to his rule, levelled the thunders of the church against the unholy traffic in human blood. Pope Pius II., in the year 1482, denounced and subjected to the severest censures, such of the early emigrants of the new world as reduced the natives to slavery. And what might not be said of the labours, more than human, in the cause of liberty, of that apostolic man—the good, the great, the renowned Las Casas? And yet, what could he have accomplished?—what could the whole Dominican order, of which he was so eminent a member, have achieved without the aid of Papal power? What other influence in the world could have even contended at that time, with the great and potent monarchy of Spain? And fortunate it was for humanity and liberty, that there existed a high priest who, true to his sublime mission, and superior to all human considerations, could dare to advocate the cause of the defenceless natives, in opposition to the most formidable nation of the time;—who could proclaim aloud, and with a voice that was not to be resisted, the rights of man, and the liberty and fraternity of all men, ages before these high and holy things became as a mockery upon the lips of those pretended sages—the philosophists of the eighteenth century.

With slave-holding, even in its most mitigated forms, our more enlightened age has no sympathy. Nor does it tolerate at all, the inhuman traffic which treats the children of certain foreign races as mere articles of merchandize. But whence has it derived these salutary and noble instincts?

From no other source than the invariable teaching of the Papal church, and from its most urgent appeals at all times and under all circumstances, in behalf of oppressed humanity.

Against the slave systems of modern times, the Popes have raised their voice with no less boldness, and exerted their influence with no less effect than they were wont to do in those early ages, when the battle for liberty raged immediately around them, and moved society to its depths.

Pope Pius II., as we have seen, towards the close of the fifteenth century, denounced the crime of reducing, to bondage, the natives of the newly discovered countries of America. Paul III., in the sixteenth century, issued apostolic letters to the Spanish nation requiring that it should respect the liberty of the people, over whom it had recently obtained dominion. Urban VIII., early in the 17th century, addressed the Portuguese, at that time a rich and powerful nation, protesting against the gross injustice of reducing to slavery the natives of their new dominions. In the 18th century, Benedict XIV. confirmed all the most humane ordinances of former Pontiffs against slavery, and addressing the Bishops of Brazil and some other countries, speaks more urgently, if possible, than any of his predecessors, in behalf of the suffering natives, forbidding that they should be reduced to slavery, or retained in that unnatural state. This most important object called forth also the pastoral solicitude of the late Sovereign Pontiff Gregory XVI., whose apostolic letters against trading in slaves, and *against holding in bondage those already reduced to slavery*, many of us may remember, having read when they were first issued on the 3rd day of November, 1839. Pope Pius VII., likewise, at the beginning of the present century, zealously interposed his good offices with men in power *for the complete abolition of slavery among Christians.*

Who now shall doubt who they were, who first advocated, and, with so much power and efficacy, the high principles of humanity and justice which in our times so generally obtain; and which, ere long, may we hope, will so completely pervade every bosom, that there will not exist a man who shall tolerate for one moment the sad and degrading spectacle of slavery.

[Note—page 98.]

ORIGIN OF THE POPE'S TEMPORAL SOVEREIGNTY.

Extract from a sketch in the Ottawa *Tribune*, of 20th August, 1859, of a LECTURE ON THE TEMPORAL SOVEREIGNTY OF THE POPE, delivered by the Rev. Æn. McD. Dawson, in St. Andrew's Catholic Church, Ottawa, on Sunday, 14th August, 1859.

"So necessary has it been towards the freedom of their spiritual state and the exercise of their high functions among all Christian nations, that the Popes should be independent sovereigns, that, by the favor of Divine Providence, they have from the earliest ages enjoyed this privilege.—Scarcely had the extreme violence of Pagan persecution ceased, and whilst the Emperors possessed, as yet, all their power, when the Christian High Priest was in reality the Judge of the Roman people.—So early as the third century, one of the greatest of the Roman Patricians observed playfully, as St. Jerome states, " Promise to make me Bishop of Rome, and I shall at once become a Christian." The Pontiff, although the subject of the Cæsars, and neither professing nor pretending to any power against them, was by all men held in such consideration, that they could not keep their ground beside him. " There was read upon his forehead the character of a Priesthood so exalted, that the Emperor, among whose titles was that of 'Sovereign Pontiff,' tolerated him in Rome with more impatience than he could suffer in his armies a Cæsar, who contested the Empire with him."* There may, indeed, have been already in the mind of Constantine a beginning of faith and of reverence, which, added to this feeling, induced him to cede Rome to the Popes. The seat of Empire is transferred to Constantinople, and the Pontiff, although still acknowledging the Cæsars, and never ceasing to preach obedience to their authority, is, in reality, the Ruler of the West. Hence, it is by no means true that he owed his temporal power to the Carlovingian Dynasty. This dynasty existed not as yet, when Gregory II. wrote these remarkable words to the Emperor Leo: "*The West*

* Count de Maistre.

has its eyes directed towards our humility.—It looks upon us as the arbiter and the moderator of public tranquility. You would find it, if you only ventured to make trial of it, *ready to proceed to the country where you are, there to avenge the wrongs of your subjects of the East.*" This same Pope, in 726, sends ambassadors to Charles Martel, and treats with him as one Prince with another.—Pope Zachary (741-752) sends an embassy to Rachis, King of the Lombards, concludes with him a peace of twenty years, *by virtue of which all Italy was tranquil.*

"When Pope Stephen came to France, Pepin went out to meet him with all his family, and paid him the honors due to a sovereign.

"What are commonly spoken of as the donations of Pepin and Charlemagne, are only acts of restitution. The Lombards, who appear to have been from time immemorial the inveterate enemies of the Holy See, were exhorted by Pepin, before he atttacked them, to "*restore* the properties of the Holy Church of God and of the Roman Republic." The Pope, at the same time, conjured them to *restore* willingly and without effusion of blood, these same properties, designating them as *belonging to the Holy Church of God and the Republic of the Romans.*

"Tuly, then, may we say, with an eminent writer of these times, that "far beyond the age of Pepin and of Carlemagne the august Dynasty extends, until it is lost in the twilight of fable." As regards the spiritual rule of the Supreme Pontiff, such an observation would only be in part applicable; for although it be true that it is by many ages more ancient than the Carlovingian Kings, it can by no means, be said, that its origin is unknown. The name and history of every Pontiff who succeeded Peter, from his day to ours, is familiar to every scholar; and the Holy Scriptures, that are read in every Church, speak of a Sovereign Pontiff, the fourth from St. Peter, of whom St. Paul declares, that his name is in the Book of Life.

But at present there is question only of the temporal sovereignty of the Pontiff. There is no sovereignty so hallowed by time, so generally acknowledged, so deeply rooted in the opinions of mankind. It is also the basis of all sovereignties, and a pattern to every government.

[Note—page 98.]
MERCIFUL CHARACTER OF THE PAPAL GOVERNMENT.

Extract from a sketch in the Ottawa *Tribune*, of a LECTURE ON THE POPE'S TEMPORAL SOVEREIGNTY, delivered by the Rev. Æn. McD. Dawson, in St. Andrew's Catholic Church, Ottawa, on the 14th of August, 1859.

"The exercise of mercy was in those days peculiar to the character of the Pontiff-Sovereigns. Other sovereigns—such as were merely temporal Princes—were strangers to this philosophy. Their greatest merit was to hold the scales of Justice even. Nor in this will they bear to be placed in parallel with the model sovereigns. The most terrible of all the Pontiffs, Julius II., pardons, the moment victory crowns his arms,—almost in the very heat of battle. The mildest of all monarchs, the *debonnaire* King, "the Father of his people," that Louis XII., of France, who was, by principle, clemency itself, acted very differently in the hour of conquest.—The garrison of Peschiera no sooner yields to his arms, than *all the inhabitants are put to the sword, whilst the Governor, Andre Riva, and his son, are hanged upon the walls.* And such has been in all time the *policy* of this earth's earthly rulers. Surely it was good for them, and more beneficial still for the nations over which they ruled, not only that the law of mercy should be preached, but that it should also find its exemplification in that temporal Prince, who, by his Pontifical character, was above all other princes, and who was entitled to say to them, "Behold and imitate the example which is set before you."

"Who could more eloquently thus exhort the nations and their Kings than the Pontiff-Soverign of our own time? Pius IX. no sooner ascends the Chair of Peter and inherits the Apostolic Patrimony, than he enters on a career of mercy. One of his first acts is to forgive the enemies of his State, and the exile returns rejoicing to the land of his birth, to the ancestral hearth. But such loving—such paternal rule does not deter from new rebellion. Men who appear to have sworn the destruction of all government, of all society upon earth, avail themselves of every circumstance (*) to disturb and, if possible, to overthrow the wise and beneficial rule of the Pontiff-Sovereign. "Let him govern the Church," say they; "that is no affair of ours. But the things of this world are our proper province, and we have no doubt of our superior qualifications for their management." If the rest of mankind could be taught to share your conviction, you might perhaps be allowed the honor of a trial. Meanwhile, until you can show your claim by right of birth, the call of heaven, your surpassing wisdom, or the people's choice, you must allow us to believe that Rome, and all other portions of the Church's States, are as prosperous and as happy under that rule which God's Providence has assigned them, as they could possibly be under any other government. What is the great source of weakness in all human governments? Is it not to be found in the vices of those by whom they are administered—their selfishness, their pride, their ambition, their avarice, their indolence, and their want of care for the people subjected to their sway? Where are there fewer of

---

*None are ignorant that on occasion of the recent invasion of Italy by the French, the Secret Socities did all in their power to excite insurrection throughout the dominions of the Pope. At Rome itself they vainly hoped to obtain the countenance, or at least the neutrality, of the General on duty there. In other cities they were successfully opposed by the municipal bodies; and the chief magistrates of six or seven towns were formally thanked by the Pontifical government for the meritorious exertions they had made against the cause of subversion and anarchy. At Perugia, however, with he aid of "sympathisers" and "filibusters" from other States, a few malcontents succeeded in raising a disturbance. For some time the Government at Rome continued to send to these rebels the most urgent remonstrances—the most friendly warnings. But they persist, and it becomes necessary to send a force against them. In four hours two thousand soldiers succeed in re-establishing peace and order in a city of forty thousand people. What better proof could we have that the inhabitants were not inclined to rebel? The soldiers were indeed exasperated by the obstinate resistance offered to them, as well as by the cowardly manner in which the rebels fired upon them from houses and other places of concealment. They did not, however, act like barbarians, as has been falsely reported, and slay indiscriminately women and children. No such act was perpetrated. And if a few men with arms in their hands were sacrificed in the houses from which they cruelly shot down the troops in the very act of doing their duty, this must be charged to the account of the rebellion and those by whom it was stirred up,—not to the most merciful of all Governments. The care of the officers and men to protect the person of a certain Mr. Perkins, whom they supposed to be neutral, could not save them from his calumnies. The columns of the London *Times* bear witness how abundantly an American citizen could repay with the utmost ingratitude all the kindness that was heaped upon him.—(See a letter from Perugia, signed by two of the most eminent citizens, in the *Weekly Register* of July 23rd, 1859.) See also Mrs. Ross' letter from Perugia, in this Appendix.

these hindrances to good government to be met with than in that of the Pontiff-Sovereign? They rule at Rome, and Rome is a great city. Their throne is overthrown. They are driven into exile, and Rome decays—it all but perishes. It is no longer the resort of the learned, the refined, the great and the powerful of all nations. Obedience and contentment are no longer within its walls, and it dwindles to a village of no account. Such, on two memorable occasions, was its fate,—when the Popes, compelled by disastrous circumstances, established their abode at Avignon; and again, when the revolutionary Emperor of France, in defiance of all laws human and Divine, drove the holy Pontiffs from their States. True, this mighty monarch did good *in his way*. There is no denying that he made expensive excavations, drained marshes, and *purified* the Churches and other public buildings of superfluous works of art. But we have yet to learn what he did for the people's good, or to encourage strangers to take up their abode in the famous city, so replete with classic and Christian associations. As was to be expected, the population rapidly decreased. It was to all appearance doubtful whether, from the moment that sacrilegious violence was done to the person of the Pontiff, Rome or its destroyer were destined to have the more speedy downfall. Events only could solve this question. And they were close at hand. The Imperial Despot is overwhelmed with calamity and hurled from his throne; whilst the unoffending victim of his mad ambition, whom he had made to drink the cup of misery to its dregs, returns with a thankful heart, to the capital of his States. It is no exaggeration to say that prosperity followed in his train, and, together with it, population and popular happiness. Let any one who wishes to be more fully informed, read in Baron Geramb's truthful work the comparative state of Rome under the Empire and under the restored sway of its Pontiff-Sovereigns; and he will undoubtedly arrive at the conclusion, that the Roman States might have a less wise and less beneficent Government than that which by the favor of Divine Providence they have enjoyed so long."

[Note--page 98.]

MERCIFUL CHARACTER OF THE PONTIFICAL GOVERNMENT.

Letter of the Hon'ble Mrs. Ross from Perugia, vide Weekly Register, February 11th, 1860.

THE TRUTH ABOUT PERUGIA.—We have received from Rome an original English copy of the letter of Mrs. Ross, of Bladensburgh, written from Perugia on the 23rd of June last, and an Italian version of which we announced last week to our readers as having appeared in the *Giornale di Roma* of 23rd ult., and which is referred to in our special correspondence from Rome this week. We really never expected that our former Perugino antagonist, Mr. Perkins, of Boston, should have turned out to be such a very *unfortunate* man. We have now a fair sample of the authorities consulted by travellers of his class to procure evidence against the Pontifical Government.

[Extract from a letter written by the Hon. Mrs. Ross, of Bladensburgh, to her husband, from Villa Monti, at Perugia, dated Perugia, June 21st, 1859.]

"Hautes Pyrenées, France.

"To David Ross of Bladensburgh.

"I wrote to you last Wednesday, 15th inst., to announce a revolution which occurred here on the previous day; now I write to relieve your mind of anxiety in case an exaggerated account of what has occurred here be given in the public papers. I have to tell you of the re-entrance of the Papal troops, which took place yesterday after a stubborn resistance of four hours on the part of the revolutionists.

"When the revolt at Perugia was known at Rome, orders were given to a body of Swiss troops to replace the little garrison which had been driven out. The revolutionary junta was well informed of what had been decided on at Rome, and immediately prepared to oppose the re-establishment of social order in the town. Victor Emmanuel, to whom they had offered the town, returned no official answer, but instead, reports were industriously circulated among the citizens of sympathy and support from Piedmont; an honest refusal on the part of Victor Emmanuel, or an open acceptance, would have prevented subsequent events, which his calculated silence brought about. On Saturday last, the 18th inst., we heard that the Pope's troops were close to * * *; and on Sunday that they had actually arrived there. In the * * * Buoncompagni sent from Tuscany, I am told, 300 muskets in aid, and waggons were despatched to Arezzo for arms and ammunition; barricades were commenced. The monks were turne ! out of their convent at St. Peter's Gate (one of them came down to us); and 500 armed men instead were put in to defend the gate and first barricade. After two o'clock, p. m., the gates were closed, and no one could go in or out of the town without an order. It was then I wrote a note to Mr. Perkins, warning and requesting him and his family to accept a shake-down with us; and with difficulty I got the note conveyed up to town by a woman who happened to have a pass. Nothing could induce any of the peasants about us to go near the town, as the revolutionary party were making forced levies of the youth of the place, and arming them to resist the coming troops.— Next morning (Monday the 20th) a body of shepherds coming up from the place, told us that they had just seen the Swiss troops at Santa Maria degli Angioli, where they stopped and had mass,* having heard that the citizens contemplated resistance. About ten o'clock that same morning I got Mr. Perkins' answer to my note; it was to this effect —that he had gone to the President (of the Junta) who assured him that the Swiss had not yet even reached * * * and that certainly they would not arrive before the next day at sunset. And the inn-keeper, (the notorious Storti) he added, said that they were not coming here at all, but going to Ancona! I cannot imagine how he could trust such people, who were all implicated in the business. His messenger, who was one of the servants of the hotel, said, as he gave the note—'Don't delay me, or I shall not be in time to kill my three or four Swiss,' showing how well informed and prepared that hotel was. I should have written again

---

* Mr. Perkins, in his letter to the Times, makes out that they forced open the houses of the inhabitants to make them give up their wine, and that they got drunk.

to the poor Perkins's to undeceive them; but it was too late, for almost immediately the columns of the Swiss appeared in the plain below, which you know we see from our villa, and the President (revolutionary Junta) and other heads of the rebellion had their carriages and horses ready waiting. They fled at the first gun, leaving the people to act for themselves after having inflamed, deceived, and armed them, and gathered into the town all the *canaille* they could get from the neighboring country. From the moment the troops appeared, all the peasants belonging to the villa flocked around us. Anxiety was depicted on every face. The countenance of one old man in particular was very striking—'Bad times,' he murmured. 'We have fallen on evil days.—Respect and awe are gone, and the people are blinded.' The parish Priest was also with us, and the monk I mentioned before. We watched with great anxiety the slow ascent of the troops up the long five miles to the city gate. There the Colonel and his men halted, and he parleyed with the people. We could see him stop and address them, and then we saw a volley fired down on them by the armed men in the convent windows. The first fire was from the people on the troops. We could see all from our villa windows like a scene on the stage; while the distance was sufficient to veil the horrors of war. Then we saw some troops separate from the main body and advance to the foot of the wall, and, in the twinkling of an eye, they scaled it, amid a hot fire from the insurgents, whom we heard shouting out—, Coraggio! coraggio!' from behind the walls. Then we saw one soldier rush up and tear down the revolutionary flag, and carry it in triumph back to the main body of the troops, and then we saw the Pontifical flag float where the revolutionary one had been.— In the mean time the rest of the troops had planted their cannon opposite to the city gate. Boom! boom! they went at the barricades, and in an hour after the firing of the first gun, they had driven out the 500 armed men from the convent of St. Peter's, and entered the first enclosure of the town. We then saw no more, but sat all that afternoon in the window, listening to the incessant firing in deep anxiety. As the soldiers fought their way up to their barracks, and as the report of the arms became more and more distant, we could judge pretty well of the advance of the troops, knowing as we did the chief points of resistance within. The first gun fired was at three o'clock, p. m., precisely, and at seven, p. m., all was silent again ; the soldiers had reached their barracks. I hear that * * * * have fled out towards Arezzo—all the *canaille* of the villages of the place were enlisted to defend the city and it was the talk of the country that had the Swiss been beaten, the city was to have been pillaged by that armed mob. They say that had they not had promises of succour from Victor Emmanuel (the 'Re Galantuomo') and of encouragement from Princess Valentini (nee Buonaparte, who resides here), that they would not have resisted as they did : thus were they deceived ! There is more in it all than one sees at first; and clearly it was an affair got up to make out a case against the Pope. Piedmontese money was circulating there just before the revolution. N—— got it, in change, in the shops.

June 22.—P.S.—Our servant has been to town to-day ; he brings me a letter from the Perkins's, and such news as is the general talk of the cafes. Our poor friends in the Hotel de France (Locanda Storti) suffered much. Deceived to the last, they had not even been told of the actual arrival of the troops, and had just sat quietly to dinner, when the roar of the guns startled them. They strove to go to another hotel, but alas ! the gates of their inn were fastened ; they could not stir.— The letter I got from them said that the troops were *irritated on account of the firing from the roof*. We knew before hand how it would be *there ;* and in fact they did shoot an officer and two men while passing the door. It was on this that the soldiers infuriated rushed and assailed the house. * * * I hear every one blames the imprudence of these people. They could not afford to be hostile ; for the hotel, if you remember, commands the street from the base up the hill. No troops, therefore, could risk going up that hill with a hostile house in that position, ready to take them in the rear.— The escape of the poor Perkins's is a perfect miracle; they, I hear, lost everything. The innkeeper, waiter, and stableman, they say, were killed in the fray. The number of deaths among the Swiss were ten, and 33 of the Perugians. Several prisoners were made. I went up on this same afternoon (June 22) with the two little boys, to see the Colonel of the regiment. The town is wonderfully little injured, only broken windows * * * * after a mob riot, with the exception of a few houses in the suburbs, between the outer and inner gates. One was burned by the accident of the falling of a bomb-shell' The other was cannonaded as being a resort of the rebels. There is great talk of how the heads of the revolution scampered off, betraying thus the tools and dupes of their faction, * * *

[Extract from another letter to David Ross, of Bladensburgh:—"There is great terror here among all the country people, who dread, sooner or later, vengeance being taken upon them by the revolutionary party, because they would have nothing to say to the movement."]

[Note page 108. and page 193, Note.]
BARON MACAULAY.—SCIENCE NOT UNFAVORABLE TO THE PROGRESS OF THE CATHOLIC CHURCH.—NUMBER OF PROTESTANTS PROBABLY NOT INCREASED.

Protestants may have increased, but not considerably, in the course of the last quarter of a century.

Let us take the opinion of a very learned Protestant writer. Baron MacCaulay says:—

"We often hear it said, that the world is constantly becoming more and more enlightened, and that the enlightenment must be favorable to Protestantism, and unfavorable to Catholicism. We wish that we could think so. But we see great reason to doubt whether this is a well-founded expectation. We see that during the last two hundred and fifty years, the human mind has been, in the highest degree, active; that it has made great advances in every branch of natural philosophy; that it has produced innumerable inventions, tending to promote the convenience of life; that medicine, surgery, chemistry, engineering, have been very greatly improved; that government, police, and law, have been improved, though not to so great an extent as the physical sciences. Yet, we see that during these two hundred and fifty years, Protestantism has made no conquests worth speaking of. Nay, we believe that, as far as there has been change, that change has, on the whole, been in favor of the Church of Rome. We cannot, therefore, feel confident that the progress of knowledge will necessarily be fatal to a system which has, to say the least, stood its ground, in spite of the immense progress made by the human race in knowledge, since the time of Queen Elizabeth."

The more progress is made in knowledge, the fewer dificulties will the Church have to contend with. True religion it may be said, is as much impeded by ignorance, as by the corruption of mankind.

VALUE OF THE POPULAR VOTE FOR ANNEXATION TO PIEDMONT.—FOREIGN INTERVENTION.—ITALIAN CORRESPONDENCE SHEWING THAT THE REVOLTED AND ANNEXED PROVINCES HAVE BEEN COERCED. PAGE 194.

THE REVOLUTION IN TUSCANY.

Sir,—The enclosed document has been forwarded to me from Florence, with a request to endeavour to get it inserted in the Weekly Registkr. It is too late for the publication of it to affect the election by which the political fraternity of Tuscany is to be decided; but it will serve to show the nature of the machinery by which the imminent annexation to Piedmont has been worked up to its present stage. The document has been forwarded by a Protestant gentleman who, though not over friendly to the late dynasty, condemns, in the strongest language, the nefarious agencies used by Sardinia, to carry out her ambitious views of self-aggrandisement. He says:—" No one that is not on the spot can imagine the tyranny of this government, which certainly keeps things quiet, but panders to all the vile passions of the people—liberty and licenses to all who go with it —terror and imprisonment for those who do not. Some of your acquaintances have been in prison for upwards of a month, without being told why or wherefore; others have been forbidden to receive certain persons in their houses.— Lent is no longer what it formerly was. ...... We have got importations of foreign preachers, of all denominations, who do not convert, but only unsettle the minds of the people. The print shops are full of the most blasphemous publications, and caricatures against religion, the Pope, and all things sacred; the press in England is bought, and the writers of the articles in the papers here are persons of small respectability."

The *Weekly Register* is admitted into Tuscany, and as no local paper dare publish this document, those who are interested in its circulation, are anxious to get it inserted in the columns of your journal. No doubt, by so doing you will greatly aid the cause of truth and justice.

I remain, yours truly, &c. J. J. B.
Leamington, March 13, 1860.

MARCH 6, 1860.—It is notorious to all Europe that the Tuscan Revolution of the 27th April, last year, was not the spontaneous act of the people, but was brought about by the machinations of a neighbouring kingdom, aided by the powerful influence of France, through the agency of an accredited minister to the Tuscan Court, and who, by unexampled perfidy and deceit, succeeded in seducing the army from their allegiance, by bribing the common soldiers with money, and the officers, by promoting them to higher grades, and, in many instances, paying their debts.

The revolution, thus inaugurated by fraud and treachery, has since been maintained by force, and now seeks to hand over our noble country to the power which has been the cause of so much misfortune to us.

The means that are in progress for that end is what is denominated a "popular vote," but such a vote cannot be taken as a just criterion of the sentiments of the people, as all persons of intelligence favourable to the dynasty of the Grand Duke deny the right of any power to call upon them to transfer their allegiance, and have resolved on a policy of abstention. The less intelligent and educated classes are utterly unable to form any judgment on this question, as only a one-sided view is presented to them, and by a system of intimidation and coercion they will be compelled to vote as they are directed by the prefects, mayors, and other agents of the Government in the various districts.

In the meantime, no one dare breathe a sentiment, or express an opinion, in opposition to the present order of things, without the certainty, if discovered, of being incarcerated, compelled to leave the country, or otherwise maltreated, whilst the state of the press is such that free discussion is not only unknown, but absolutely prohibited; in fact the newspapers are merely the registers of the decrees and wishes of the Government.

Some minor publications, however, have the license to abuse, and hold up to the vilest ridicule the most sacred and highest personages. Foreign journals not in accord with the existing Government are not permitted to enter the country, and persons bringing them in are subject to fine and imprisonment by virtue of a decree of 23rd Feb., 1860. We therefore object and protest against these so-called elections for the following reasons:—

1st.—Because we ignore and repudiate the principle of the people to dethrone their sovereign.

2nd.—Because we see the annexation of Tuscany to Sardinia will be fraught with many evils, and will reduce our country to a province, and our metropolis, full of proud traditions and historical recollections, to a provincial town.

3rd.—Because the Sardinian system of conscription applied to Tuscany, will remove from the soil numbers of the young and most active of the country population, and thus the land in many places will be thrown out of cultivation, and ultimately become a desert.

4th.—Because the benevolent and paternal Government of the Grand Dukes of Tuscany is so impressed on our minds, that we desire no dynastic change.

5th.—Because the progress of improvement, both social and material, under the auspices of the grand Ducal Government in all parts of the country, as well as the embellishment of the cities, are so manifest, that we cannot view its annexation to a state so overwhelmed with debt as Sardinia, otherwise than as a pernicious and retrograde step, which will eventually lead to nothing but ruin.

10

We have no means of making ourselves heard in our unhappy country, and giving publicity to our names would draw upon us the vengeance of our present rulers. We are therefore obliged to have recourse to the medium of a foreign press, in the hope that our sentiments, once in print, will find circulation, and Europe will hear the truth from

A VOICE FROM TUSCANY.
[*Weekly Register*, March 17, 1860.]

POPULARITY OF PIUS IX,—LETTER FROM ROME.

March 15th, 1860.
(*Weekly Register*, March 24, 1860.)

If the Romans were left free from all foreign intervention, and from the deadly influence of the secret societies, the Holy Father would have nothing to fear. Yesterday, as is the custom on the Fridays in Lent, the Holy Father went to St. Peter's, accompanied by some of the Cardinals and the principal members of his household, to venerate the relics exposed there. This was thought to be a happy moment for the loyal subjects of His Holiness to express their feelings of love and sympathy for him. Accordingly, with one spontaneous movement, the nobles and gentry of Rome thronged the magnificent Basilica, to the number, of at least, twelve thousand; these prayed for the prosperity of their sovereign, venerated the sacred relics with him, and then returned quietly to their homes.

The Piazza, and in fact the whole space leading to the bridge of St. Angelo, was thronged with carriages, and the Church itself was as full as St. Peter's ever is,—as full, it was remarked by many, as it is, on Christmas or Easter day. Owing to the inconvenience of the hour, the working classes, and the numerous class of employees here, could not attend, otherwise, without doubt, the numbers would have been immensely greater.

This one fact must at once put an end to the idea that this demonstration was a thing got up in any way by the government, and will prove it to be the heartfelt expression of loyal sentiments entertained by the people of Rome towards the Holy Father. The number of strangers there, was but few, the demonstration being begun and carried out almost entirely by Italians.

H. W. W.

VALUE OF THE POPULAR VOTE FOR ANNEXATION TO PIEDMONT. FOREIGN INTERVENTION.

Extracts of the Note from the Holy See to the French Government, of 29th Febuary, 1860, in reply to the despatch of M. Thouvenel, addressed to the Papal Nuncio at Paris.

* * * * "It is sufficient to have resided in Italy for the last four years, or at least, to have followed with attention, its various calamitous phases, during that time, to know by whom and by what means the revolt was prepared, accomplished and supported, and the *cui bono*, which is ever a most important guide in penal matters, can be applied here in a manner the more evident from the patent manœuvres of the party which does all in its power to gain possession of the provinces, of which it is desired to deprive the Holy Father, or rather, which it is desired to abstract from the patrimony of the Catholic Church. From what is intended to be done in the end, it may easily be understood what was intended to be done from the beginning; and long beforehand, were foreseen and prepared the very difficulties which are now represented as insurmountable, and beyond all provision. Nor do I believe myself wanting in due regard towards any one, if, compelled by the necessity of maintaining my assertion, I am obliged to recal facts, and even individual names, but both of which are notorious from one end of the Peninsula to the other, and here, not to go farther back, I shall confine myself, for the sake of brevity, to point out that, when Count Cavour, in the Congress of Paris in 1856, issued a kind of Programme relating to what ought to be done in Italy, and declared afterwards, in the Pidemontese Chamber, that he wished to carry out by all means in his power, its execution, then began in Central Italy, an increase of activity in that slow working, which had been undertaken long before, and which aimed at preparing the much wished for annexation.

It would truly be long and tedious to enumerate all the means which were adopted for the purpose; but the emissaries who overran it in every direction, the gold which was amply distributed, the clandestine prints which were circulated, the suborning the military, especially latterly, were among those chiefly used. In the same manner as was practised in other towns of the state, by persons emboldened by important connections, so in Bologna the Marquis Pepoli constituted himself the head of that party, held in his own house their meetings, surrounded himself with some hundreds of assistants, and gathered arms. The Government, who knew all this, was on the point of securing his arrest, when, for considerations easy to be understood, it contented itself with giving notice of it to the ambassador of France in this capital, who, subsequently to an interview he had with Pepoli in Leghorn, gave assurances, not confirmed most certainly by facts, that all could be left at rest, on this account. But what will be a most rare example in history, if not the only one, is what the diplomatic agents of Sardinia did to the detriment of the other Italian States, to second the ambitious views of their own government. The conduct of the Commendatore Buoncompagni in Tuscany either has no name, or deserves such an one as I shall guard myself from using; and, nevertheless, with the exception of the last of his steps, the action of Messrs. Migliorati and Pes Della Minerva in Rome, was scarcely different. The first of these stooped even to going about during the summer months, in some Provinces of the State, to organise there, clubs in favour of the Piedmontese party. Stimulants so active and constant were necessarily to have their effect, and they produced it, in reality, either by creating or by increasing to some extent, the small party which perhaps existed there, and around which were gathered nearly all the disaffected, who are always found in every country, without there being any want of individuals under the illusion and seduction of the aspirations for an Italy, one and independent, but, both the former and the latter ever were far from constituting the people,—that people, so

uerate all the
but the emis-
ie gold which
s which were
cially latterly,
ne manner as
y persons em-
Bologna the
of that party,
unded himself
ed arms. The
point of secur-
to be under-
f it to the am-
equently to an
ve assurances,
l could be left
most rare ex-
the diplomatic
e other Italian
 own govern-
oncompagni in
n an ono as I
eless, with the
f Messrs. Mig-
scarcely differ-
about during
e State, to or-
nontese party.
sarily to have
either by creat-
ll party which
were gathered
ound in every
lividuals under
or an Italy, one
the latter over
at people, so

honest, moral, and christian-like, especially in the country, who arose with such exultation, and, in so many thousands, when the Holy Father visited it, hardly three years ago. But has not such a class of people, which in substance, forces the immense majority on account of its very honesty and tranquility, found itself and remained, many times, in other parts of Europe also, exposed to the violence of a party, small but audacious, which from circumstances often unforseen, prevailed over and oppressed it? Such circumstances seem not sufficiently to have been taken into account, in the above mentioned despatch, when in it it is said that by the mere fact of the Austrians having withdrawn from Bologna, "the population found itself independent, without having need of any special impulse." The truth is, that the population, as in a hundred similar cases, know little or nothing of it. But the Austrians having retired too suddenly, and that city having remained, almost completely without troops, the party, which was already prepared from previous intrigues, and rendered the more audacious from certain proclamations of one of the belligerent parties, laid hold of power, and imposed it on the real people, who, to its own inestimable injury and grief, has still to support it, and, perhaps, it would not be too far from the reality, to believe that, were a certain capital suddenly abandoned by the garrison which guards it, something similar would take place, without, nevertheless, that any conclusion might be drawn from it, either of bad government or present incapacity." * * *

THE VOTE FOR ANNEXATION TO SARDINIA BY NO MEANS THE VOTE OF THE PEOPLE OF THE LEGATIONS.

* * * "And although the above mentioned party was strengthened by the promises, the encouragements, the subsidies, and the thousand other means which came necessarilly from Piedmont, it, nevertheless, on the day of its success, found itself so small and weak as scarcely to be able to bring together a few hundreds of adepts on the public square of Bologna; and even to these, when the Pontifical arms were taken down, Marquis Pepoli was obliged to pre-

tend that it was done to remove these arms from any possible insult, which, nobody at the moment was disposed to inflict, and in the same way as it had been prepared out of the state, so, as soon as the rebellion was accomplished, from outside the state also came, to maintain it in strength; all the supplies of ammunition, money and men, either in a military or a civil capacity; and, among the latter was seen to figure, as Intendant of one of the four Legations, the very Migliorati, of whom mention has already been made. *But the population took no other part in all this, than to abstain, to the number of fifty-nine-sixtieths, from all voting, supporting every kind of pressure, even to the extent of seeing themselves denied the manifestation of their own feelings; and that, by such means as threats, imprisonment and proscriptions, which prevailing factions know well how to use.*" * *

COMPLICITY OF FRANCE.

(*Note of the Holy See continued.*)

* * * "I am very far from accusing the French arms, and much less France, from which so many distinguished services have been received by the Holy See and the Church. But I cannot refrain from recalling to the recollection of your most illustrious and Reverend Lordship, (the Nuncio at Paris), 'that inevitable logic of facts,' in virtue of which the Emperor of the French said, in his last letter, that "he cannot deny a certain solidarity of the effects of the national move provoked in Italy by the war against Austria." Now, amongst these effects, must not the revolt of the four Legations be reckoned?" * * *

WHETHER FOREIGN AID MIGHT NOT BE LEGITIMATELY APPLIED TOWARDS THE SUPPRESSION OF REVOLT IN ROMAGNA.

(*Note of the Holy See continued.*)

* * * "I do not wish to conclude this despatch without proposing to you a last consideration touching the impossibility which, it is said, exists, of the Romagnas being restored to the legitimate rule of the Holy Father without foreign intervention, or to keep them without renewed occupation,—things which are declared to be impossible, insurmountable. But if it is true, and it is impossible to doubt it, that the revolt of the four Legations was made, and is maintained by the means of a party which owes its power to foreign help, and to hopes of still greater assistance, I do not see why a rebellion made by iniquitous foreign aid, should not also be supported by legitimate foreign aid. Again, can it be said that aid given by Catholic nations to their common Father, and in the interest of the whole christian universe, can be styled foreign assistance?

"At any rate, if all that is to be found of foreign in the Romagna was removed, in the shape of men, money, influence and assistance of every kind, there would be room to hope, that the Government of the Holy Father would succeed, with the resources it possesses, in maintaing in order, *the small amount of revolutionary element which is to be found there,* in spite of the increase it has received from the serious disorders which are so long prolonged in it." * * *

(Signed,)

G. CARDINAL ANTONELLI.

Rome, Febuary 29, 1860.

THE MARQUIS OF NORMANBY. — VALUE OF HIS TESTIMONY.—
PAGES 179, 180, &c.

"If we were to sift the pretentions of all our public men to discover that one person who is necessarily best informed of the past and present state of Italy, and the causes and means that have produced the anarchy which now prevails over the greater part of that unfortunate Peninsula, Lord Normanby would inevitably be the man for our purpose. His long residence in Italy, his intimate acquaintance with all that is there distinguished for literature, science, art and statesmanship, and his unquestionable liberality of sentiment, as a politician, give him a paramount claim to our respectful attention, and even to our confidence, when he comes forward to enlighten his countrymen, with respect to Italian affairs,—a claim, to which no other member of the Legislature can have the slightest pretentions. He has, too, throughout a long public career, always maintained such an independence of Character, and so nobly and generously subordinated his personal interests, to his sense of public duty, as to entitle him, as a right, to our confidence when he unbosoms himself, either in print or in speech, of that knowledge which he has acquired by long study and experience in official and non-official life, and tells us important truths which it is necessary for us to know, in order to be able to form a correct judgment upon momentous passing events."—*Weekly Register*, *February* 11, 1860.

ADMIRABLE SENTIMENTS OF GOOD PROTESTANTS. PAGE 193.

It is no new thing that Protestants should protest against injustice, and in favor of the Pope. John Francis Maguire, M. P., in his eloquently written and most instructive book, which I regret not having met with until the last pages of this work were in the press, states that when, in 1848, the Pope was in exile at Gaeta in the Kingdom of Naples, "sympathy conveyed in every living language its sweet consolation to the wounded heart of Pius IX., and perhaps one of the most touching letters received by the Holy Father was one sent to him by a Lutheran Protestant, named Christian Freytag, of Lubec, enclosing thirty Ducats, and concluding in these words:—

"Permit me, Holy Father, who am penetrated with the most profound respect for your Holy person, to continue my prayers for you to our Saviour Christ Jesus. Deign, in return, to bless my family, who, although Protestant Lutherans, implore for you the choicest blessings from the hands of our Father in Heaven, who himself is love and holiness."

Recent newspapers inform us that Protestants join with Catholics in sending subscriptions, as well as verbal expressions of sympathy, to the Pope. Let one instance more suffice. It may not sound so high as the magnificent donations of such wealthy Protestant nobleman as his Grace the Duke of Hamilton, but, it is equally, and even more significant. At a great meeting held at Cork in the middle of April, for the purpose of raising funds in aid of the Papal treasury, the Bishop of Cork, who was in the chair, handed in a subscription of £10 which he had received enclosed in the following note:—

"LONDON, 24TH FEB., 1860.

"MY LORD,—I beg leave to enclose £10 towards the fund raising for his Holiness the Pope. Although I am a heretic, and have no right to offer an opinion, yet I cannot help thinking that the good, amiable old gentleman has been rather hardly treated."

A FRIEND.

THE END.

www.ingramcontent.com/pod-product-compliance
Lightning Source LLC
Chambersburg PA
CBHW021012240426
43669CB00037B/629